From Peac

With my mother.

From Peace to War

A Study in Contrast

1857-1918

Oliver Lyttelton

Viscount Chandos

PC, DSO, MC, LLD

THE BODLEY HEAD

LONDON SYDNEY

TORONTO

ACKNOWLEDGMENTS

Permission to quote copyright material is gratefully acknowledged as follows: Macmillan & Co, Ltd for brief extracts from Morley's *Life of William Ewart Gladstone*; John Murray, Ltd for extracts from *The Diary of Lady Frederick Cavendish*, edited by John Bailey; A. Tilney Bassett and A. P. Watt & Son for two versions of an epitaph from *The Gladstone Papers*; Winant, Towers, Ltd for extracts from *The History of Underclothes*, by Cecil Willett Cunnington and P. Cunnington; Mr. Kenneth Young, the Earl of Balfour, and G. Bell & Sons Ltd for an extract from *Arthur James Balfour*, by Kenneth Young.

© The Trustees of the Chandos Literary Trust 1968

SBN 370 00321 7

Printed and bound in Great Britain for

The Bodley Head Ltd

9 Bow Street, London WC2

by William Clowes & Sons, Beccles

Set in Baskerville type face

First published 1968

TO MOIRA, ANTONY,

ROSEMARY, JULIAN, AND ADRIAN

CONTENTS

LIST OF ILLUSTRATIONS

FOREWORD

This volume is divided into two books, which differ entirely in subject.

The first book gives some glimpses of Victorian and Edwardian life, and of the people who lived it. They are seen partly through the eyes of the Lyttelton family, partly through my mother's, and in its later years partly through my own.

The second book gives some glimpses of the First World War from the letters which I wrote to my mother from the Front. Beyond suppressing some trivialities, mainly about food or clothes, and some French expressions, I have not edited them nor even corrected the grammar.

The volume is intended only to entertain, but it cannot avoid drawing attention to contrasts with present-day Britain. These contrasts do not lead me to hanker after times past, nor am I sad at having spent my life in a world of convulsion and change. It seems to me that there is as much to praise as to condemn in both the past and the present. *C*

Book One
1857-1914

THE LYTTELTON FAMILY

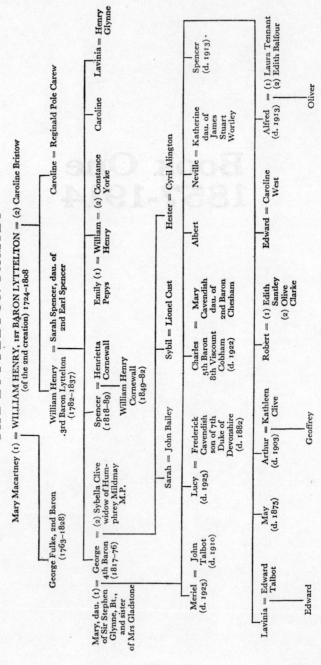

Mary Macartney (1) = WILLIAM HENRY, 1st BARON LYTTELTON = (2) Caroline Bristow
(of the 2nd creation) 1724–1808

George Fulke, 2nd Baron
(1763–1828)

William Henry = Sarah Spencer, dau. of
3rd Baron Lyttelton
(1782–1837)
2nd Earl Spencer

Caroline = Reginald Pole Carew

Mary, dau. (1) = George = (2) Sybella Clive
of Sir Stephen   4th Baron   widow of Hum-
Glynne, Bt.,   (1817–76)   phrey Mildmay
and sister   M.P.
of Mrs Gladstone

Spencer = Henrietta
(1818–89) Cornewall

William Henry
Cornewall
(1849–82)

Emily (1) = William = (2) Constance
Pepys   Henry   Yorke

Caroline

Lavinia = Henry
Glynne

Meriel = John
(d. 1925) Talbot
           (d. 1910)

May
(d. 1875)

Arthur = Kathleen
(d. 1903) Clive

Geoffrey

Lucy = Frederick
(d. 1925) Cavendish
           son of 7th
           Duke of
           Devonshire
           (d. 1882)

Sarah = John Bailey

Charles = Mary
5th Baron Cavendish
8th Viscount dau. of
Cobham   2nd Baron
(d. 1922) Chesham

Robert = (1) Edith
           Santley
         (2) Olive
           Clarke

Sybil = Lionel Cust

Hester = Cyril Alington

Albert

Edward = Caroline
           West

Neville = Katherine
           dau. of
           James
           Stuart
           Worley

Spencer
(d. 1913).

Alfred = (1) Laura Tennant
(d. 1913) (2) Edith Balfour

Oliver

Lavinia = Edward
           Talbot

Edward

1

The Lyttelton family of the mid-nineteenth century was typically 'Victorian', as the term is now understood. Since my grandfather had fifteen children, eight sons and four daughters by his first wife, and three daughters by his second, the various relationships are sometimes baffling even to one of their descendants. The table opposite may, however, help the reader.

I have in my possession a book the first page of which has this inscription:

M.L. 1857

This book records the last day of his dear
mother,[1] and was made and given to Alfred
Lyttelton[2] at his confirmation by his loving
aunt and godmother, E.L.

The book, which was written by Lord Lyttelton, four other Lytteltons, Mr and Mrs Gladstone, Henry Glynne and Anne Smith, seems a saddening gift on such an occasion.

My grandfather's first entry runs:

I believe that Mary's days of vigorous health may be said to have ended before the birth of Edward, the eleventh child, in July 1855: every exertion was a little trying to her. On her return [from a concert in Stourbridge] she had a disagreeable adventure from the drunkenness of the post boy who had driven the carriage. . . . It was a matter of special anxiety to watch whether no ill effect followed thereupon. . . . All her strength was given to her twelve children . . . and the twelfth baby was the last gallant effort of the high mettled racer. . . . It is the bare truth that there were not more than two or three of the children connected with whom a day's serious anxiety of any kind was sent to her. Such a

---

[1] My grandmother, Lady Lyttelton.
[2] My father.

life, to be continued to anything like the full term of an existence, is not for man. The sure alternatives were what has happened, or some real sorrow to her, if she lived.

There is a Christian sense to the heathen saying, 'Whom the Gods love dies young'. But apart from the religious view, I am inclined to believe that she was not physically fitted to struggle with suffering or adversity, bodily or mental. She would have borne it with entire meekness, and holy resignation; but her bloom and brightness and elasticity would have gone.

Two years after the birth of Edward, on 7th February, 1857, my grandmother gave birth to my father. The book records that her confinement was 'wonderfully easy'. She was indeed fortunate to escape being bled, which was the treatment prescribed to a contemporary for weakness after giving birth to a son.

The text continues: 'She was fit to move to Brighton on the 6th April and to go to Communion on Easter Day, 12th April, but showed increasing weakness.' She was given a 'highly stimulating treatment, quantities of port wine, steel, etc. The strength that accrued was an artificial one, and the constitution rebelled against it. The high stimulants may have over-exerted the circulation and so caused the disease of the heart.'

Although she did not die until August 1857, nearly six months after giving birth to my father, there is little doubt that the cause was exhaustion from continual childbirth. My wife's grandmother also died in giving birth to her thirteenth child. My grandfather's comments on my grandmother's last illness seem strange to modern eyes and, considering his devotion to her, curiously detached and almost complacent.

It seems miraculous that my father, Alfred, the twelfth child, was one of the most richly endowed men of his time. No one before or perhaps since has ever excelled at games as he did. At cricket he was the first choice for England after W. G. Grace; he was Keeper of the Field and Fives at Eton; he was the real tennis champion for many years, and the racquets champion for nearly as many. He played association football for England. Unlike some athletes, he did not lack intellectual powers, for they brought him in later life a large and thriving practice at the Bar. In politics he rose to be Secretary of State for the Colonies in 1904, just fifty years before his son retired from the same office.

1. My grandmother's twelve children. From left to right: (standing) Lucy, Neville, Arthur, Charles, May, Spencer, Edward, Albert, Robert; (sitting) Alfred, Meriel, Lavinia.

2. My grandfather, Lord Lyttelton, from a drawing by George Richmond, R.A.

3. My aunt Lucy, Lady Frederick Cavendish, from a portrait by George Richmond, R.A., painted about the time of her marriage.

I am an advocate of the planned family, both because it is the imperative necessity of our time if we are to avoid 'Standing Room Only', and also because of the intolerable burden upon women of bearing and bringing up a large number of children. If applied, however, in this instance, the country would have been deprived to their loss of the services of my father and uncle Edward, who were the last born of twelve.

When my grandmother realised that she would not recover, but would not die immediately, she said, 'Don't let's sit tight for it to be directly.' Mr Gladstone visited her on Sunday, 16th August, and carried her in his arms from one room to another. He records in the book: 'She seemed to be as one preparing for an ordinary journey,' and later, 'She is already half an angel.' 'Soon her increasing weakness made her talk chiefly of the consequences of her death.' 'She talked to her sister [Mrs Gladstone] of how much she too would miss her, and to us both of what she knew would be Lord Lyttelton's grief. She said a little later, 'How sad it will be to see all the children in mourning', and later, joking, 'I can't imagine anything poorer than Sundays at Hagley without me.'

She talked also to Catherine Talbot[1] about the girls. She thought there might be a danger to Lucy of indulging in a sort of luxury of grief. She said, 'They had better come out together. Meriel would be kept back a year, and then Lucy would be old enough. I should not like them to be buried in the country, but to go to London occasionally and make acquaintances with nice people—people I like—*good* people.'

In early August she sent down a request that she might have a little music, 'and so all the young performers sang several choruses'.

A little later she saw each of her children and said goodbye to them. She exclaimed more than once, 'I think the idea of seeing our Saviour in Heaven ought to make up for all one is losing.' She frequently asked for some prayers to be read, and Catherine Talbot read one from the Visitation of the Sick, and her husband read prayers and passages from sermons.

Of my uncle Neville my grandmother said: 'She was much pleased with him and was very glad to see how he had conquered

[1] Daughter of Lord Wharncliffe, married to John Talbot. She was my aunt Lavinia's mother-in-law.

his temper.' In parenthesis, I remember him as one of the sweetest-tempered of men, and certainly the sweetest-tempered general whom I have known.

Meriel records: 'As I was kneeling by the bed she exclaimed, "Mind you are kind to the neighbours. I don't mean just now, but afterwards, the little civil things I used to do."' And again, "'You know what sort of things you can be useful to Papa in, things like Mackie and the pines, and what is to be done with them.'"

On Sunday, 16th August, Lucy Lyttelton writes: 'Uncle Billy[1] administered the Holy Communion to her (in the bedroom) at 6.45 a.m., together with Papa, Mrs Gladstone, Mrs Talbot, Uncle Henry, Meriel, Agnes[2] and me.' Her mother-in-law, Sarah, Lady Lyttelton, continues:

He read the service most nobly, with his most heavenly look and manner, and loud enough to be heard in the next room, where many of us were kneeling. She sat up, supported by pillows— white and thin, grave and altered indeed!, but looking grand and gentle too, like a Christian matron soon to leave us. I spoke to her after she had communicated. She was holding herself up, and showed no weakness, her appearance and expression were most striking; full of a calm holy dignity, as if her mind were raised above this world.

Her voice was firm, eyes large and clear. The look was graver, less young; it inspired reverence and heavenly hope. She said to me: 'Now don't fash yourself about the children; you are too old for that. Your province is to look after him [George] and to comfort him.'

On Monday, the day on which she died, she talked to Meriel and Lucy. Soon after, Lord Lyttelton said to her, 'My darling, you can smile on me once more? She turned her head, looked on me, and smiled. I saw no change in any part of her aspect, from the smiles of bygone days.'

In a few seconds after this smile, she died.

When the family assembled at Hagley for the funeral of my grandmother, my great-grandmother said that the doctor had told her that if her daughter-in-law had another child she would very likely die. A younger relation exclaimed, 'But why didn't

[1] The Rev. The Hon. W. H. Lyttelton, Rector of Hagley.
[2] Mr Gladstone's eldest daughter.

18

you tell Lord Lyttelton?', to which she replied, 'My dear, we never spoke about anything so nasty' (the 'a' being pronounced short, as in 'crass'). This story, which I believe to be authentic, used to comfort me in the First War. I thought that if my father's very existence hung by so tenuous a thread as the prudishness of a Victorian lady, it would surely not be the divine will that his son should be cut off in his prime.

I knew all my uncles very well except my uncle Arthur, who died young. My eldest uncle, Charles, restored the family fortunes, which were in disarray, and by careful and parsimonious management freed the estate of debt and mortgages. My uncle Neville became a full general, and was the first Chief of the Imperial General Staff. My uncle Arthur was Bishop of Southampton and a brilliant scholar. My uncle Robert was a solicitor, though with more knowledge of music than of conveyancing: he was an authority on cricket, and carried his revision of the lbw rule against a somewhat reluctant M.C.C. Another uncle, Spencer, at one time private secretary to his uncle, Mr Gladstone, was a dilettante, and very musical. His hobby was travelling, and as he was possessed of a substantial private fortune, he indulged it to the full. He and his wizened old Italian valet were known to every purser in the P. & O. My uncle Albert was a clergymen of eccentric nature, and still more eccentric appearance; my uncle Edward a canon, and successively headmaster of Hayleybury and Eton; my father a Queen's Counsel and a Cabinet minister.

Of course stories collected round these eight brothers. Some of them concerning the most distinguished are well known, and repetition will not improve them: but others concern one or two of the less well-known brothers.

Uncle Spencer was one of the best-looking men of his day, but contrived to remain a bachelor all his life. 'I don't suppose, Spencer,' said my mother to him once, 'that you have ever kissed a woman in your life.' 'Once—on the brow,' was the abrupt reply.

One day, at Lord Pembroke's dinner table in London, a biological discussion of a desultory nature was being carried on. Spencer was about sixty at the time, rather gaunt, with a grey beard and a piercing eye. Someone said: 'It's always seemed extraordinary to me that whales are mammals.' 'Oh well,' said

a young lady, 'if it comes to that, I suppose we are all mammals.'
'I'm not a mammal,' said Spencer. No one dissented.

It was said that late one evening, in the Red Sea, he was patrolling the boat deck with an attractive lady. He became so enchanted with the velvet Eastern sky, the moon, the stars and his companion that he determined to propose marriage, and carried out this uncharacteristic purpose by writing her a formal letter. At about four in the morning the purser, disturbed by some unusual sound, got up to investigate and found an aristocratic-looking man lying full length in one of the companion ways. He was surprised when he saw that this man was probing underneath the door of one of the cabins with a button hook, and not a little relieved when a letter, not a diamond necklace, was extracted. Uncle Spencer—for it was he—had repented, and taken direct and successful action.

I was devoted to my uncle Neville, the general, who, after he had retired from the Active List, was Governor of the Royal Hospital at Chelsea. He was essentially a commander and leader, rather than a staff officer. He was the only infantry general in the Boer War who emerged with an enhanced reputation from Sir Redvers Buller's command.

Traces of another age, and of the squirearchy, left discernible marks even upon these highly cultivated men, most of whom moved in polite society with graceful ease and distinction. They had a certain robust, even rumbustious side to them.

The paternalism of a Victorian landlord can be traced through the pages of George Eliot or Trollope, and my grandfather, who it is said was rather feckless in financial affairs, was no exception to his class. He collected his rents when his tenants found it convenient to pay, and when they found it difficult to pay, he did not collect.

In him, too, in spite of his great scholarship, there was a strain of antique horse-play. He used to drive about the park and estate at Hagley, the family home, in a dog-cart. When he met one of his tenants on the road, he nearly always flicked him with his whip, and the sturdy and independent Worcestershire yeoman always took a stone and threw it at the Lord. My grandfather used to hunch his shoulders until the stone had hit him or missed him. The greeting with the whip and the retort with the stone were an established and well-liked practice. He was a popular landlord, but the back panel of his dog-cart was dented in many places, as I can testify, for I saw it many years later in the coach house.

This horse-play was carried on amongst his own family. After dinner, as soon as the ladies had left the dining room, my grandfather used to take the soft, uneaten part of his roll, knead it into a ball and throw it at the youngest son as hard as he could, whereupon all eight sons rose up and bombarded him with similar missiles. Port and claret were then circulated.

My aunt Lavinia was the wife of the Bishop of Rochester, afterwards Bishop of Winchester. She must have been very pretty when young, and although she had become almost stone deaf she took a lively, almost a worldly interest in the life around her. In her again you could trace the faint imprint of days when bishops were great figures in the State, and when they dispensed temporal as well as spiritual guidance.

The bishop himself was a saint and a scholar, but he embarrassed his nephews, and indeed many others, by his habit of dropping to his knees in the drawing-room to render thanks for blessings received, and to pray for others to be vouchsafed. It seemed to us that if '*dulce est dissipere in loco*', there should be a similar adage relating to prayer. We felt gauche to be found kneeling on the carpet when the footman announced a visitor, perhaps a stranger.

My eldest aunt, Meriel, married Mr John Talbot, for many years the Member of Parliament for Oxford University, and afterwards a Privy Councillor. This left my aunt Lucy, then nineteen, to act as a mother to the younger children, and particularly to my father, the youngest. She died in 1925, when she was eighty-four and I was thirty-two. I saw and talked to her many times, and though she was pious almost to the point of bigotry, I never felt the slightest constraint in conversation with her, because with me she chiefly spoke of the secular and political part of her life in the great world. From her I learnt that Lord Palmerston's good looks were spoiled by his slate-coloured false teeth. After she had turned into a Liberal she detested Disraeli. When she walked behind him on his way to the House, she says in her diary, 'a grisly sight he is, with his blue grey colour and sham old black curls: he was drest like an old clo' man, in a long light grey coat and loud trousers'.

A witty lady wrote about her: 'Church is Lucy's Public House, and unfortunately no one can get her out of it.' One entry in her diary[1] sheds some light on what devotions could mean in 1863.

> Whenever in London I generally hear but one sermon in church. Today I have heard three. Papa came as usual, and we all went to Whitehall, where Canon Stanley preached beautifully on the Triumphs of Death. St James's in the afternoon: the Bishop of London preached on the use of the historic books of the Bible. . . . Went at 7.0 with her [Mrs Talbot, my aunt Meriel] and Lady Wharncliffe and daughter to a delightful hearty Congregational Service at St Peter's, Windmill Street, where they have just set up a new organ. Good sermon by Mr Kempe on Church music. Papa dropped me at home and so it fell out that I came in for prayers here and a fourth sermon—a short, striking one, Uncle W.'s own, on the Ascension.

When Maid of Honour to the Queen she made her first visit to Osborne early in 1864, and wrote:

> To my satisfaction, we all attended the whole service at Whippingham (except President Hohenlohe) in the morning. Nobody went to church again, so I missed the second service for the first time since I recovered from the fever. Was glad I brought Aubry's sermons and Arch. Leighton with me, but O dear, it doesn't feel much like Sunday.

In 1864 Lucy Lyttelton married Lord Frederick Cavendish, second son of the Duke of Devonshire. She then spread her wings into a wider world and into an environment surrounded with riches and possessions far beyond the scope of her own family.

The Duke of Devonshire had a number of noble houses. In London he inhabited Devonshire House, which stood back from Piccadilly on the site where the Rootes showroom is now established. I remember going to a ball there in 1912 or 1913, and even in those spacious days being impressed by the army of footmen.

A few miles away, near the river, he owned Chiswick House, in which both Fox and Canning died. The Victorian wings which he added have been pulled down, and the building the passer-by now sees is the original Palladian rotunda. With the

---

[1] *The Diary of Lady Frederick Cavendish*, ed. John Bailey, John Murray, 1927.

gardens, it was made over to the municipality in modern times. Chiswick was a sort of villa residence, to which the duke could retire in hot weather, or when oppressed by the excessive hospitality of the London season.

Another ducal place was Bolton Abbey, which the duke used chiefly for shooting. I sadly recall that I was asked there on August 12th, 1914, but had to chuck for obvious reasons. Then there were Holker and Hardwick, and Lismore in Ireland, a smaller house at Eastbourne, and finally Chatsworth, the duke's principal home.

After her marriage in Westminster Abbey, on June 7th, 1864, it was at Chiswick House that my aunt and her husband spent the first days of their honeymoon. She arrived about four o'clock, 'into peaceful summer loveliness and the singing of birds'. Here, the day after their wedding, the young couple began *Westward Ho!* and Carlyle's *French Revolution*; also, 'I spouted to Fred the *Allegro* and the *Penseroso*, and other bits of poetry. I didn't find him utterly unworthy.' And on Friday the 10th: 'We sat and spouted *In Memoriam*, and he to me Canning's "Letter from Lord Russell to Lord Cavendish", with its liberty and patriotism-ums.[1] Also Carlyle. Walked in the Horticultural Gardens after luncheon.'

No two people could have been happier together than Lucy and Frederick Cavendish. She had only one sorrow: she had no children. In all other respects life seemed to them perfect. When Lord Frederick had to go on yeomanry training for a fortnight she writes down the day of his departure as a black day, and wonders how she is to live alone through the fortnight.

Lord Frederick devoted his working life to politics and, if not much of an orator, he justly earned a reputation for thoroughness and integrity in all the affairs or offices in which he was engaged. Through the Lyttelton family he became an intimate of Mr Gladstone, who learned to value his gifts and virtue very highly. In the Sixties Irish affairs were, of course, seldom out of the Prime Minister's mind, and Lord Frederick had made a study of them.

It was in the eighteenth year of their marriage that the Prime Minister, to some people's surprise, appointed him Chief Secretary in Ireland. No one dreamt that this was to prove a sentence of death.

[1] One of the Glynnes' bogus superlatives or suffixes.

Lord Frederick left to spend a day or two in Dublin, and bring himself up to date on Irish affairs before taking up his post. On the morning of Saturday, 6th May, he was sworn in as Chief Secretary. In the evening he decided to walk back through Phoenix Park, and was joined by Mr T. H. Burke, the Permanent Under-Secretary. It was about seven o'clock on a warm spring evening. The two men had much to talk about: the new policy, bringing a new hope to Ireland. They were in deep and earnest conversation, and in sight of the Viceroy's Lodge. They passed through a small group of men, apparently idlers: then, suddenly, there was a shout and both of them were struck down 'and died under the slashing, merciless blows of great knives wielded with fanatical force'.[1] The assassins were members of a terrorist group known as 'The Invincibles'.

The news of the murder first reached the Prime Minister and Mrs Gladstone. It fell to Mrs Gladstone to go round to Carlton House Terrace, Lucy and Frederick's house, and tell Lucy that her golden days were over, and that her happiness was in ruins at her feet. An hour or so later the Prime Minister himself came round. The heroic widow found it in her heart to say to him at once, 'You were right to send him to Ireland.'

A month later Mr Gladstone sent her a poem, '*In mortuum et in memoriam, F.C. multum delecti.*' Two verses of this poem read:

> Another doom perchance is ours
> The subtle touch of chill decay
> The palsying sense of crippled powers
> That ebb, yet will not ebb away.
>
> All this was spared him: from his feet
> He shook the dust away: he trod
> The upward path, with ending meet
> And gave his duteous soul to God.

She replied:

And now, in the midst of all your own heavy and weary struggle, you have gathered all the blessed hopes into these beautiful lines, which will to the end of my life speak peace, yes even joy, to me. I don't know that you can have remembered that I should receive them on our wedding day: the day which I used to note down year after year in my journal as 'our golden day'.

[1] *The Phoenix Park Murders*, Tom Corfe, Hodder & Stoughton, 1968. Mr Corfe has written a brilliant and scholarly book on Irish politics and the events leading up to the murders.

2

My father was twice married, first to Laura Tennant, who died within a year of their wedding, and secondly to 'D.D.' Balfour,[1] whom he married seven years later. I am the only surviving son of his second marriage. Amongst my papers are twelve slim volumes[2] in which my mother has described how the lives of four people were interwoven. The four were my father, Laura, Doll Liddell[3] and my mother. Almost all the letters which passed between them, and some extracts from Doll Liddell's diary, are filed or embodied in my mother's book.

The story of my father's two marriages as it unfolds is so strange and unlikely that after reading it no imagination or quirk of coincidence in a novel would seem to be impossible.

Laura Tennant was the daughter of Sir Charles Tennant, a great figure in Victorian finance who had multiplied his inherited fortune many times. She had three brothers and four sisters living. The Tennant sisters of the time suffered much less constraint than some other young ladies. Margot and Laura Tennant, and for that matter Miss Balfour, belonged to a set known as 'The Souls': they were classed as intellectuals—not so ugly a word as it is today—and some unconventional tendencies were forgiven. They were allowed a freedom which began or forestalled the wider emancipation of women which followed. They talked to young men on a variety of intimate subjects without the presence of a duenna or chaperon. In moments of emotion, amongst The Souls, suitors or sentimental men friends were allowed, and even encouraged, to clasp and kiss ladies of gentle birth and unquestionable virtue in a way which in our

[1] To avoid confusion I have referred to her as Miss Balfour in the narrative up to the date of her marriage to my father.

[2] Some of the quotations in this chapter are from these volumes, which she entitled, 'Interwoven'.

[3] A. G. C. Liddell.

times would have been the prelude to deeper or more lasting attachments.

My maternal grandmother was also a pioneer of liberty for her daughters, and permitted them to ask men to her house and to indulge in *tête-à-tête* conversations, provided that the men were either asked to tea with her, or other methods of vetting them had been adopted.

At the time when Laura first met my father, she was twenty-two and he twenty-eight: she had a suitor called Doll Liddell. My mother described him thus:

Adolphus George Charles Liddell, always known as Doll, was tall and slim. He had a good figure, moved well, and held his handsome head upright. His hair was pale and straw coloured and he had a silky, almost golden beard worn very short, and a moustache nearly hiding his sensitive mouth. His whole appearance was distinguished and unmistakably well bred. One would have recognised him as an aristocrat immediately, indeed he was rather too inbred looking, as he once expressed it to me. He had a way of throwing his head back when he was going to say something tinged with his curious rather sardonic temper, expressed in choice but naked language always touched by humour with a slightly bitter tang. He was born an artist in temperament; books, pictures, poetry, above all beauty in landscape and sea-scape, clouds, stars and moon, transported him and lifted him above the world. For him beauty was religion. If he possibly could he always left the company after late dinner and in any weather went out of doors for a few moments, communing, so he felt, with some remote essence of life. All these things were an intoxication to him, but his exhilarations made him aloof and silent in company, and often he did not speak at all. I have been long walks with him in my time when not a word was uttered. He had a great bevy of friends, both men and women, he loved shooting and fishing and golfing and bicycling with his male companions, and he loved sketching and reading and talking with his female ones and often played the schoolmaster to those young women with whom he was a favourite. His diary is full of his various visits and parties, but every page ——almost—— notes the weather and some aspect of beauty in the street or countryside. Also in cypher there are brief accounts of his loves which were sometimes rather transient.

Doll met Laura through Lady (Frances) Horner. He writes:

26

'Miss T. [Laura Tennant] at dinner [at her father's house] told us about the *Grantully Castle* trip.'[1] This was one of their first meetings and the friendship ripened. He wonders whether 'under her ultra-vivaciousness . . . lives "a good fellow". I haven't yet made out.'

On 26th May: 'Drew Miss Tennant in the morning, water-colour. Something Leonardesque about some of her lines.' From this time onwards there are certain passages in Doll's diaries, in a transparent cypher, written in Greek letters. They are mainly an account of some amorous passages. He fell completely under Laura's spell. My mother wrote:

Few could resist her wonderful charm, her wit and gaiety, her sudden storms of emotion, her sparkling mind which could not conceal the depths in her stream of life. . . . Laura must have read him easily, except I think in one direction. I doubt if she suspected his suspicion. He often told me how her unrestrained manners, her affectionate gestures, her freedom from convention, made him misjudge her.

He was a visitor at Glen in Peebleshire, her father's house, and wrote:

September 24th. Was shown the Doocot. The Doocot was the girls' sitting room, furnished with many books and pictures, a good fire and windows looking on the garden—green lawns and hills beyond . . . a long talk with occasional fondling—an attractive time. Saw Miss T.'s room, very pretty, hung round with old sporting prints—between the two little beds (Laura's and Margot's) a box for East London poor, then a small turret with a writing table and little shelves about in odd corners with books, altogether a unique apartment from the extraordinary mixture of sport, literature and virtue, like the wonderful little animals themselves. . . . After lunch tennis in the covered court: pretty to see the two little T. marmots play. After tea walked in the dark avenue of firs, talked about the smell of the trees, the sighting of the wings and the darkening twilight, sat on a trunk and held each other, a sweet time, so novel to me to be caressed by anyone I care a bit about.

[1] Actually *Pembroke Castle*. Laura wrote: 'Never was such a menagerie on board, poets, toadies, doctors, cads, and humdrummers worshipping old Gladstone, with which mixture very suddenly poured at Copenhagen three or four kings and about four of their families and suites. . . . The humdrummers have been bores ever since.'

27

They arranged to meet at the house of Laura's cousins. Her brother was a tactful chaperon.

Walked with B.[1] down the Fells towards the wild brown river ... a glorious sunset, the sky above Blackburn Fell was in stripes and bars of black through which glowed a great lake of red gold, a wild west wind roaring through the sky like the wind in *Villette*, a sounding spacious sight sending the blood through the veins and filling the whole soul with a sort of high exulting. We sat on a trunk under the hedge in the twilight, while the wind surged above us and the red gold deepened in the sky and the black drew upon it till at last it went out, or nearly so, leaving an ochre flame in one place above the hill. I looked into the strange grey eyes and saw the oval face close to mine with its knot of twisted hair on *the* day of my life.

Many other incidents of this kind made Doll believe that he had won the day with Laura and that he could regard himself as nearly engaged to her. The affectionate and intimate nature of her letters to him reinforced him in his belief. She christened him Larry, for some unknown reason.

Sunday night. Stanway[2]

Here I am in the same room you may have had, Larry, and I hope you had the picture of Queen Elizabeth by Kirk Patrick Sharpe dancing and a Johnsonian gentleman opposite and a darlin' little crib with a balcony front and pink curtains. Isn't it a divine place Larry? I think I could be happy here if I were Hugo's[3] wife and never 'saw Larry. It is saying a great deal. Today the sun shone brilliantly and the trees looked like cathedral windows traced against the bluest sky.

The Bina [her abbreviated nickname] came down yesterday with the Brodricks, Alfred[4] and Arthur,[5] all nice in their way. Of our conversation Alfred was the salt, Arthur the pepper, St John [Brodrick] the bread and Hilda [Brodrick] the dessert. I felt rather like the milk. We found Hugo and Mary in good form. He is v. amusing and completely unscrupulous.

[1] Her nickname for herself was Bambina.
[2] The beautiful house in the Cotswolds where Lord and Lady Elcho were the hosts.
[3] Lord Elcho, afterwards Lord Wemyss.
[4] My father.
[5] Arthur Balfour.

Arthur is the most interesting of them all . . . because he lives with his windows shut and has a few false windows. He is v. amusing. I don't think he would like me: we are so rectangular—he has a lot of background behind the curtain of flippancy and is grave sometimes. . . . I feel he looks upon me as a strange paradox (partly from Gerald's[1] account of me, partly from self-betrayal—a slight and accidental love of flirting), but that I have got some qualities below the dust heap of frivolity, eccentricity and enthusiasm. . . .

Mary (Lady Elcho) is a dear. Everyone is v. kind. Alfred is quite a support but I am alone. Will you take the little tired Bina in your arms and lay her gently down. . . . Promise whatever happens to help me, though you will have to be very unselfish. . . . Goodbye till Saturday . . . dear, dear old Larry. Goodbye, bless him, from his own B.

From Glen

I had an odious journey—an accident at Leicester which detained us there three hours. . . . The cruel fact was that I slept through the accident and all the glory, being in great danger and knowing it denied me.

Don't you pity me, Larry? We are alone here excepting for a vile man called Richard Drummond, a great tenor with the most horrible decolleté collar. I can see his socks down his neck. . . . As soon as I hear him humming his Italian airs on the stairs I hastily snatch a flannel petticoat from my workbasket.

We are friends, Larry, and you will never cut the string will you—never—and I'll never bite it. You are my Romantic friend and, Larry, don't ever not be it. I love to feel that whatever happens I have one Friend who will not forsake me.

Your own Bina

Towards the end of November Doll was full of fear that Arthur Balfour had proposed to Laura and hardly 'dared to look at an evening paper'.

The day after this entry in his diary he went to stay with the Horners at Mells.

Felt somehow she would be there and sure enough I saw her small figure—pretended not to see it and went out to the brougham: delicious drive, the dear little arms once more round my neck.

[1] Gerald Balfour (brother of Arthur Balfour), who was also in love with her.

29

Two days later, on 1st December, he recorded, 'She won't marry me: she says I am too near herself: odd things females: that she should like all this caressing and not be able to go beyond.' And on 3rd December 'The most miserable day since Feb. 7' (apparently the day he asked Evelyn Charteris[1] to marry him). 'Why I don't know because I have known all along that marriage with B. was not possible.'

During the next few days he hung between despair and hope, and when he was summoned once more to Grosvenor Square[2] and was told that Gerald Balfour had proposed to her on the doorstep and that she had refused him, 'the little flame burnt again. Wonderful little animal.'

By the 1st of January 1885 Laura had returned to Glen. He was at Gosford—the Wemyss' house in East Lothian—and against his better judgment yielded to his longing to see her again and accepted an invitation to go to Glen. He did not enjoy finding the house full of guests. . . . Alfred had arrived the day before.

My heart sank . . . I walked up the glen over the icy road . . . a wonderful night, still as the other world except one faint whisper of waters. Happy, falsely so, a glass of water in the torments.

On 2nd January he writes:

Walked with B. into the wood. We sat down together though it had begun to snow. I took her in my arms: a quaint time and place, the grey night falling in and the snow dripping on us through the trees. Going back she said she kissed A.L. I was torn with jealousy and folly—we both made ourselves very wretched and kissed and almost cried. Very low. I shiver with self-contempt at the thought.

The next day was the date which ended this part of the strange story: it was this very day which was for ever printed on Doll's mind, because on it his hopes and dreams of marriage with Laura vanished. It was not till the evening that he was to know it.

He does not seem to have been suspicious that Alfred Lyttelton was his most dangerous rival. He still hoped and had cause to

[1] Sister of old Lord Wemyss, afterwards Lady De Vesci.
[2] Sir Charles Tennant's house.

hope, but it is true that his hopes were less substantial and that fears and doubts had intruded. He wrote on this day:

After lunch it came down dark, wild and sleety, the great bare hills groaned and the wind wailed. Never so wretched since 1872. Sat with B., she occasionally smiling with tears hardly restrained. . . . One long last kiss. For five minutes I sobbed— very nearly missed the train.

That very evening Alfred had to leave for London. He proposed and Laura accepted. The news of the engagement was published three weeks later, on 28th January. They were married on 21st May 1885.

No one could have had more friends than Alfred. For all his success, his great prowess at games, the promise of a great career, he remained modest. He was gay and sparkling, he was sensitive to other people, and heard the whisper amongst the leaves.

Laura trod lightly across the stage of life: sometimes her foot-fall seemed from another, unearthly world. Here was a creature who opened like a flower to love and life, and she found in Alfred the fulfilment of her longings.

A great many of her letters to her husband are among my papers. He was building up his practice at the Bar and was obliged to be often out of London. When he was away they corresponded almost daily. For example, she wrote from Glen:

My darling sweet. . . .

I am so full of you and myself that I can't begin or end my letter. I can't help thinking nothing of it is true and that I have been sleeping under a lilac tree in full bloom, with the swallows swimming in the blue and roses over the world and sky, and the sweet far-off sound of summer in the air, and a new rush of something never known before in my heart.

He wrote from Newcastle on another occasion:

I don't know how I should have got through another of these most exhausting days if I had known that there was only a telegram instead of one of the winged messengers which bring such delicious freight of love and softness and wit and fire. . . .

I cannot find it in my heart to quote more of the letters, for blowing dust from them and quoting them is like 'watching people dance without hearing the music', and 'Tread softly, because you tread on my dreams' must be my guide.

The idyll was short-lived. The jealous Fates cut off the threads. Just eleven months after her wedding Laura died in childbirth.

Miss Balfour had met Laura before Laura was engaged to my father, and she too had fallen under her spell. She heard from Laura's own lips of the strange physical attraction of Doll Liddell—though his name was not disclosed—her rejection of it, of the feeling that she would not marry him, of the pangs of sorrow and remorse that she should be obliged to hurt him so grievously. When Laura died, my mother wrote, 'Her death was the first real grief I had ever experienced.'

Godfrey Webb now appears briefly on the scene. Like many others, he had been in love with my Balfour grandmother, a beautiful and gracious lady. After she married he took an avuncular interest in her children, and even walked with the two Misses Balfour, aged twelve and thirteen, to their day school. When they grew up he helped to launch them into the great world, where he had innumerable friends, and watched their social success with some of the pride of an impresario. It was at a dinner in his house that Miss D. D. Balfour first met Doll Liddell in 1888, two years after Laura's death. The beginning of their romance followed the pattern of a novelette.

On her return from this dinner-party, Miss Balfour wrote: 'I was unaware I had even made a friend: he got out at Pont Street [her father's house], said good night, and did not even wait to see my door opened.' However, 'the strange, aloof Mr Liddell' had left his 'rugs' in the cab. Clearly they had to be returned, and letters were exchanged. He wrote, in the style of the day, 'It appears that your little green jacket bewitched my coats and persuaded them to hide themselves in order to be longer with it.' He wrote in his diary : 'Filled for the last two days with idiotic fantasies about D.D.: surely signs of incipient insanity.'

They next met at Woodmans, Cobham, Mrs Earle's[1] home. Aunt T., as she was called, was a cousin of Doll's. Her food was the most appetising, her beds the most comfortable, and her flowers the most profuse that I can remember. Doll wrote:

[1] The famous gardener and author of *Potpourri from a Surrey Garden*.

4. My mother as a young woman.

5. My father in middle age.

After dinner strolled about with Miss B.: not a bad business, night in June, scent of spring, stars, attractive young female.

The next day he was annoyed when Harry Cust[1] arrived, but as she was passing, she said she would like a walking stick, there being none other present but mine. After this Miss B. said she would like a walk, so we sallied forth. She put her handkerchief in my pocket. Query: is this derived, or a common dodge? It gave me such a start when I felt a hand putting a handkerchief in my pocket.

Many years later, when she read Doll's diary, she disclaimed all coquetry over the walking stick and the handkerchief, and attributed her apparent forwardness to 'girlish inexperience and crudity'.

He was next asked to stay for a few days in a house near Guildford which her family had rented for the summer. He accepted and the friendship ripened. Two days later he proposed, and was refused. 'Although she kissed me on the lips deliciously, her eyes were as hard as flints: it did so remind me of old days with Bina.'

Miss Balfour wrote: 'Though I was twenty-three . . . and had many ardent friends, like Spencer Lyttelton, Lord Pembroke, Harry Cust, I had never been kissed before. It was a shattering experience, I mean to my self-control, and I longed to see him again.'

He was greatly in love. At this time a crisis broke in the Balfour family: the executors of a rich man who had financed my grandfather's firm demanded immediate repayment of the capital—the firm would fail, the family income would fall to £1,000 a year, the daughters would have to earn a living as governesses. Miss Balfour wondered if her feeling for Doll 'might not grow into the kind of love I know I can give. Why should I throw it away . . . to go and be a governess? I wrote him a letter in which I plainly hinted that I would give him a different answer if he asked me again.' Once she had posted it she had a violent reaction and telegraphed to him that he was not to open the letter. After the letter had been returned, 'I could not feel that

[1] Heir of Lord Brownlow, athlete, scholar and wit, at one time editor of the Pall Mall Gazette. Also a noted philogynist.

I had very nearly married a man as an escape . . . which seemed to me the basest treachery.'

A month or two after this telegram my grandfather averted the crisis by selling some forests and other property in Sweden which belonged to the firm. It afterwards prospered under his control.

At this time Miss Balfour was unhappy, and at odds with her life, but in spite of the great affection which Doll had for her she knew that she could not marry him: 'Something tougher and stronger than my passion held me back.' Despite this, the romantic friendship continued.

Doll paid a visit to the family, who were spending a Scottish holiday at the Spalding Arms, an hotel in New Galloway. One day he walked up the glen with Miss Balfour. He wrote:

D.D. said she was thirsty and went down to the burn to drink. She took up the bright water in her hand and I kissed her pretty wet lips. It was a wonderful evening . . . the sun going down threw a golden veil over the purple hills, the river dark but touched here and there with yellow flashes: the air soft and still. I never thought I should have tasted this sort of thing again: so like the old Inverinat days only the hills are not so high.

Miss Balfour left for the south a day or two later, and his diary reads: 'Two long letters from D.D. which made me think it was all up—very uncertain whether to stop the whole thing.' If he had followed his instinct he would have saved himself much suffering, for the lady wrote, long after:

I see how wide was the gap of age and experience. Doll always chose to treat me as a child, but although very immature and ignorant for my age, when I write of Alfred, I shall perhaps be able to describe the haunting sense I had during the whole of my relationship with Doll that another kind of love and life were waiting for me, though not at this time did it include any image of Alfred.

It was in this same year, 1888, two years after Laura's death, that Miss Balfour came to know Alfred Lyttelton well. She had gone to Schwalbach to take a cure for migraine, and there made friends with him, Mary Drew (Mr Gladstone's second daughter), Lady Helen Shaw Stuart, Violet Dickinson and others. It was

34

under Mrs Drew's influence that she became, for a short time at least, a Browning addict. She was invited by Mary Drew to Hawarden,[1] and accepted. She wrote:

Undoubtedly the visit and the friendship with Alfred which began there was a turning-point in my life.

When it came time for me to leave the others at Crewe I wished a hundred times I had never said I would go to Hawarden. I caught my train by an inch, found my evening gown at Chester and arrived at Sandycroft with nothing left behind. There was a Whitechapel[2] waiting for me and in fear and trembling I drove up. The house looked most imposing in the half-light, and I wondered again why I had ventured to come. Miss Helen[3] met me on the stairs with the news that Mrs Drew had been obliged suddenly to go away for one night.

Now Mary Drew was the only member of the whole family whom I had ever seen before—it was a daunting moment.

A sort of courage of despair came to me and I followed Miss Helen quite composedly. No one in the long book-filled library. She was as kind as possible and told me that no one was staying in the house except Alfred Lyttelton—a good unexpected piece of news to me—and her brother Herbert. Then she shewed me my room, large and old-fashioned with a fascinating little round turret room out of it where all the washing things were.

When I came down to dinner I found Mrs Gladstone sitting on a sofa dressed in lilac plush with lots of diamonds. I took to her directly, she was so kind and natural. First Mr Herbert came in, not very distinguished looking, but with nice firm brown eyes. Then came in the old man like a strong suppressed light somehow—he and I sailed in to dinner.

Alfred told me afterwards that he felt so sorry for me having to cope with such a formidable neighbour among people all unknown to me—I had not seen him since his marriage or his sorrows, but we had at least met before—that he resolved to rescue me. Mr Gladstone had been roused to fury by a pamphlet by one Ingersoll, so Alfred—I can see him doing it now—leant forward and said, 'Who is this Ingersoll, uncle William, you have been crossing swords with?' The Grand Old Man responded at once—he was like a tiger who has been flicked by a

---

[1] Home of the Gladstone family.
[2] Apparently a two-wheeled spring dog-cart.
[3] Mr Gladstone's youngest daughter.

whip by his keeper and roared at once. 'Ingersoll,' he exclaimed, 'most paltry mean fellow.'

He abused Ingersoll pretty roundly and altogether got very animated and excited. As I had never heard of Ingersoll before, I confined myself to listening and watching the extraordinary variety of expressions which writhed their way over the wonderful face. I have never seen a head with honour so visibly stamped in every line and turn, and his eyes seem to be always gripping something. Now and again I wondered whether I was in the way, but I was too much interested to worry. After dinner HE disappeared into his own room and we sat talking over the fire— chiefly Alfred and I about Carlyle, and I told him of our visit to Craigenputtock until it was time for bed.

Wed. Sept. 26th '88. Hawarden Castle
No one had told me when Mrs Drew was to be back but by now I felt completely at home. Breakfast was amusing as Mrs Gladstone explained to me all sorts of things about HIS health across his very nose. I could hardly keep serious. 'I have always heard, my dear,' (with a wink) 'that after a certain age the tissues get weak, and I am so afraid,' etc.

The next day, after tea I sat in the library with Alfred and we had a long talk about 'the old engine' as Alfred called him, and then we branched off into a talk about the sort of strength which is most wanted in life, and he quoted Bagehot (I must read the essays). We talked on and on till long after the dressing bell rang and I only managed to be punctual by the skin of my teeth.

I had only originally been invited for two nights and Mary did not arrive till very late but I had telegraphed home to know if I might stay on, as Mary and the rest wanted me to and the answer came next day while we were at breakfast giving me permission.

Arthur and Kathleen Lyttelton[1] arrived and my tremendous friendship with both began then, and of course had a compelling influence on my life.

Kathleen had told me the night before that she couldn't help staring at me because of the extraordinary likeness between us.[2] Laura, she said, had influenced her enormously, little as she had seen of her, 'and that she felt her individuality perpetually'.

The next day was Sunday and I walked to church with Alfred. We were a little late but we marched into the pew behind the old man. He read the lessons in a splendid impressive way with his

---

[1] My uncle Arthur and his wife.
[2] That is, between Laura and D.D.

36

deep sea-beating voice. When the sermon time came he went and sat near the pulpit and listened intently. It was curious to see his wonderful old head against all the others. He looked as if he belonged to a different race, the forehead twice as broad and high, the eyes full of contained fire, the mobile strong scornful mouth, and the passive strength of the chin all starting out by the contrast.

Alfred and I walked home again together—it was a lovely morning. We talked about Mr Gladstone and he said he could not help feeling that G.'s long parliamentary life had debased his argumentation. If there is any doubtful question he sends out whole troops of side skirmishers and fills the air with dust and blinds his antagonist.

We sang anthems after dinner—I was ashamed of my faulty reading. No secular music allowed because Mr G. is a strict Sabbatarian, and Mary said he would notice it in a minute in the next room.

There was another long talk over the fire between Alfred, Mary and me, and I felt sad that this enchanted week was over, for the next day I had to go home. I finished the diary of my Hawarden visit like this: 'When I got home I found that I had been nicknamed "The Grand Old Maid".'

In spite of the letter in which Miss Balfour said she would never marry Doll, they met constantly; though this is perhaps an ill-chosen adverb. His diary is full of expressions such as, 'I am always thinking of my darling child' (October); 'I hear she is getting quite the fashion, dining at the H. of C. with all the crack young men. It makes me sick at heart' (December); and 'My child constantly with me and the pain as bad as ever' (December).

The next year, 1889, Miss Balfour went to Stanway. She found a large shooting party and many friends, Lord and Lady Pembroke, Lord and Lady de Grey, the Bankes, Doll and George Curzon. George Curzon paid court to her. She wrote:

I wish I could reproduce George's swelling eighteenth-century manner and phraseology. 'I had heard of you,' he said, 'as a great addition to our circle, clever, brilliant, a good talker, and I had imagined to myself a woman of a certain age, without any other charms but those of intellect. What do I find? A young buxom creature, charming. . . .'

37

Miss Balfour, from modesty, suppressed the description of her other seductive features.

During the rest of the visit his attentions were explicit and enthusiastic. . . . He and I were alone at the breakfast table for a few moments. . . . I got up to go, but before I had reached the door George got there in front of me, shut it and kissed me with fervour. I was rather bewildered but not displeased and got away—he had no physical attraction for me.

There were other amorous passages on his part in which he was repulsed, but the repulses were forgiven and they remained friends for life.

Doll was wracked with love and jealousy. They walked together.

I had her hand in mine in my pocket, so warm and clutching mine tight. I stopped sometimes and put my arm round her neck and walked or else kissed the dear childish face that looked up at me, half softly, half sadly.

She wrote him a letter which puzzled him; 'it was full of passionate expressions of love for him', but then went on to explain that the affair could go no further because one should not kiss unless one was 'ready to pass the rest of life with one's lover'. She added: 'I wanted my cake of sensation and thrill and have it also intact.'

Later in the year Doll regained his influence, and a continuous stream of letters passed between them. He wrote to her in May, about Laura:

She loved me to the last . . . in the true sense of the word, more than any man, though she looked up to and worshipped a fair being like A.L. more. . . . Close as we have been we have never felt like that, though I have had great and genuine love for you, and a higher one in the beginning for her.

And later:

There is something very strange in the connection between us three. I have once or twice seen Laura looking out of your eyes . . . perhaps she left a part of herself in you to take care of me.

begging me in pathetic terms to be quiet, and yet this morning she was more ready to kiss than usual: so strange are females. I have a kind of weariness coming over me of the hopelessness of the enterprise: she will give no reasons, yet it seems clear she loves me dearly.

Doll had not given up, in her words, 'the idea that he might eventually break down my resistance to our marriage'. His letters generally began 'My sweetest child', and she replied 'Dearest'.

In 1890 the same pattern can be seen: first a compact that nothing more than friendship was to be permitted: then a breakdown of a treaty, then a final parting, daily correspondence, friendship again, then another scene and another parting.

Miss Balfour's mother asked Doll to spend three weeks with the family (which numbered seven at the time), and their numerous guests in a house she had rented in the Tyrol, under the impression that he was an accepted suitor. This impression was no doubt confirmed when they read German together, Faust and Heine and Paul Heyse: surely more proof than a ring.

She was very angry when she discovered that there was no engagement and heaped reproaches on her daughter, and once more there was another final parting, moonlight, copious tears, and on his side hopes fanned by such sweet sorrows. Evan Charteris,[1] writing in November 1889: 'Doll has returned from the Tyrol, and Miss D.D. is still in the market.'

In the middle of this year, 1890, the fourth actor in the drama, Alfred Lyttelton, begins to take the stage. In June he was writing 'My dear Miss Didi', and sending her some books. The letter reads: 'The charm of seeing you so well and happy frame them [these two days] for me in gold. Yours ever faithfully, A.L.'

Miss Balfour, however, still regarded him as a man set apart by his sorrow, though she feels 'the curious conviction that whatever I did or thought I should end by marrying Alfred began to grow'.

Meanwhile Spencer[2] and I were constantly meeting, and when I added Arthur and Kathleen to my Lyttelton circle of friends

[1] Younger son of Lord Wemyss.
[2] My father's elder brother.

there were many opportunities between Cambridge, Mells, Oakdene and my own London home for meetings between Alfred and me. I very soon realised that Kathleen and Arthur and I think Spencer also wished Alfred to marry me, but I also knew that Charty Ribblesdale[1] and Margot did not like the idea at all and in many trivial ways did what they could to prevent it. This may not have been a conscious so much as an instinctive process, for Margot with her exaggerated Tennant egoism felt no one in the world could be mentioned in the same breath as her sister Laura. I remember her slightly absurd phrase, 'Laura had an intellect second to none.' It was fortunate for me that I had loved Laura so dearly for it saved me from any form of resentment—indeed my own feeling in a way echoed theirs. I knew that Alfred was subject to those rapier-like thrusts of criticism which Margot's brilliant wit was supremely good at, but I did not seek to mitigate them, or indeed greatly to fear them. The curious fact remained true, that Laura's great friends were my great friends—Frances Horner, Doll Liddell, Godfrey Webb, Kathleen Lyttelton—among minor friends Harry Cust, George Curzon, old Sidney Colvin, Theresa Earle and so on. The only thing I scarcely realised until I was engaged to Alfred was the interest and love Charty had for him and the devoted affection mixed with gratitude and sympathy which he gave her. I do not know how he would have got through those first years of loneliness except for her constant companionship. The situation was not without its dangers, and I think at times Charty suffered greatly and dreaded the possibility of his second marriage. I only allude to this because it was one of the reasons I think why Alfred and I lingered apart so long.

At the end of 1890 the doctors advised that Miss Balfour and one of her brothers, Archie, should spend the winter in a warm climate, and a party was made up of Spencer Lyttelton, Mrs Jekyll and her small son to take a trip to Egypt.

Before they left Miss Balfour plunged into Egyptian history with gusto. Mr Colvin sent her two enormous volumes in French on Egyptian monuments by Perreka Chipiez, and on her last night in England she read till 4 a.m. and finished in triumph. These studies gave her a lifelong interest in Egyptian scarabs, inscriptions and monuments.

The party returned through Sicily and Rome in April. Letters

[1] My father's sister-in-law, Lady Ribblesdale, *née* Charty Tennant.

are exchanged, 'Dear Mr Alfred', 'Dear Miss Didi', but they grow longer and more intimate.

Although he dined several times at Pont Street [she wrote] I saw hardly anything of Alfred that summer. . . . I had begun to wonder whether this curious certainty I had experienced for two or three years was merely a delusion. My pride was a rescuer. . . . I had no intention of engaging in a struggle for him, and I said to myself that if he chose to prefer the Tennants—well, he must. I was not going to put out my hand.

At the end of 1891, the doctors again decided that she should avoid the cold spring and it was arranged that she should join Mrs Jekyll and her son at Bordighera. It was on the eve of her departure that Alfred consulted Frances Horner, who told him he need have no fear. She in turn advised Miss Balfour to be less reserved.

Their meeting began in a stiff and embarrassed way, but suddenly he put all to the test, and there they were in one another's arms, engaged.

She wrote:

Now began again that curious sequence of parallels between Alfred's marriage to Laura and to me. She had also spent the weeks before Easter at Bordighera, and it was mere chance that I should be going to the same place at the same time of year. At least it seemed like a mere chance. . . . For me it had a strange significance.

My mother, with her strong psychical bent, saw the whole story as preordained.

One of the four characters in the story had died. Since 1888 Doll's score in this strange symphony, little did he know it, had been marked *da capo*. Once again he had entertained the same beguiling dreams, once again he had hoped to have won the lady to whom he was passionately devoted. Once again the cup had been snatched from his lips; once again the same man had carried her off; once again the bride wrote to him on her wedding day. He was left alone. He wrote, 'I should have hated Alfred Lyttelton, but I could not.'

41

3

I just remember being taken by my mother, at the age of five, to see Mr Gladstone, my great uncle. I was fascinated by the profusion of his white whiskers. He seemed full of fun and kindness, and did not frighten me at all. No doubt at other times his Olympian gravity may have been a trifle oppressive.

One day my uncle Edward, then about seventeen, was walking in the grounds at Hawarden with the Grand Old Man, who was wrapped in brooding and statesmanlike silence. They came upon a walnut tree over fifty feet high and the boy, who had felt some constraint, thought he should breach the silence, and said, 'That's a magnificent walnut tree, uncle William.' Uncle William came out of his reverie, paused a moment, and then in rolling tones replied, 'I haven't eaten a walnut for thirty and a half' (pronounced 'haf') 'years'—pause—'nor indeed a nut of any kind,' and relapsed once more into silence.

This anecdote must not be taken to demonstrate that silence was a habit to which uncle William had frequent recourse. In society his conversation was lively and copious. His letters too, a vast number of which were in his own hand, were of a Ciceronian complexion, even when writing to friends, or to his wife. Thus, in 1857, when hearing that there was no hope for Lady Lyttelton (my grandmother), who was very ill, he wrote to his wife: 'I have been in many minds about my duty today, and I was all but ready to break the bonds of the high obligations that have kept me here with reference to the Marriage Bill.'

Mr Gladstone's armoury in debate was truly formidable. Lloyd George, himself one of the great parliamentarians (and I like to remember that I sat in the House of Commons with him), told me one evening that when he was first a Member he made a somewhat flippant and disrespectful speech about Mr Gladstone. The reader may imagine that the story lost nothing in the telling. 'It was a naughty speech, Oliver, but brilliant you know, the sort of thing I can do. When the old man rose in his place, he devoted quite ten minutes to tearing this cheeky young Welsh attorney to pieces. When he had finished there was nothing left of me. I sat in the gangway riveted by his supreme parliamentary gifts, and was as lost in admiration as if I hadn't been the victim.'

Mr Gladstone introduced the Budget of 1853 on a Monday. On Sunday he went twice to church, and read the *Paradiso*: he acknowledges with some contrition that he had given several hours to his figures even on a Sunday. He read Shakespeare at night, and on Budget day drove and walked with Mrs Gladstone in the morning. He went to the House at 4.30, and spoke for four-and-three-quarter hours.

He received many congratulations. Lord Aberdeen wrote to Prince Albert: 'The display of power was wonderful: it was agreed in all quarters that there had been nothing like the speech for many years.' Lord John Russell wrote to the Queen: 'Mr Pitt in the day of his glory might have been more impressive, but he could not have been more persuasive.' The Queen applauded the speech, and Prince Albert wrote in characteristic vein: 'I have just completed a close and careful perusal of it and should certainly have cheered had I a seat in the House.... Trusting that your Christian humility will not allow you to be dangerously elated, I cannot help sending for your perusal the report which Lord Russell sent to the Queen.'[1]

Is the reference to Christian humility a somewhat wintry joke, or an admonition? The answer must be left in doubt.

It should not be forgotten that his orations were good-humoured, and that sarcasm and wit were brought into play as lightning to set off the rolling thunder of his eloquence.

As today's taxpayer writes a cheque for his income tax, his grimace may be a little less sour when he reads that the Chancellor of 1853 exposed its defects. Thus: '...The inquisition that it entailed: the frauds to which it led: the sense in the public mind of its injustice in laying the same rate upon the holder of idle and secured public funds as upon the industrious trader, as upon the precarious earnings of the professional man.' The grimace may quickly return when he realises that the income tax imposed

[1] For this and subsequent passages cf. Morley's Life of Gladstone.

43

at that time was 7d in the pound and that, for the reasons out-lined above, it was to be abolished entirely in seven years.

The description of Mr Gladstone when Chancellor, 'Heroic in economy', does not seem misplaced. There is a story upon which I have been brought up that he issued an instruction to government departments that no one under the rank of assistant secretary[1] was to put coals on the fire after 4.30 p.m. At the time the price of coal was about 6s per ton at the pit head. The Civil Service, it is said, proved equal to this challenge and issued a counter-measure laying down that the temperature in govern-ment offices was not to fall below 65° Fahrenheit. I believe this story to be authentic.

Mr Gladstone said: 'A Chancellor is not worth his salt if he is not ready to save what are meant by candle ends and cheese parings in the cause of the country.' He appealed to the Foreign Office for a retrenchment in fly leaves and thick folio sheets and so forth.

As one who has conducted many a battle with the Treasury, his great-nephew thinks that these principles have come to be over-rigidly applied. Tens of millions of pounds, for example, have been lost by foolish economies made by the parsimonious alliance between the Treasury and the Office of Works over the sites of our embassies abroad. Some great intentions of state have also been frustrated or greatly delayed by niggardly regard for the present at the expense of wide and fruitful gains in the future.

If there is a clash between the need for economy and wide matters of public policy, the nation must rely upon the wisdom of ministers to strike the balance. In doing so the minister will find the Treasury case, thanks partly to the Gladstonian tradi-tion, argued with force and cogency by men of high intellectual capacity, nurtured upon the delaying strategy of Quintus Fabius Cunctator. On the other hand, this fierce scrutiny over a few hundred pounds provides a striking contrast to a govern-ment department of today (July 1967) which is found to have been over-charged by an aircraft company by about £3,960,000 on a single contract. Nor is this an isolated or unique example.

A bond between my grandfather and Mr Gladstone was the classics. In the midst of his parliamentary duties Mr Gladstone found time to write a massive work on Homer, and many dis-

[1] i.e. about the rank of a full colonel in the Army.

44

quisitions upon classical subjects. My grandfather used to put a
Homer or a Virgil into his pocket before going to the House of
Lords if he thought that the debate was likely to be tedious. He
excelled in translating the classics in both directions. As a
distraction he translated *Samson Agonistes* into Greek, to my mind
a rather superogatory exercise.

An apposite quotation from the classics took the fancy of the
House of Commons. Hear again Mr Gladstone.

He is referring to the remission of £250,000 by the Turkish government—yes, £250,000—which rescued the British government
from an unbalanced budget by enabling some bills to be retired.

Mr. Speaker, Sir,
> ... *Via prima salutis,*
> *Quod minime reris, Graia pandetur ab urbe.*

(A rough translation of these Virgilian lines might be: 'Our
first path to safety, little though we may think it, is held out to
us by a Dago city.' *Graia* in this context is a pejorative word.)

The last classical allusion which I personally heard in the
House of Commons was made by Sir John Anderson. He said,
somewhat ponderously, 'As Horace has it, "If you drive out
nature. . . ."': the rest was drowned by ribald and Boeotian
shouts of the then Labour Party, 'Good old 'orace!' Today he
might be outquoted by his opponents. Be that as it may, the classical tag is as dead as is the custom in my father's day of pronounc-
ing Monsieur as 'Mownseer' in the House of Commons, lest
perchance the speaker should be dubbed Frenchified. Perhaps
we are on the way back to this quaint conceit.

I remember, when criticising some proposal of Sir Stafford
Cripps from the Opposition front bench, saying that if I had not
known of the austerity of his habits, I should have described it as
a 'tipsy dixit'. Only Mr Pickthorn laughed, and I stuck to
English for ever after.

Mr Gladstone was an inveterate versifier. He asked Tennyson
whether he did not consider Carlyle to be a true poet. The answer
was, 'Certainly he is a poet to whom Nature has denied the
faculty of verse.' Speaking of one of his own poems, Mr Gladstone adds, 'I find the case exactly reversed: it is versification
without poetry.'

It is certainly rather engaging to find him rendering the well-known epitaph on Robert Lowe into Italian and Latin. The English is:

> Here lies the body of Robert Lowe;
> Where he's gone to I don't know.
> If to the realms of light and love,
> Farewell to happiness above.
> If, haply, to some lower level,
> We can't congratulate the Devil.

Mr Gladstone's Italian version runs:

> *Qui di Roberto Lowe giace il frale;*
> *L'alma non saprei dir se scenda, o sale:*
> *Se vola in ciel, ne' cieli qual fracasso!*
> *Se in altra parte, quai a Satanasso.*

And the Latin:

> *Roberti Lowe hic corpus jacet;*
> *Qua sit ipse, Musa tacet.*
> *Ad superna si volabit,*
> *Pax e coelis exulabit;*
> *Sin ad Orcum praeceps eat,*
> *Sortem Ditis quis non fleat.*[1]

* * *

I look back to the days of the country-house parties in some of the great houses in England, Scotland and Wales—I have been but seldom in Ireland. Though there are still exceptions, a list of them would now look like extracts from a catalogue of the National Trust.

Some of the rooms and corridors, though not all, of these great houses were cold enough in the winter to have killed off quickly an American of our days. I remember 'seeing over' Belton with the grandfather of the present Lord Wimborne. It is a beautiful house near Grantham, by Christopher Wren, and belongs to the rich Brownlow family. Lord Wimborne said that when he was

---

[1] *The Gladstone Papers*, Cassell, pp. 40–41.

last in the house—about 1912—for a shooting party, the ladies came down to dinner carrying fur rugs.

Whether from mere modesty—and the sight of an ankle was thought provocative—or to prevent death from exposure in country houses, Victorian and Edwardian ladies were clothed in several layers. They were well upholstered above the waist and had reinforcements of shawls always at hand: below the waist there were several petticoats: drawers protected their knees as well as their thighs: in Victorian times pantaloons for the young ladies extended nearly to the ankles, and were visible without scandal.

The tendency towards mere wisps of clothing is quite modern, and did not become marked until after the Great War. For example a popular song, sung by a well-known artiste in about 1913, had a refrain which as far as I can remember ran:

> I've a little pink petti from Peter,
> And a little red petti from John,
> And one blue and yellow
> From some other fellow,
> And one that I haven't got on.

Crinolines and their adjuncts must have been purgatory. A specialist in this subject writes: 'Contemporary advertisements indicate a wide variety of design and material. Thus "woolsey petticoats with patent steel springs and flounced, 10s 9d" (1858), and in the following year "the Victoria crinoline lined with flannel, 25s" would have been for day-wear. The "eighteen-hoop watch-spring petticoat with silk band and tapes, 16s 6d" (of 1860), and "watch-spring skeleton petticoats with ten to 100 springs, 6s 6d to 31s 6d" (1861) would be light enough and large enough for ball dresses. The "Sansflectum crinolines, the hoops covered with refined gutta-percha, 10s 6d–25s" served for wet weather, while "puffed horsehair jupons, 21s–33s" of 1864 indicated that the "cage" was declining in favour.'[1]

In 1860, thick, dull fabrics were à la mode. Ladies equipped themselves for London with bombasine, plush, linsey, kersey and tartaleen (whatever that was). My aunt Lucy, who was a Maid of Honour at the time, arms herself for the Court at Osborne by

[1] From *The History of Underclothes*, by Cecil Willett Cunnington and P. Cunnington, Michael Joseph, 1951.

buying velvet and cloth cloaks, a hat, flowers, a bonnet, boots and shoes, gloves, collars and cuffs, a canezon,[1] a sealskin muff, a linsey petticoat, a set of jet, a buckle, a set of studs and a new gown.

During the less felicitous periods of fashion, in the 1860s, some of the ladies' clothes sound drab indeed. In 1863 my aunt writes 'Lou's[2] trousseau has arrived and causes great excitement. She showed off to us a specially charming plush gown, in colour very like a mouse-coloured Scotch bullock.'

The clothes worn by Victorian ladies of fashion, their insulation in my own family from the erotic influences of the valse or the ballet—the unmarried daughters in the Lyttelton family were not allowed to valse, nor would my grandfather take them to the opera if it included a ballet—the strict rules of chaperonage, the footmen that accompanied them in the street, may give rise to impressions that they lived in a sort of zenana. In one respect at least this was not true, for they equalled and sometimes exceeded the ration of exercise which ladies allow themselves today.

Riding is perhaps the first example. In the country, my aunt thought nothing of going out for a four-hour ride with my grandfather. When at Hagley she was constantly on horseback, and in London she rode very often in Rotten Row at half past twelve, the fashionable hour.

Although it might no longer be true that ladies thought nothing of walking six miles out and six miles back 'to buy a thimble', like Dorothy Wordsworth, they often went on foot about their duties, and for pleasure would sometimes walk for four or five hours across the fields. My aunt walked to church at Witley, five miles out and five miles back. Riding, hunting or walking, they were tougher than might be thought. The father of the present Lord Lovat was born after his mother had returned from a day's hunting.

Though in the Lyttelton family no one would have dreamed of paper chases for both sexes, we hear from Lady Eleanor Stanley (1859) that they were the latest fashion at "fast" country-house parties. She writes: 'The Duchess of Manchester, in getting too hastily over a stile, caught a hoop of her cage in it and went

[1] Apparently a corsage made of lace.
[2] Lady Louise Egerton.

One of my father's letters from Lady Wemyss. The drawing shows Doll Liddell (with club raised), and below, Lady Wemyss.

7. A sketch she did of Lord Rosebery.

regularly head over heels, lighting on her feet with her cage and whole petticoats remaining above her head. They say there was never such a thing seen—and the other ladies hardly knew whether to be thankful or not that a part of her underclothing consisted in a pair of scarlet tartan knickerbockers (the things Charlie shoots in)—which were revealed to the view of all the world in general and the Duc de Malakoff in particular.'[1] The duke's subsequent exclamation, '*C'était diabolique*', seems hardly adequate to the occasion.

In their more sedate manifestation, ladies walked long distances in London, to and from church, or to luncheon, or out shopping. 'I must have walked seven miles today,' writes my aunt.

One of the reasons for such exertions was because they seem to have preferred walking, when the family carriage was not available, to going in an omnibus or a cab. Neither Lady Lansdowne nor Lady Wolverton, nor for that matter several young women whom I knew, had ever been in an omnibus or a hansom cab in their lives. Even in this century Lord Spencer, father of the present Lord Spencer, was caught in a thunderstorm in Piccadilly while walking towards his luncheon. He hailed an omnibus and said to the conductor, 'Put me down, if you please, at 8 Berkeley Square.'

Although they certainly became less colourful, the contrast in men's clothes is not so striking. One of the greatest changes was from the huge chokers of the Regency fashions to the Gladstone collar of mid-century, and the soft, turn-down variety of our own times. Portraits of my immediate ancestors look like a history of the collar, a theme marked *diminuendo* which perhaps had not yet spent itself.

Top hats were a necessary piece of equipment and were the custom, for example, when skating. Again, a man usually carried his top hat into the drawing room when calling on a lady, and this custom persisted into the twentieth century. I remember M. Cambon, the French Ambassador and a friend of my father and mother, sitting in our drawing room with his top hat beside him on the floor, and his gloves laid across it.

The Edwardians admired French cooking as we do now, and the main differences were the vastly greater number of courses

[1] Also from *The History of Underclothes*.

and varieties of food. The mere sight of a menu in a great house of those days provokes an indigestion.

Huge meals were not confined to the rich. We hear from Mr Kilvert[1] that at a time when his total wealth was 'a sovereign in the world, and I owed that', he and three friends had for dinner —no doubt a special occasion—some soup (sent from the vicarage), a leg of mutton roasted, a couple of boiled chickens and bacon, a brace of pheasants from Llysdinan, an apple pie and an apricot jam tart.

My son-in-law's grandfather was Lord Chaplin, 'The Squire'. I remember him well and saw him, in my father's house, put a gold sovereign in the dish, saying, 'Excellent. Give that to the chef with my compliments.' He had a fall out hunting when of advanced years, and broke a rib. Since he weighed nearer 300 than 250 lb., in order to guard against pneumonia the doctors insisted on him sitting upright in his chair and not lying in bed.

He was living at the time, as the guest of his son-in-law, at Londonderry House. The chef reported to Lady Londonderry that he had ordered for dinner some soup, a sole, a pheasant, a jugged hare and a snipe. Lady Londonderry expostulated with her father, and after some argument he gave in rather unwillingly, and said, 'All right, Edie, cut out the snipe.'

Edward VII himself was a trencherman of Olympic class. Two months before he died, when in failing health, he gave the last of his private dinners, and was seen to do full justice to turtle soup, salmon steak, grilled chicken, saddle of mutton, several snipe stuffed with *foie gras*, asparagus, a fruit dish, an enormous iced concoction and a savoury.[2]

Formal entertainment in the 1860s and '70s was provided by dinner parties, balls, drums and breakfasts. Dinner parties did not differ much from those of today, except that they were larger, more formal and I suspect, on the whole, duller. Balls were more magnificent, and the waltz, the quadrille, the lancers and other round dances were the fashion. In my times the valse predominated and a spare collar was useful.

In the evening I wore a tail-coat and white waistcoat three or four times a week in London in the season, almost up to 1939, but I cannot shed many tears that they are no longer *de rigueur*

[1] Kilvert's Diary, ed. William Plomer, Cape, 1964.
[2] Philip Magnus, *King Edward VII*, p. 449.

for the opera, the theatre or the ballroom. Nevertheless, some of the panache, some of the sense of occasion, some of the respect due to the performers on the stage has vanished. Some price has been paid for the comfort of the dinner-jacket or the 'lounge suit'.

When jazz and modern dancing arrived after the Great War —some foxtrots had been introduced in the era of Ethel Levy before the war—Foch, looking at a ballroom, said, '*Je n'ai jamais vu des visages si tristes ni des derrières si gaies.*' Today's dancers seem sometimes to conform to this description, but they probably enjoy themselves just as much as their predecessors.

Although I have attended a 'drum' in my day, they became obsolete before the First War. A drum was a term for an evening party without dancing: guests then were not immune from songs, sometimes sung by the daughter or by a relation of the host and hostess.

A Victorian 'breakfast', and there were many in a season, does require explanation. My aunt Lucy's account of a breakfast at Ashridge in 1859 should induce some sentiment of gratitude that such parties are now extinct, although we have invented the most barbarous of all entertainments, the cocktail party, as a partial substitute.

On 7th July 1858, my aunt left Lord's 'in a raging state of disappointment' because Charles (her eldest brother) had been bowled third ball by a shooter. 'Home a little past two, luncheon, dressing.' She continues:

We went by the four o'clock train to Lady Marian Alford's beautiful breakfast. The train was twenty min. late, and the journey horrid with the dust, which grievously dirtied my new gloves. At Tring, where carriages were to be provided by Lady Marian, we had to wait an hour before they came, then such a scramble for them. We got off at last in a brake with Lady Clarendon and the Villiers, but didn't arrive till seven. Such a beautiful drive, and the place glorious. Eight hundred people were there in the course of the day: heaps that we knew. We sat, walked and talked, ate some cold dinner and listened to the splendid Grenadier band. At dusk, the band moved under the windows and some dancing began.

After some charming interchanges with the Comte de Paris,

with whom she was obviously much taken, she was unable to find Mrs Gladstone, under whose wing she had come.

His Royal Highness says, '*Mais je voudrais vous ramener à Mme Gladstone.*' '*Monsieur, je crains gêner votre Altesse.*' '*Pas du tout. Mais où resterez vous donc?*' '*Ma soeur est ici, Monseigneur.*' '*Ah! C'est bien donc.*' A beautiful bow, a deep curtsey, and that most exciting and delightful transaction was well over. We stayed till about 10.30. We crammed thirteen into a brake, with Lady Schomberg Kerr and Lady Constance Grosvenor, the others invisible in the dark, and had great fun bumping down the long steep hill, feeling very near upsetting now and then. We waited in the train an hour before it set off, with the nice Wilbrahams who were with us, then everyone went to sleep except me, who only succeeded in getting muzzy and uncomfortable, and we arrived home at two on Sunday morning, feeling wicked.[1] Ate some cold mutton at that dead hour, and went to bed, everyone hideously tired except me.

When a marriage took place, or an eldest son came of age, the festivities and hospitality were generous and widespread. When my uncle came of age there were thirty-eight to dinner at Hagley, and a ball for 500 for the quality. The next day there was a dinner for all who worked for the tenants, a mere 250. Fifty tenants dined at the Lyttelton Arms, and two days later a servants' ball was attended by all the Stourbridge tradespeople and Hagley farmers.

Those who have lately re-read *Can You Forgive Her?* will remember that an engagement to be married was thought as binding on the parties as marriage is today. Jilting was a social crime more heinous than adultery in 1967. It is all the more melancholy to read of the cruel case of the eldest Miss Brougham, who (at Brougham) 'poor thing, poured out to me[2] all the griefs of her nine years' attachment and one year's recognised engagement to the clergyman, Mr Edwardes, brother of Lord Kensington: they are to wait for a better living' (after ten years!).

If so strict a standard was maintained on important matters such as engagements, the protection provided for ladies against other misadventures was even stricter. Young ladies did not walk

[1] For breaking the Sabbath.
[2] My aunt Lucy.

in the streets alone, and my aunt even thought it daring when 'Aggy and I walked along with Herbert' (aged eight) 'and a footman'. Again, when the same two walked from Downing Street to Stratton Street (their grandfather's house), accompanied by a footman, she says, 'Rather scampish, but it was early and the streets empty.' When this is remembered, the impropriety of driving alone in a hansom cab needs no emphasis. Indeed this bizarre prohibition extended in some families into this century, although four-wheeled cabs, for no apparent reason, were permissible.

In the mid-nineteenth century, poverty, unemployment, starvation and squalid homes were amongst the horrors which beset the unfortunate. Domestic service in 1867 was one of the means, not the planned or conscious means, by which some distress was relieved. Families far down the economic scale still employed servants. Even Mr Underwood,[1] whose poverty is described by Miss Yonge as 'grinding', had two servants: one, it is true, 'a scrub'.

In Victorian times the numbers of servants increased very rapidly with the economic scale. The Lyttelton family of those days was not, and rightly, counted rich: yet when my grandfather rented a house at St Leonard's, to give the children the benefit of sea air, besides Lord and Lady Lyttelton and Mrs Talbot there were nine young people and, in addition to Mr Hook (the butler), Numeny (the head nurse) and Amelia (the nurse maid), there were two maids on the third floor, and 'some three or four maids' on the top floor.

When Lord and Lady Frederick Cavendish moved from Holker to Hardwick, in October 1864, she writes:

Fred and I came here alone, under the ducal circumstances of a special train, twenty-two servants, six horse boxes and two carriages.

(No wonder my aunt described Cliveden, at that time the property of the Duke of Sutherland, as 'grand, but not large'.) Reaching the top-most scale, we learn that the royal household, numbering nine, (the Queen dined alone), were served by eight noiseless servants.

[1] In *Pillars of the House*, by C. M. Yonge.

Wages were, to our ideas, shockingly low: indeed they would have been intolerable if the conditions outside had not made lodging, food, clothes, security and, on the whole, good treatment, a refuge and a boon. £8 a year was not an abnormally low wage for a house-maid, and even in 1919, £18 or £20 a year was about the standard wage for maid servants.

All through my grandfather's and grandmother's correspondence, all through my aunt's diaries, all through the literature and fiction of the period, 'good works' loom large. We read of soup kitchens and free meals, help for old people, visits to the sick, schools in which they taught. Mrs Gladstone, even when wife of the Prime Minister with two large houses and a family to look after, found time for good works, which she pursued with unflagging energy for many hours almost every day. Everyone was aware of the heart-rending conditions under which part of the inhabitants of these islands lived; everyone, for example, knew of the workless, the starvation and near starvation in Lancashire when there was a shortage of cotton as a result of the American Civil War; everyone knew when bread was scarce.

The aristocracy and the Church did their best to relieve suffering, but it did not appear incongruous to them that great riches and numerous houses in one ownership should exist side by side with stark poverty. Yet they were on the whole a deeply religious and Christian class. Why did they not realise that what they did fell far short of what was needed?

As this book has no pretensions to be a social history, I can only advance one reason, and that with diffidence. The landowning class was slow to understand how completely the Industrial Revolution had changed the country. Landowners in the past had been accustomed by tradition—and not an ignoble tradition—and by paternal interest in their tenants and farm labourers, to relieve the hardships of the unfortunate, whether caused by age, accident, illness or failure of crops. Broth and a joint, and a bottle of port were carried by the ladies of the house to the cottages of those who were suffering. It was also quite usual for them to spend hours reading to the aged in their homes.

In an agricultural country such as Great Britain was at the time of (say) the battle of Blenheim, supporting a population of under six million, this sort of relief was much more effective than would appear to our modern eyes, first because it was spread over so few people, and secondly because some subsistence can always be wrung from the land. The labourer grew his own vegetables, kept a few hens and some livestock, which gave him a start against starvation, and help from the the great house, the manor or the vicarage did not, so to speak, start from scratch. Once, however, the Industrial Revolution had gathered momentum, it was amongst the new urban and industrial population that the most grievous cases of suffering arose, and relief and help, which had done something for six million people living mainly on the land, now did little or nothing amongst more than twenty-four million, most of whom did not. But England was always a generation too late, as Trevelyan says.

One of the main roots of paternalism in the pejorative sense of the word was the convenient doctrine, apparently endorsed and even preached by the Church, that men and women had been called by the Almighty to their fitting stations in life, and it was a Christian duty to accept these instances of the divine will with resignation and humility. This doctrine also did something to erode the sense of responsibility of man towards his neighbour.

With all its complacency, and sometimes with a hypocrisy which falls little short of the nauseating, here was a society deeply influenced by Christianity and the Church, stable and courageous, which could be moved to indignation by Armenian massacres and Turkish misrule, in which the seeds of liberalism had taken root and were being nurtured: a society, in short, with a compass by which to steer. Those who mock at them should rather turn to the study of the convulsions, the violence, the mass murders, and the materialism of our own times before they can permit themselves a sneer.

It may be asserted that what I have written about the Victorians only portrays the more admirable characters of the age, and paints society as a whole in too favourable colours. I should deny this. The Court, the Church, the Cecils, the Cavendishes, the Stanleys, the Aberdeens, the Spencers, the Gladstones, the Glynnes, and even the Lytteltons, to name only a few, represent a considerable segment of the then national life. Their standards were looked up to and widely followed.

No one would, of course, claim that the society which revolved round Lord Palmerston or Disraeli was either so strict or so pious. The strange case of the free-thinking Lord and Lady Amberley would point to at least one noble family which defied the conventions and rejected the dogmas of the day.

Looking back at my father's family, I can only assert that their rules of conduct, their religious observance and their piety gave them a strong inclination towards virtue and truth.

The Victorians and their immediate descendants no doubt paid a price for the preservation of so many impeccable principles. The worst of them were self-righteous, inhuman and un-Christian towards weakness and misfortune. In general, their stern and unforgiving commination of vice, their threats of ostracism in this world and damnation in the next if a foot slipped from the path of virtue, are not far removed from that most repellent human failing, intolerance.

This attribute persisted up to the end of Queen Victoria's reign, and could even be discerned in the laxer days of Edward VII.

In the comparatively tolerant Lyttelton family, a rebuke was administered to my mother for 'calling' on a lady who had been involved in a serious scandal with Harry Cust, and even my father was doubtful if my mother had not carried tolerance to the point of condonation.

Many pious, church-going Victorians were stuffy and complacent, and could sing without a snigger words which would have rightly shocked Mr Kaunda:

> Can we, whose souls are lighted
> With wisdom from on high,
> Can we to men benighted
> The lamp of life deny?

There was, too, in the upper reaches, a reliance on the unspoken eleventh commandment—not to be found out—which was at least a refuge to those who had broken some of the other ten. But if we are to pass judgment on this age, we have probably more to learn than unlearn.

4

Nearly everyone has examples of how far he can see back over the years. In Norfolk, in the 1920s, I read in the local paper that a man had been charged with stealing flowers from a neighbour's garden. His plea in defence was that he had stolen them to lay on the grave of his brother, who had been killed at the battle of Waterloo. If he had said his half-brother it would have been true.

To me the most vivid link with the remote past was Lord Wemyss—his sobriquet 'the Brigadier'. He was born in 1818, and in 1912 he displayed almost undiminished vigour and alertness. He died in 1914. His Scottish home, as I have described, was at Gosford, near Longniddry in East Lothian. It was a large house, with an imposing marble staircase and a collection of pictures and china of some distinction. As a boy I frequently stayed there, and when my father built a house a few miles away, at Muirfield,[1] visits were constantly exchanged. To the young, Lord Wemyss was a formidable figure. At the luncheon table he would suddenly rap out, 'Sit up, boy!', and if you did not obey at once, the peaches were disallowed. When well over eighty he used to shoot pigeons from a wooden tower forty or fifty feet high, with no rail round the top. Although smokeless powders had already come into vogue, he preferred the old black powder, and I can still remember his face, framed in white Dundreary whiskers, emerging from a mephitic cloud after he had fired. He was reported to have shot snipe in what is now Belgrave Square, and considering his age this seems possible.

His first wife died, and a few years later he married Grace Blackburn, much younger than himself and very good-looking. She adapted herself readily to being the hostess at Gosford, an exacting position in the autumn, because the Firth of Forth was

[1] Highwalls, afterwards Grey Walls, a Lutyens house and now an hotel.

then fashionable, and society with a large 'S' poured in and out of Gosford by the dozens. For example, Lord and Lady Dudley arrived for the shooting with five servants, two ladies' maids, a valet, a keeper and a chauffeur. The Brigadier was annoyed, and sent one or two of them into the village.

Grace Wemyss used to sketch with facility, and often interlarded her letters to my father or mother with portraits. Facing pages 48 and 49 is an example.

Bicycling was a fashionable exercise, but about this time motor cars began to be taken seriously as a means of transport, and not just as curiosities. One of the pioneer owners was Arthur Balfour, a neighbour. I took my first ride in a car in his tiller-steered De Dion Bouton, driven by Mills, his celebrated and revered chauffeur. It had tube ignition, and my pleasure as a child was slightly spoiled when Mills told me that the tube was due for replacement and that we could expect a loud explosion at any moment.

Lord Wemyss went in for steam cars. One, if my memory serves me, was a Serpollet, and another a Locomobile. The boiler of one of these cars was under the front seat and it was the practice, before tackling a steep hill, to stop and gain some increased pressure in the boiler. The posterior of the passenger in the front seat became very hot, and if he or she had followed the modern style of dress it would no doubt have turned a golden brown.

Lord Wemyss' eldest son, Lord Elcho, had early in life got into some financial scrape by speculating on the Stock Exchange. After the account had been settled he had been disinherited, though not cut off with the proverbial shilling. A trust fund of £100,000 had been formed for his benefit, and the income from it was intended to keep him from positive destitution. My father, Arthur Balfour and Maurice Yorke were the trustees. Much later in my life, after my father had died, though I was still in my twenties, A.J.B. said he wished to retire and asked me to act in his place.

Any embarrassment that I may have suffered from being the trustee of a man thirty-six years my senior were many times compensated for by getting to know him intimately. He was one of the most amusing men to be found, and he would be on my short list of 'Charmers I have known'. He was rather a scamp, made no bones about his indiscretions, one of which was a rather formidable mistress. I became much attached to him, at least between financial crises. We never had a hard word, and seldom a dull one.

During my father's lifetime my mother, whose health at this period of her life was not robust, led a social life. When he died she was prostrated by grief. She left the lighted candles without reluctance and her three great interests lay in psychical research, approached from the scientific angle, in her work for the League of Nations,[1] in the drama, in the foundation of the National Theatre, and in writing plays. She had many other interests less dominant than these three. The English Speaking Union, of which she was chairman (Lady Brice being the president), was one. She worked hard in its interest and was still active in promoting it when she died.

She led almost two different and distinct lives. Talking of the early part of her life she often described to me the sinking feeling with which she faced a Victorian shooting party in those unhurried days. The guests did not sweep up in motor cars to Panshanger,[2] Bolton[3] or Powis,[4] and sweep out again with the gravel sputtering when the last shot was fired. You arrived on Monday by train and probably did not leave until the following Saturday at the earliest. The ladies came down to breakfast in one toilette; they perhaps joined the shooters in the field for luncheon in another, they changed into tea-gowns for tea, and swept in to dinner in full fig.

'I'm tired of this buttoning and un-buttoning,' said the small boy who tried to do away with himself, and his sentiment must have been echoed by many a Victorian lady, as she was pressed by her maid into her majestic corsets before dinner after three previous changes during the day. The long meals and succession of courses were not—at shooting parties—illuminated by the conversation of only the best brains. Naturally some of the men guests were asked for their shooting rather than for their wits, and although there were generally guests of influence, taste and education, a whole week of a shooting party tended towards the

[1] For which she received the Grand Cross of the Order of the British Empire.
[2] Home of Lord and Lady Desborough.
[3] Bolton Abbey, Yorkshire home of the Duke of Devonshire.
[4] Powis Castle, home of the Earl of Powis.

59

ponderous. Moreover, the ladies had mostly to be content with their own society.

Shooting was quite a business. During one party at Panshanger my mother slept ill and woke early. She had finished her book, and at about half past seven put on her dressing gown and went down to the library to seek another. There she found Lord de Grey, the greatest shot of the time, drilling his two loaders and assiduously changing his three guns.

He was not pleased to be discovered, for in those days it was considered more praiseworthy to excel by natural and unforced aptitude rather than by hard work and assiduous training, the lack of which is often censured in our own times. 'Unfortunately, Dexter has allowed political ambition to interfere with his cricket,' is in the style of today's comment.

One of the ingredients of charm in a friend to my mind lies in the feeling that you have not got to compete, that you need not strain to keep up: it is difficult to form long and abiding friendships with those who are cleverer, better read and better informed than you, and whose conversation lets you know it. Part of the charm of Arthur Balfour seemed to arise from his presumption that what you were saying was at least on the level of his own thoughts, whether it accorded with them or not.

He could, at the same time, deliver a rebuke so delicately poised that an insensitive recipient, unless on guard, might well miss the deadly nature of the riposte. Winston had asked, on one occasion, whether the whip was to be withdrawn from him, as some report in the *Daily Telegraph* seemed to indicate. He was indignant. No doubt a mistake had been made by the newspaper, wrote A.J.B.

'However,' he continued, 'the mistake was not without some plausible justification. A hasty reading, for example, of such a phrase as "Thank God, we have an Opposition", which occurs, I think, in one of your speeches, is apt to lead to misunderstanding. It was rashly interpreted by some as meaning that the policy of the country would be safer in the hands of the Opposition rather than in the Government's, a meaning clearly inconsistent with Party loyalty. Obviously, it is equally capable of a quite innocent construction. It might, for example, be a pious recognition of the fact that our heaviest trials are sometimes for our good. Or, again, it might mean that a world in which everybody was agreed would be an exceedingly tedious one; or, that an effective Opposition made the Party loyalty burn more brightly.

'There are, in short, countless interpretations, quite consistent with the position I understand to be yours, namely that of a loyal though independent supporter of the present administration.

'Exegesis is a harder task to perform in explaining, or explaining away, a letter which you seem to have written to the electors of Ludlow apparently advising them to vote against the Unionist Candidate.'[1]

The word 'exegesis' is not used from pedantry. If he had written 'explanation', it would have conjured up in the mind of the recipient the phrase 'calls for an explanation'—and nobody ever called for an 'exegesis', a nice neutral word that takes the pus out of the sentence.

I dearly liked Maynard Keynes, but he certainly lacked this particular attribute of not inviting competition or causing strain. He presumed, in an alarming fashion, that you had formed and expressed an opinion only after having absorbed most of what had been written or said upon the subject. 'Ah,' he would exclaim, if you propounded some economic idea—as you thought, of your own—'You have been reading Casel, or the article in the *Revue des Deux Mondes* by Professor Dupont.' You had at once the feeling of a long-distance runner, when the pace set by the leader after a lap or two was likely to prove too fast for you. His omniscience detracted from Maynard's powers as a negotiator. Morgenthau, and the Americans with whom he negotiated after the Second War, were terrified of him, and felt sure that not only were they about to be outsmarted but, worse still, that any resistance that they offered might be opposed by ruthless and unanswerable logic.

'It takes me about a week to recover from a ministerial meeting—my dear Oliver—on an economic subject: I often feel like a woman outraged, and must retire for a while to solitude and reflection after the attempted rape of my reason.' When you yourself are one of the ministers referred to, these remarks apply a certain strain, and give rise to the hope that you will not be engaged upon a discussion about—say—the velocity of circulation with your friend. Would it not be better, you reflect, to

[1] From Kenneth Young's Life of Arthur Balfour, *Arthur James Balfour*, Bell, 1963

confine your friendship to those who are not likely to raise this topic at all or, if they should perchance do so, to know that you could at least keep them at bay?

I think that both my father and my mother had the gift of charm. Reading the letters written to them by friends, I am struck by the warmth of affection which they seem to have evoked—the reward of the flame of friendship kept from the wind by kindly, sheltering hands.

Who would at first sight guess the writer of this letter to my father, written on August 19th, 1891?

My dear old Alf [no one except the writer of this letter ever called my father Alf]:

In your letter is the ring of that true and deep affection upon which, now for twenty-one years, it has been one of the greatest delights of my life to rely. I cannot say how often, as I have been defending arguable policies, or executing rhetorical capers, the sight of your dear old face aglow with sympathy—as I have turned round to the benches, has cheered and helped me to go on. It, with D.D.'s, must come and shine on us in * * *, which we hope to make a pleasant autumnal retreat for jaded politicians.

By the way will you thank D.D. for one of the dearest letters I ever received? I am lying flat in bed, and letters are piled like haystacks around me. She must excuse me since I can only get through a very small proportion. . . .

. . . Love to all your party. Mary keeps well: but the expected guest is tardy in arrival.

Your ever affec
* * *

Again on June 28th, 1899:

Dear old boy,

Your handwriting last week was the next best thing to the sound of your beloved voice and the pressure of your affectionate arm. It is so good, once a week, in the ceaseless, inveterate, almost mechanical throb of official life, to get the life-touch, the electric impulse, of a reminiscence from home. Days and weeks speed by here. Every day is full; every hour devours its successor as well as itself. Six months have gone: and I am still only at the beginning. All this is vastly absorbing to me. I think it, in my narrow concentrated sort of way, the biggest thing in the world.

And therefore it is good now and then to hear a trumpet note from the outside world both to rouse one from the ceaseless labour, and to remind one of other things and fond souls elsewhere.

Won't you and D.D. ever come out here and see for yourselves how wise you were not to be legal member and memberess although, by the way, the former is a post of no small dignity and influence. Which is your year? This next or next after? No one is an Englishman who has not been to India. It is a vast mystery, a prodigious experiment, a genuine glory. But I do not honestly think that the romance is what appeals to me most. It is all duty. I hate to see a British official not slaving his heart out: a department slack or careless: society frivolous or rotten: Tommy Atkins coarse and contemptuous: the English ideal shattered or impaired.

But oh, dear me, why should I bother you with all this? It is all my life but it is not yours. Therefore let me for one second float out of it and back to the good old times and the dear devoted hearts at home. I follow you all in *The Times* and in such letters as we get from those who do not forget. I think you were too sensitive about the Mahdi's head.[1] Kitchener's action did no harm to a single living human soul. Can one say the same of one-tenth of the political acts that one supports or condones? Write to me again some day, old boy.

Give my love to D.D. and to the past; and believe me,

Your ever affec. GEORGE

Yes, the writer was none other than George Curzon, afterwards Marquess Curzon.

A great deal of the unsung qualities of the man come through the pages of these two letters to my father. I have in my possession a dozen or more which show how affectionate, warm-hearted and loyal a friend he was.

St John Brodrick had been Secretary of State for India when the clash between the Viceroy and the Commander-in-Chief in

[1] When Khartoum fell, the Mahdi had General Gordon's body decapitated, and the head exhibited as a trophy to his followers. In 1885 the Mahdi died of smallpox. His tomb was a grandiose building with a white dome, ninety-three feet high, in the centre of Khartoum.

Four days after his victory at Omdurman, Kitchener gave orders that the tomb was to be razed to the ground, and the bones of the Mahdi thrown into the Nile. Someone presented the Mahdi's skull to Kitchener, who thought of giving it to the Royal College of Surgeons, or to a museum. This drastic example of oriental symbolism caused an outcry in Great Britain.

India led to Curzon's resignation. He had, whether from his office or his convictions, supported the Army against his friend. They were not on speaking terms. My father's help was invoked, I believe by St John Brodrick, and he composed the quarrel although the wounds of it were never completely healed. I am now dipping my pen into an inkstand given to my father by St John Brodrick to commemorate the successful issue of his diplomacy.

It is now often forgotten that Lord Curzon when in form, and in form might perhaps be written when not in much pain, was of the 'best company' in the world. I knew him myself quite well: he treated me like a nephew, almost like a son. One day soon after the end of the First War, I went to a ball given by him at Carlton House Terrace. As I shook hands with him at the top of the stairs, where he was receiving the guests, he said, 'Ah, Oliver, good evening. It is my dearest wish, as I know it would have been of your dear father, that you should be affianced to one of my daughters.' I was fairly taken aback. When I told this to Irene and Cimmie, his two eldest daughters, who were great friends of mine, they were enchanted with this old-world wish, and the Trollopian terms in which it had been expressed. It is true that we were great friends but if I had pursued Lord Curzon's wishes and opened a siege, I have to confess that I should certainly have been repulsed in the outworks before even reaching the main fortifications.

I was once lucky enough to hear Lord Curzon recount the story of one of his journeys in the east as a young man. Although the scenes were described in rolling and majestic periods, they were illuminated by humour, and sometimes by almost schoolboy jokes. If only tape recorders had been invented, the replay would have given to posterity a very different view and a more endearing memory of his Lordship than that usually entertained. The fact, too, that his wit was ready and spontaneous was concealed to the casual observer by the excessive formality of his manner and the antique nature of his diction.

One day, the annual dinner of—if my memory serves me—the King Edward VII Memorial Fund was being held. His Royal Highness the Duke of Connaught was in the Chair, and the top table coruscated with Garters, ex-Proconsuls and Ministers. Just as H.R.H. was obviously approaching his peroration, the

64

8. At Eton.

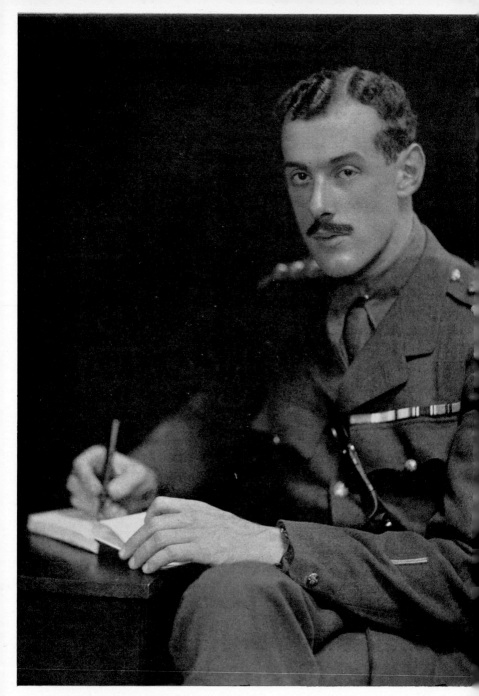

9. In 1918

Secretary realised that F. E. Smith, Lord Birkenhead, who was to propose the vote of thanks, was not in his place. In a panic he hurried down the table, found Lord Curzon, explained the horrifying vacuum and asked him to fill it.

Almost at that moment H.R.H. finished his speech and sat down. Lord Curzon rose from his place, the iron corset which he was obliged to wear creaking, and began in orotund tones: 'Your Royal Highness, my Lords and Gentlemen, the Lord Chancellor,[1] who seldom misses a duty and never a pleasure, has on this occasion missed both.'

Even between the wars life retained many of its formalities, which often served a more useful purpose than would be credited to them today by young ladies in leopard-skin pants and pony tails.

For example, you gave your right arm to the lady whom you were to take in to dinner, and naturally when you sat down you started to talk to her first. Now that this seemingly ridiculous custom has disappeared, how often does the conversation telescope, so to speak, at the soup and leave on each side of the table one stranded guest, not usually the most entertaining. The process of natural rather than formal selection of a mate at dinner is all the more embarrassing when the two guests who must run mute for a time are opposite one another and are man and wife.

Another friend of my mother and father was Henry James. His letter of congratulation to my mother on her engagement contains some characteristic turns of phrase.

'As soon as I knew that you were beyond all hope or help, a victim of matrimony,' it begins, and continues, 'I dedicated to you, mentally, a modest nuptial offering and sent it to the binders (it was a book) that he might give it some little external grace to make up for all it should inwardly lack.' These volumes of short stories, bound in morocco, are now in my library. I am pleased to have them, because Henry James is an author whom I particularly admire, and have lately been re-reading with enhanced pleasure.

Of course there are pieces of *petit point* in his work, but he has wonderful evocative powers of a more impressionist nature. For example:

[1] The 'a' pronounced short, as in 'can'.

The Venetian footfall and the Venetian cry—all talk there, wherever uttered, having the pitch of a call across the water.

That sentence could only be the work of a master craftsman. You see Venice in your mind's eye more sharply and clearly than you would even by looking at a Canaletto.

Behind his delicate irony you can hear a chuckle. I am fond of:

Mrs Varian thought highly of literature, for which she entertained that esteem that is connected with a sense of privation.

And also from *The Portrait of a Lady*:

Madame Merle, I am always kind to those with good Louis Quatorze.

When he moved to Lamb House in Rye, he was no farther than four or five miles from my parents' house at Wittersham. He came over several times when I was at home, and I remember well our first meeting. A small, rather tubby man, with a round head, he was dressed in an impeccable Lovat mixture, topped up by a stiff wing collar and a bow tie. Country clothes, yes, but not such clothes as would have condemned the wearer to any more countrified pursuits than a stroll in a well-paved garden. He had a rare twinkle. He had arrived at one o'clock, for luncheon at 1.30, and found only me at home, and in the library.

He started to talk about receptacles in the characteristic vein belonging to his later period. 'Even when objects, like that box on your mother's table, are empty, the imprint, the impression, yes, perhaps the aura of what it contained or might have contained, seems to cling to it, Oliver. Even empty receptacles have a certain eloquence for those who wonder what gracious or what malevolent hand once filled them. And what did they put there, what gentle potpourri, or skeins of Italian silk?'

Started upon this theme, he wove and rewove a pattern which I can remember, though some of the threads are lost. I was slow to realise that he was marking time, or treading water, to fill in the twenty minutes or so before my father and mother appeared, and that he was trying to avoid embarrassment or effort on my part.

At luncheon he embarked upon a description of Rye society, and the great place in it of the Hennessys. He spiced his account of the climbers and aspirants towards the *bon ton* of Rye with only a distilled drop or two of malice. He elaborated upon the hopes and fears, the savour of success or the tang of snobbery of the members of this little provincial set.

To me the characters in his long novels seem like old friends. I have long known Roderick Hudson, and Isobel, and Ralph, and Lord Warburton. I should recognise them without an introduction if any of them walked in. The only other author whose characters to me are as clear-cut is Proust. It is curious that someone whose style is so obscure should nevertheless flood the scene with light and leave in your memory not puppets but human beings of real flesh and blood, and real thoughts and talk and silences.

Henry James in his very late life was rewriting some of his books and I believe adding things which he had left unsaid, or partly unsaid, rather than in pruning and polishing. It is a blessing that he had not gone far before he died. He too, in his later works, was weaving himself into obscurity, but at all times the actors are living, not-to-be-forgotten persons.

One of my mother's friends was Mrs Patrick Campbell. As a boy I can remember her vividly. She had glorious beauty, black glossy hair, and a voice in the contralto range which stirred your blood.

One August, when she was staying with my father and mother at Muirfield, it came about that she had to go into North Berwick, four or five miles away. A carriage had to be hired, and Mrs Campbell asked me to ride with her. At this time, North Berwick was a fashionable resort, where the rules for dress and deportment were only slightly relaxed. When Philip Sassoon was asked about North Berwick, he had answered 'Rrather rrustic', which was thought an amusing comment on this Deauville of the Firth of Forth.

Mrs Campbell and I went off in our open Victoria, clip-clop down the road to Dirleton. (I was about eleven years old.) She addressed some disintegrating remarks to the coachman, whose shoulders began to heave, and to one or two of the passers-by, who did not seem to appreciate them so much. We talked about the horrors of sea-sickness, and as we approached North Berwick,

Mrs Campbell produced a deer-stalker cap, stuck it on top of her long and luxuriant hair with a couple of enormous pins, and said she felt sickness about to overcome her. Her whole face was overcast with impending tragedy, her gestures became listless, her very complexion seemed to pale, and as we reached the more frequented parts of North Berwick, she leant out of the Victoria and emitted some groans which would have wrung the heart of a family doctor. Amid the spasms, she turned a luminous wink upon me and, when the passers-by averted their gaze, she murmured, 'You should look sick too. You can do it, I know.'

It is not hard to imagine how this production, with a most beautiful woman friend in the principal part, affected a boy of eleven. I remained her abject and devoted friend till the day of her death, although a lot of strains were put upon my affections later in life.

Her romance, and the word seems felicitous in at least most of its varieties, with Bernard Shaw produced at once some of the most intriguing and ridiculous scenes, and drove him to spell out his exasperation to my mother. I have no doubt myself that Mrs Campbell played the whole incident as if it was a passionate romance, in which the deepest feelings of both the leads were inextricably engaged. She was certainly shocked if G.B.S. did not always repeat his lines with at least the dramatic intensity of a grand passion.

It is difficult to think otherwise than that the whole affair was a charade, or a dramatised imitation of real life. I certainly regarded G.B.S. as a *farceur*. Her nickname for him was Joey, Joey being the stage name for a harlequin in the pantomime.

When I was much older I often heard G.B.S. at my mother's table discoursing upon serious subjects, and my impressions of him as a highly entertaining, paradoxical bit of nonsense were enhanced. He talked once—by then I was twenty-six—about *The Intelligent Woman's Guide to Socialism and Capitalism*, and gave vent to a number of epigrams and sophisms of such astonishing naivety and—to commit an oxymoron—of so profound a superficiality as to increase my liking and to decrease my respect for him until it almost disappeared.

I do not believe that in divorce court terms the 'affair' was serious. G.B.S. corresponded with my mother upon the subject. It should be explained that of all the artists whom I have ever known, Mrs Campbell had the least idea of money or expense, and that is saying something. When earning £400 or £500 a week—of Edwardian money—she succeeded in having no more than £30 or £40 left on Monday.

Thus G.B.S. to my mother:

10 Adelphi Terrace, W.C.
22nd Dec. 1912

I hear, O beautiful and gracious D.D., that Stella has made you angry by accusing you, on my behalf, of narrowness of mind. Don't believe it. Not that Stella is a liar (at least to you—we are all liars to people we don't care for); but she is an Italian savage as far as about nine-tenths of my—of *our*—activities are concerned, and cannot be tamed to admit that the least part of her dignity consists in the opinion of other people. Let me illustrate, in the Italian manner, by a diagram. [Here he drew a large circle, blacked in except for one segment which he left blank. In the middle of the circle he drew two hearts.] The two hearts in the middle are yours and mine. The circle is our whole range of interests and activities and sympathies and ties and knowledges. The white segment is that part which is common to us and to Stella; and you will remark that it goes right into our hearts, and that it is flooded with light. But the rest of the circle is darkness to her—doesn't exist for her.

Consequently, when I was rash enough to point out that if I abused Stella's reckless hospitality I should not be treating her quite respectfully, and that (for instance) you would think so, and that I really could not bear that, the fat was in the fire directly; and—well, you know better than I do the form in which my conduct was reported to you.

I don't know what's going to happen now, with all that black part of the diagram building in the part that she understands. It was clear, wasn't it, when she had nothing to do but lie there staring at the ceiling and waiting for what she calls, with her barbarous humour, the tureen, that nothing could occupy and distract her and give her an interest in life but a thrilling love affair. And you will admit also that a more desperate enterprise for an elderly gentleman of fifty-six than to make himself the Romeo of such an affair could hardly be imagined. It was like Richard III and Lady Ann. However, I plunged in head over ears and literally wrote off my fifty-six years, and talked my whitening hairs red again. I never before deliberately tried to make any woman fall in love with me. With Stella I tried all I

69

knew—or rather all I could desire. When the hour for that threatened operation came I was like the lady in *Man and Superman*: I concentrated all my magic. I guessed mystically that with your wonderful gift of affection and my Irish power of weaving love spells we could kill the poison in her blood and raise her out of her illness by a sort of apotheosis. And we have done it: and the glory of the cure justifies the desperation of the remedy.

BUT—what next? No sooner had I succeeded in interesting Stella than she resolved that I should not only fall in love with her—for of course I had done that already—but that all my poor little tricks should be trumped and all my snares tied round my own neck and heels by *her* enormously superior enchantments. When she was ill she was half a child and half an angel: all the mischief in her was dead; and no feeling for her was possible except one of anxious affection. But now that she has sprung into complete life again, the reaction is tremendous: her witcheries and devilries are inconceivable: she plays cat and mouse with me: she teases poor Helen[1] fiendishly: she asks her unlucky brother to play for her and then rolls him in the mud because she has used me to make him nervous; and if one of the worms dares to turn, she is noble and sincere again in a flash, and—since one cannot shut eyes and ears and hammer her with the poker as she deserves—everyone is not only disarmed but infatuated.

This is a nice situation for a respectable married man, whose wife, though neither so beautiful (to other people) nor so subtle nor so delightful nor so lots of other fascinating things as Stella, is none the less a part of himself. I have no scruples about breaking up marriages that are mistakes (perhaps all marriages are, by the way); but if I break with Charlotte I break with everything that holds all of us together. But Stella is such an utter individualist that she would eat up all the faiths in the world as she would eat a Neapolitan ice, if she took a fancy to the ice. However, I haven't the very faintest intention of breaking with Charlotte, nor of cooling one jot to Stella, nor of risking one atom of your regard. How I shall trample my way through, goodness knows; but I shall manage it somehow. Forgive me for burdening you with my confidences; but I want you to know authentically.

G.B.S.

P.S. By the way I am bound to add that Stella seems to have cured *me* of my headaches; so the balance of benefit is on my

---

[1] Her daughter-in-law.

side. She knows too—the witch!—that she has loaded me with debts of this kind.

P.P.S. Why don't you let me read your plays sometimes, since I seem never to hear of their performances until too late?

And again:

My dear D.D., *27th Dec. 1912*

Playing Romeo has given me an ill-divining soul: I cannot foresee the happy ending. It is a delightful game, and oh! so beautifully acted; but she makes me feel my part so deeply that I sometimes forget that I am on the stage. She is so horribly improvident, or rather so shortsighted (Henry Arthur Jones[1] once told me that she could see more clearly than any other woman alive for just six inches in front of her nose); and I, though as improvident as you please, just live in the future. Think of all our fortifications! You with your Alfred, and your social position, and your income, and your deeprooted home; and I with my work, my copyrights, my home, and the lady she elegantly called 'my old Dutch'. And she a widow, unprovided for, an actress, fortyeight, with a man's responsibilities and more than a man's work, dancing on precipices! Who is to be responsible if her heart and her pockets find themselves empty? For a long time yet there will be adorers and worshippers and even offers of substantial salaries; but where is to be the cornerstone of her home? Charles II will die affectionately saying 'Don't let Nelly starve'; and Nelson will die heroically saying 'I bequeath Emma to my country's care'; but what good is that, especially to a proud woman like Stella? I am no use: I am, as you kindly say, kind, or at least not unkind; but my powers force me to a savage selfishness, since I must get my appointed work done before I die or decay much further; and I simply feed on her to nourish my own soul. I am going to get replunged into Socialism by this new paper of Webb's—replunged even into journalism, perhaps: a horror at my age. I have a book on Socialism to write —*the* book on Socialism. I may have plays to write which will be of no use to her—in fact, I *know* that I must give up writing Fannys and Lizas and become again commercially impossible. She is, people think, perfectly able to take care of herself; but I feel, outside all the romance (or perhaps inside it) that she is a starving, unprotected, resourceless daughter or mother or sister of mine whom I must provide for or else be a monster. So it is

[1] The contemporary playwright.

71

perhaps lucky for me that I *am* a monster, capable of sprite-like heartlessness. At least I used to be; and the leopard does not change his spots.

There! You see that the game has possibilities of earnestness; but we—you and I—cannot stay the march of destiny; therefore let us not be in a hurry to bid the devil goodmorning; for 'thy kindness shall not depart' from her; and I can amuse her for a time yet.

You got me into a terrible row by showing her that letter (don't show her this); for she does not like crumples in her rose-leaves; and I had to scud close reefed before the storm, for a full hour before the sun shone again.

As to the boots, that was the Italian savage. She wanted to know where my telephone is (could anyone hear me speaking to her?) and I thoughtlessly explained that it was on the wall between Charlotte's bedroom and mine, and that I had to resort to railway telephone cabins and to the club for our more private conversations. Then, great Heavens! what a storm! To the Italian savage, separate bedrooms are mountains of ice, insults, cruelties, ingratitudes, contemptible impotences. I was overwhelmed with ridicule, and accused of and pitied for never having known any women but suffragettes. In a feeble attempt to explain I said that a woman must have some room into which a man had not a right to burst without knocking and throw his boots about. The scornful audacities which this provoked she has apparently reported to you. For the wretched dastard who would hesitate to fill her bed with his muddiest boots she had nothing but derision. I pity the man who ever presumes on these bravuras; but the suffragette comparison was sincere and significant.

Now may I devote two lines to you? I am not anxious about you, and hope I never shall be; but if I can be of any use in your theatrical projects, come in at any time without knocking and throw your boots about without ceremony if you want to play read or anything else done that is within the power of your devoted

G.B.S.

Italian savage! I have studied these letters carefully. They are capable of other interpretations than my own, which remain, in one word, play-acting.

A superb actress and mistress of the craft, every word, intonation, movement, studied and perfected, Mrs Campbell was not over-critical or jealous of those who she considered were her equals. Thus, she had a genuine affection for Sarah Bernhardt. In *Pelléas et Mélisande*, when they interchanged parts on alternate nights, they tested one another's technique and composure with some practical jokes. Sarah had a horror of frogs, so Mrs Campbell put a clutch of them at the bottom of the well. Sarah Bernhardt as Pelléas peered into the well, caught her breath at the sight of the frogs, but avoided a recoil. The next night Sarah Bernhardt put a large convex mirror at the bottom of the self-same well, so that when Mrs Campbell looked in, she suddenly saw a gigantic mongol-like face gazing back at her. She too did not miss a cue or falter over a line.

I had come across a line of the Poet Laureate, Alfred Austin, and once asked Mrs Campbell if she could make anything of it.

We kiss and part,
Leaving the beloved behind to feel the smart.

Much to my youthful delight, she failed to put them over, and confessed that they were beyond her.

The other day I tested Larry Olivier with the same lines. I guess he could have managed them without more than a titter from the gallery. Sir Laurence, by the way, is another great artist who does not seem to feel jealousy for his rivals. 'What a beautiful, peerless performance of Michael Redgrave in *Uncle Vanya*,' he exclaimed with ringing sincerity.

The last time I saw Sarah Bernhardt was when Moira and I were invited to her dressing room in a London theatre. She had had a leg off, played her part in the play on a chaise-longue, and had a young man in slavish attendance. She had a youthful mouth painted on above her own. Grotesque: until the *voix d'or* gave you a note of the past.

The friendship between Sarah and Stella seemed to me in those days to pass mutual admiration into warm, mutual sympathy. Someone may produce evidence to the contrary, because such lack of jealousy—rivalry, if that is a preferable word—is not an invariable feature of relations in the life of the stage or the opera.

Sir Seymour Fortescue, an equerry of Edward VII, had, I believe, a romantic attachment to Nellie Melba in his early life. He happened to be with his royal master at Monte Carlo and, after a bad Epsom, was short of cash with which to gamble. To his delight he saw that Nellie Melba was singing in *Bohème*, and he forsook the Sporting Club and went to hear her. As soon as the last note had been sung, he sent his card to Nellie, was admitted to her dressing room and, embracing her with fervour, exclaimed, 'Darling Nellie, you were *wonderful*. Your purity of tone, your command of every inflection, your glorious, soaring voice is an unbelievable experience—and the new tenor!!'

'Oh,' said Nellie, *and her face fell.* 'You like him? I don't think much of him myself.' Seymour added: 'I then realised that a new star had appeared in the operatic firmament.' The new tenor was Enrico Caruso, so the courtier was nearer the mark than the *diva*; but then he did not sing.

It is not for me to discuss whether Mrs Campbell's drawers really fell off in *The Second Mrs Tanqueray*, although the modern dramatic scholars would probably say that they did. I remember how shocked I was when George Cornwallis West, after they had married, said in mixed company, 'Darling, do tell the story of how your delicious drawers came off on the stage, and how you recovered them and your composure, without bringing the house down with them.' So you would have thought she could have managed 'leaving the beloved behind to feel the smart', but she failed, and we must therefore continue to regard the line as undeclaimable.

The project by Mrs Campbell to publish all G.B.S.'s correspondence with her led to some exhausting scenes in which unfortunately I shared. It is certain that some of the letters would have been judged by the public to be in bad taste. Phrases like 'Let us jump into bed and perish scandalously together', which were mere *badinage*, would clearly have earned the strictures of the Lord Denning of the day.

Unfortunately Mrs Campbell was very much pressed for money and my mother, having no loose cash at the time, had pawned her diamond tiara and had handed over £1,200 or so to Stella to satisfy her more pressing creditors. This made matters more difficult when we tried to persuade her to suppress some passages which no doubt would have swollen the sales and would have had some *succès de scandale*.

I remember all too clearly one night at 16 Great College Street, when my mother, my wife and I struggled with the great actress until nearly 4 a.m. At least we had a partial success, but if the storm somewhat subsided, the ground-swell continued. Thus Mrs Campbell to my mother in February 1922:

There has been *great trouble*. Joey having heard the book was 'amateurish' and an opinion expressed about Charlotte—revoked—causing no end of awkward feeling between the publishers and myself. The letters have been cut so that there is no 'story' or sincerity of any kind, and the four or six best ones taken out entirely.

Whatever it was you said, caused a revulsion—or convulsion—unfortunately the publishers had the MS (carefully cut by you and me and their reader) in their hands. The whole affair has been intensely boring. I was *absolutely* to blame for having read any of my MS or told anybody at all about the letters.

I was to have gone through the revised proofs *with* Joey, and together we would have decided, independently of all outside opinion, what cuts were necessary. All this is now made *impossible*.

I know it will be a grief to you, and you will realise the immeasurable amount of difference to the interest of my book. So far as I am concerned, I had to learn the lesson to keep my affairs to myself, and if I haven't learnt it now, I deserve to be hanged.

The book will be out quite soon—the serial rights in America first. I am sorry you have had such a lot to do and sickness in the house. I hope baby Oliver is all right. . . . [I was twenty-nine.]

. . . A few days ago I was ill and had to stay in bed. The local clergyman came and sat with me!

Poor Millicent Stone died. She seemed so restful and happy, and smiled as though she were going to a party. Odd that her death didn't upset me.

The birds are singing like mad—I hope you will come here some day.

Your loving Stella.

My mother and Bernard Shaw remained friends until her death. I know that my mother was greatly comforted and her friendship deepened by a letter he wrote to her when my father died. It is in my possession, but I am disinclined to quote from it since it deals with deep emotions. It ends with these words:

And come and close *my* eyes too, when I die, and see me with my mask off as I really was. I almost envy him.

Yours, dear D.D., still marching on

G.B.S.

75

5

What I have described so far would be, in modern jargon, the environment in which I was brought up. I have written elsewhere of my life at Eton. I left with a leaning towards the Classics: was strong in translating Greek and Latin into English: weak in turning English into Greek and Latin.

I still believe that the Classics are a fine discipline. If a boy has to struggle with these ancient and often obdurate languages, he begins to discover how many of our modern ideas and expressions are smoke-screens. He finds out that imprecise thought in the twentieth century leads to imprecise language, and that the chain reaction of imprecise language leading to imprecise thought sets in. The Greeks, after all, did not permit much, if any, difference between reason and words: they made do with the same word for both. Today we should include, of course, other forms of words, musical notation, mathematical formulae and so forth.

I cannot claim that when I put on my cap and gown and became a member of Trinity College, Cambridge, I took life or my studies very seriously. The increased freedom which the university brings to freshmen often manifests itself in large meerschaum pipes, too much beer or port, noise in the streets, even broken lamp posts and plundered policemen's helmets. I indulged in most forms of freedom, though lamp posts and policemen have never appealed to me as targets.

These outbursts are less excusable from an Etonian, because in his last year or two Eton is very like a university.

Freshmen at Trinity live in lodgings, and my rooms were in Hoop Chambers in Bridge Street, opposite the gate of Whewell's Court. My first year's routine went something like this. A marvellous breakfast, beginning with porridge and cream; the newspapers, a careful study of the form book, half an hour to begin an essay for Walter Fletcher, my tutor, on with the cap and gown, and to a lecture. I remember particularly lectures on Theocritus, an author whose Greek I always found elusive and difficult, but one whom I thought I should like if I could get guidance. Luncheon at the Pitt Club. Back to my rooms. In the summer, train to Mildenhall with the Cambridge golfers. Back in Cambridge at 7 p.m. Waved a cap in Hall;[1] dinner at Pitt Club. Bridge and laughter till midnight.

This regime was varied by racing at Newmarket, a little more reading and a little less of lectures. I regret to this day not having had a wider contact in my first year with the social life of the University. When I was asked to a meal with a don I immensely enjoyed myself. To look out of a man's rooms on to the Great Court of Trinity, and to engage in some disputation with a mixed company of dons and undergraduates, till midnight took the outsiders back to their lodgings, was Heaven to me, because I love society, beautiful buildings and furniture, have as good a head for liquor as Jack Dempsey had for a punch, and have seldom turned from the decanter with disgust. Happy but worthless; *carpe diem* my motto: lots of friends, mostly Etonians, Harrovians and Wykehamists.

My father's death in 1913 changed my life and thoughts. Up till that time I had the careless and comfortable feeling that upon any matter of judgment I could fall back on his advice. It would not be true to say that I was very eager to tell him of bookmaker's bills, or overspending when the bank became sullen, but I knew that the kindest and wisest of men was behind me.

Now everything was changed. I was about to come of age, and began to regard myself as head of the family. I worked a little harder, but not enough. Meanwhile, life at Cambridge continued agreeably. My greatest friend was George Llewellyn Davies, adopted son of Sir James Barrie, and we were like brothers. Sometimes we talked with Barrie in his rooms at the Adelphi. He was a sad, little man and smoked a huge disproportionate pipe. He was not whimsy in conversation, and with us he was unexpected and affectionate.

I read in a desultory way, mostly in fields not related to my formal studies, played a little cricket, and in the evening put the world straight as only undergraduates can.

[1] This showed that you were there, but were not going to eat in Hall.

In my second year I was reading Law, and looked down the long avenue which might eventually lead to a practice: a degree, Bar finals, eating dinners, chambers, no briefs, two-guinea briefs, and in the perspective the spire of an income could hardly be discerned in the far background.

I did not find the law uncongenial: it is in the family blood. My father's allegiance to it was deep and warm and he had passed on, as only he could, some of his enthusiasm to me. I was twice marshal to Mr Justice Lawrence, afterwards Lord Trevethin and Lord Chief Justice, and began to see the law at work. The judge had been in chambers with my father and was one of the wisest and kindest men that ever lived. He was the father of Lord Oaksey, who presided at the Nuremberg Trials, and grandfather of Mr John Lawrence, the well-known amateur rider and racing correspondent of today. Horses and the law seem the two predilections of the Lawrence family.

When he was still a Q.C., Lawrie, as he was known, was persuaded by Mrs Lawrence to promise that he would ride in no more steeplechases. One day Lawrie and my father were on circuit together, and were having breakfast with Mrs Lawrence in their lodgings. A parcel of suspicious size, and apparently sent by Wetherbys, was lying on the sideboard. 'What's in that?' she asked. 'Well, never mind, darling, it's for me.' 'Open it, Lawrie, please.' He gave in, and reluctantly revealed his racing silks. 'Oh Lawrie, you promised me faithfully never to ride in another steeplechase.' 'I did, Jessie, and I shall of course keep my promise, but I never said I wouldn't ride in another point-to-point.' It should be said in mitigation of sentence that the difference between a steeplechase and a point-to-point was then much sharper than it is today, when point-to-point courses have so many made-up fences.

Lawrence, my judge, never pretended that he did not know all about life, and its seamier side at that. He never asked, 'Pray what is a tic-tac man?', or, 'May I ask what the phrase "Steady as she goes" may signify?' This convention was started, I believe, by Mr Justice Darling, and arose from the over-rigid application of the rule that judges should read newspapers very sparingly, for fear that they might refer to matters *sub judice*.

One day, at Cardiff, he was trying one of the cases of illicit carnal intercourse with a girl under the age of consent. In sea ports this charge is regarded with great suspicion by the Bench The sailor with his pay in his pocket gets a bedroom in the lodging house; the girl is sent to see him, and at the critical moment in comes the mother, and says 'Pay up, or I shall ring the police.' The defence was in the hands of an inexperienced counsel, who was laboriously cross-examining the girl's mother, the keeper of a lodging house frequented by sailors.

'I wish to ask the witness a question.' 'If it pleases your Lordship.' 'What age was your daughter?' 'Fourteen, m'Lord.' 'Did you allow her to use rouge and lipstick?' 'Yes, m'Lord.' Almost at once he ruled that the case should not go to the jury. I asked the Chief Constable if he was likely to be right, and he said, 'Oh, that's certain: she's tried this on before.'

There was also a Turf fraud case, and at one moment my judge asked a witness, who was a bookmaker, what his book was on the race. '7/1 bar two, m'Lord.' 'Then either you are not telling the truth, or you don't know your business.'

Another case has remained in my memory ever since. A strapping country girl was charged with illicit concealment of birth, a charge which is preferred when evidence of infanticide cannot be laid. The circumstances were extraordinary. A tree had been felled, and in the fork of it, several feet from the ground, the skeleton of a baby had been found. The police started to make enquiries, and eventually found a farm labourer, who, a year before, had been working in a field not far from the tree and had noticed a woman shelter behind it. He knew her name and saw her walk away an hour or two later. No one knew that the girl was *enceinte*, and she had returned to her work the same evening. She broke down under examination, and confessed. She pleaded that the child was still-born.

I still remember the judge's words when he sentenced her. They were an example of humanity and compassion, expressed in simple English: the eloquence of the heart. The girl was in floods of tears, and no one in the court was unmoved. She had been punished enough for this serious offence, he said, and when passing a sentence of one month's imprisonment, he added that as she had been awaiting trial for a month, she would go free at once.

These are not the cases that make the headlines, but everyone there that day benefited from hearing the quality of mercy.

I became restless with my life. I am not naturally studious, and though I have always worked very hard, the work has to come to me with some practical object in view if it is to engage my energies. I always longed to be up and doing, and seek action.

I therefore tried to enlist in Shackleton's Antarctic expedition, but with little hope of being selected, for apart from being very healthy, with an outstanding circulation, I had no scientific knowledge to qualify me. I was of course rejected. If I had not been, I should hardly have heard of the war, and, supposing I had survived, I should have returned to find the war half over and most of my friends dead.

Book Two
1914-1918

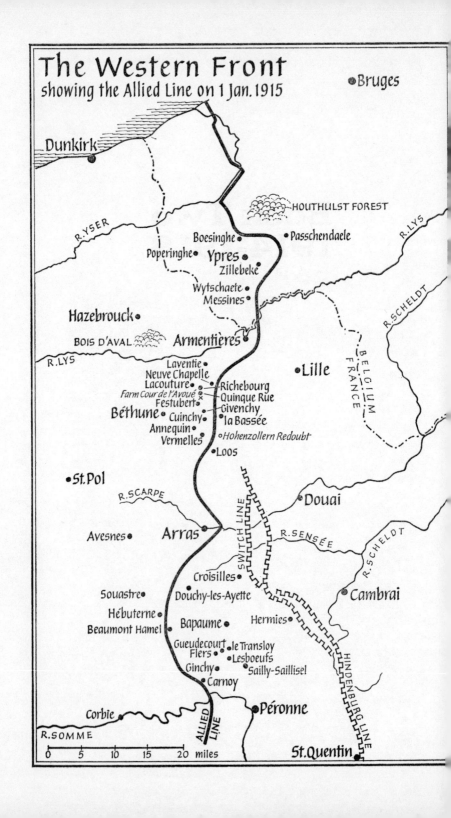

1

I published a book of memoirs in 1962. I was surprised that chapters about the First World War evoked so much interest. It may have been because they described war as seen with the eyes of a regimental officer, and in the closing stages with the eyes of a brigade major. In my experience brigade majors see as much of the line as anyone, and although their place is not in the first wave of an attack, they get their fair share of being shot at. In open warfare they get more. In spite of this I had cut down those pages about the First War. I should have remembered that although I have been a serious student of military history all my life, I had also read with avidity books like *The River War*, *The Memoirs of Sergeant Burgoyne*, *The Letters of Private Wheeler* and the like, which are personal memories of the campaigns in which the authors took part.

Moreover, since I last laid down my pen, the B.B.C. has shown to the public the wide panorama of the First World War. I admired it greatly, in almost every respect, as an historical work. *The Centennial History of the American Civil War* had already shown me how even a few photographs available to the historian can illuminate the subject. For example, the reader no longer has to make his own mental picture of Lincoln or Jefferson, of the military leaders such as Grant, Lee and Jackson, or the naval leaders such as Admirals Faragut and Porter. These photographs, these powerful, rugged, generally bearded faces, bring the American heritage and some of its architects into the very room with us. And here was the B.B.C., with most of the resources of the modern cinema and television at its disposal.

Looking at the B.B.C. production with the eyes of a regimental officer I had many times to exclaim, 'No, it wasn't quite like that.' We, by which I mean both officers and men, did not feel so doom-laden, so utterly disenchanted. We thought we were fighting in a worthy cause, and had no idea that our efforts would one day appear to Miss Littlewood as merely absurd. No one who has not experienced it can know the heart-beat of a battalion, or its discipline and corporate spirit, and how they sustain the individual man, and how the whole greatly exceeds the sum of its parts.

In short, and for these various reasons, I have succumbed to advice and have added to my previous reminiscences. I have drawn almost entirely on letters written to my mother from the Front. I have, of course, selected those that appear to me of interest, but apart from suppressing one or two French expressions, some trivialities, generally about food or clothes, and a name or two, I have not edited them nor even tidied up the grammar.

I joined the Army in August 1914, and served for a few months in the 4th Battalion The Bedfordshire Regiment (Militia), at that time commanded by Lord Salisbury, before being gazetted together with Lord Cranborne, his son, and Arthur Penn to the Grenadier Guards. We were stationed at Dovercourt, and to me there were only three incidents that broke the routine of our garrison life.

The first was the arrival of about a thousand men, in civilian clothes, to be trained. This I have already described in my earlier book.[1]

The second was a visit to the destroyer flotilla at Parkeston, not far from our hotel. I wrote this letter:

We went over to Parkeston yesterday where the destroyer flotilla had just arrived after their battle. It was the most thrilling thing I've done. We went or rather were dragged on board the *Laertes* by a red-bearded young naval officer who said he had enough of the fun of naval fighting, and when I saw the shell-holes, one of which went through three cabins and then burst, I was not surprised. He gave us a full account of the fight which was in broad daylight, though there was a bit of mist. 'We sent in our submarines,' he said, 'to bring out their destroyers, then attacked their destroyers to bring out their cruisers.' Something went wrong then and the destroyers had to engage the German cruisers for an hour, which they were not designed to do. This particular destroyer, the *Laertes*, had a rough time.

[1] *Memoirs*, p. 34.

Four of them[1] 'wheeled across the cruiser to discharge their "mouldies" (torpedoes). The first two got by untouched but they had given the Germans the opportunity of getting the range and the *Laertes*, just as she got off her mouldy, which took effect, was hit twice and disabled.' The fellow said: 'They put a shell in front of us, then one behind, then they hit us twice but the mouldy had taken effect and their cruiser was sinking, so in spite of the fact that we could not steam a knot being broken down we looked all right. God,' said he, 'another cruiser steamed up abaft, getting nearer every second, and we were done: their first shell was a bit short. It was all up. I went aft to talk to the captain (a characteristic touch). Meanwhile we got out a hawser and hitched up on the *Laurel* but at the critical moment it broke and we were left with the cruiser bearing down on us. As the tow rope broke the fellows on the *Laurel* cheered. I shook my fist and cursed them, thinking it was a farewell, then looked round and, by God, there were four of our cruisers steaming x-ty knots an hour out of the mist. Boom whroo-oo-zip. The *Crécy* let off her broadside and one funnel was all that was left on the cruiser's deck. God, I cried like a child', and upon my word he nearly wept again at the mere description of it. Another minute, less, another thirty seconds, and they would have been at the bottom. It must have been a marvellous moment. They swear they sank at least five destroyers.

The third incident was trifling. I had been writing some letters in a small sitting room in the hotel where we had our mess and was taking them to the desk for posting. As I passed through a larger room I saw three officers and a civilian playing bridge. I stopped to watch the play and stood behind the civilian. He had a very poor hand, with one queen and no suit. He had apparently not heard me, and I saw him take a card from the top of the other pack and add it to his hand. The card was the nine of clubs. His opponents were in a fair way towards the game in no trumps when two nines of clubs fell on the same trick. 'Here,' he said, 'that won't do. A fresh deal', and threw his cards on to the table. The officers, who clearly did not know the rules, did the same and the cards were re-dealt. I am glad to say that the civilian still lost the rubber, the last of the evening, and the players dispersed. I said to the civilian, 'Would you care for a drink?' 'Oh, thanks,' he said, 'a whiskey and soda.' I waited till it was half-way to his

[1] Our destroyers.

85

mouth, and then said, 'I saw you cheat at cards just now.' He spluttered, and showered me with some of his drink. 'How dare you? I'll have the law on you.' I repeated the accusation. He then calmed down a little, and said, 'It's only your word against mine.' 'True,' I answered, 'but you will find mine a good deal better than yours. Unless you are out of this town and this hotel by ten tomorrow I shall send for the police.' He went. On the whole I believe in this method.

I remember once driving Harold Macmillan home from the House about ten o'clock. We were taking part in a debate the next day and wished to discuss the line which we were to take. I was opening and he was winding up. I left my car outside his flat in Clarges Street, and after an hour or two came out to drive myself home.

I was somewhat surprised to find a young lady of the town sitting in the back seat. 'You're a nice boy,' she said. 'I'm afraid you're a very bad judge of age.' 'Oh well, I've got a nice warm flat round the corner: what about it?' To which I said, 'You're right, it is cold: I'm tired and I recommend you to buy a bottle of whiskey', pressing two quid into her hand, 'and keep it out with that.' She got out and addressed me through the window. 'I must say it's nice to meet a reel gentleman. Bless you, darling. Sleep well', and off she went.

This is the same method in a more advanced instance. If I had given her in charge, some clubman would surely have said, 'To hell with that for a tale: tell that to the Marines. He's always picking up tarts, I'm told', and so forth. So, a well-spent two quid in my view, and everyone happy: and not an excessive fine for being so careless as to leave my car un-locked.

I pass over our time at Wellington Barracks and our training as Grenadiers to the day when we left for the front.

At this moment the odds against a subaltern in the Brigade of Guards being intact in six months were very long indeed. Those who are left behind have none of the excitement of those who go to the fight, but are left to ponder upon the dread chances. Even those who go, professionals eager for promotion, or temporary officers anxious to fight in a battle before the war ended, feel a lump in their throat at Victoria station.

I wrote these two letters: one from Havre, the other from the trenches (the date of the second is clearly wrong):

As we went out of the station we agreed the worst of the war was over. It certainly was for me but perhaps for Arthur and Bobbety[1] the crossing held something at least as bad.

We arrived at Southampton and reported to a gold-hat of an embarkation officer—a good tempered fellow in spite of all the army form E.B. 1111s on his table, and his telephone. . . . We retired to the hotel where we dined rather indifferently amongst the old dug-outs with white bands on their arms labelled 'Embarkation'.

Bobbety and I after having deposited our kit—a very considerable task—on the boat started to explore Southampton more particularly with a view to pyjamas. Every shop was shut but we eventually rang up an unfortunate fellow, got the garments, made ourselves very genial, and retired, reminding him over our shoulders to vote for Herbert.[2]

Next to the boat, a smallish dark-hulled channel steamer, her decks dripping from the recent rains, and her bar reeking of territorial officers and their hearty 'cheerios'. Bobbety and I to the deck and looking out upon the shipping and lights and cranes fell into a vastly philosophical mood. And so to bed, B. and Sartoris in one cabin, Arthur and I in the other. After finessing got the top bunk, very lucky too. Woke at seven to find us just pushing off down the Solent. Slept again and woke at nine, the ship rolling and pitching like the devil. Asked Arthur if he would like steak and kidney pie—disastrous result. Every time the ship rolled a particularly big roll, Arthur groaned, all the bells in the passage rang at once, the steward shouted, 'Coming, Sir', and in spite of A.'s agony I could not help the most hopeless giggles which gave a very macabre tone to that sickly welter. Arrived greenly at Havre, we reported to another officer and were told to go and stay at the base camp.

Bobbety and I collected the baggage whilst the other two went off to the camp. The kit was twice as large as when we started—a good deal of irritated French from me. Then coffee at the hotel with Major Thornton, a friend of mine, a staff Officer with an abominable French accent and a still more abominable Chinese cur. After dinner and a two-hundred-yard run after to settle it, we arrived at the bottom of a steep and muddy hill which we climbed, sweating. Found ourselves near some huts labelled 'Officers 2nd Division Only', so got in. No valises

[1] Lord Cranborne's nick-name.
[2] Sidney Herbert.

which were to have been sent on. A mile walk after these, nevertheless successful.

Very little to be seen except a row of poles with lights along a rough road cut in the hillside with some tents and huts.

B. and I got into our hut, about fourteen by seven, made of canvas with mica windows, and got to sleep in our valises. Next morning disclosed the camp, all down one side of the valley. I should judge the camp to be about a mile long and 400 yards deep. Our bit consists of about forty huts, about 200 tents and a lot of grey corrugated-iron houses, some for washing, some stores, offices, etc., others messes like this where I write. All very well made and dry, the drainage being an elaborate network of small ditches cut zig-zag down the hillside. Telephones and electric light everywhere.

It froze very hard last night and B. and I were most uncomfortable and cold. This morning had to break the ice with a stick off the bath. Most unpleasant but B. so much amused by me and I by him that hopeless laughter again indulged in. To church at eight in a Y.M.C.A. barn. Faint giggles because A., B., and I were the only present and were addressed by the ecclesiastical but none the less inelastic term 'This congregation here present'. Arthur started it too!! B. and I much shocked!!! The day turned out superb, frosty and clear and a lovely view across the valley.

Now I must be off to re-pack my kit, putting more in my valise and less in the pack, etc., etc. I have got a man's belt and straps[1] but am keeping my pack. We are off via Rouen. Via means anything from forty-eight hours to four weeks.

2nd Battn. Grenadier Guards, 4th Guards Brigade,
British Expeditionary Force
Feb. 21st

To continue. We got into the train at Havre, in which we had two first-class but dirty carriages allotted to us. It was a long drive to the station and rather an extraordinary sight when we got there. Masses of rolling stock, not much light except from the lamps of the A.S.C.[2] men and a good deal of whistling and shouting. Well, we said good-bye to Sartoris, who was for the 1st Battn, and put our valises into one carriage but ourselves into the other. We took all the cushions from the valise carriage and piled them in the middle of the other. Long before we had finished this operation the train had pushed off and to get our

---

[1] It had become an order that officers should wear the men's webbing equipment, to protect them from being picked off.　　[2] Armoured Service Corps.

sleeping bags necessitated much climbing (by me) to the other carriage which vastly amused A. and B. Eventually the order for the night turned out to be O., B., A., this after tossing. Sleep. About six woke up to find us bumping along in a hard frost and thick mist. Felt obliged to wake up B. to tell him that A. asleep looked like a calf's head in a butcher's shop except for the slice of lemon. B. though woken much appreciated this and, chuckling, returned to slumber. We elected to get up about ten. You can imagine what the carriage was like. Paper, smuts, books, boots, sponges, anything all over the floor. However got some sort of order before reaching Abbeville, where we descended upon a bleak world of shunting. Walked stiffly along the platform, met a Grenadier R.T.O. (railway transport officer) who lived in a wagon-lit that didn't move, with three others and several telephones.

Next to the buffet, where we discussed a very good omelette in a very bad atmosphere. Then got some very dirty hot water from a very dirty cold soldier and washed on the plank of the carriage. Great difficulty was that being more or less clean we had to climb in again by the iron rail which made us more dirty than ever. On we went, A. and I shaving from the spirit lamp.

Next lunched, cold turkey, smuts, jelly finding its way into the holes where the cushion buttons should have been, your behind-the-brooch[1] highly developed, very poor soda-water from the sparklet, etc. A long afternoon stopping for an hour here and there, notably on the heights about two hours after Boulogne. About 10.30 arrived Choques, the rail-head, where we reported to a young blear-eyed weary R.T.O. who told us a lorry would call for us at 7.30 next morning.

Another night in the same carriage, another wash (and shave) in even dirtier water, a very smutty pack up and there was the lorry (a motor one) waiting. In we got and then a drive of about five miles, very shaky over the *pavé*,[2] to Béthune,[3] where we breakfasted rather ill in a beastly little room with a fat French officer with button-boots and two cut-away chins who ogled the maid whilst he dipped his bread into his coffee and his face into the sop.

Next, with somewhat of a going-to-sing-at-a-concert feeling to the refilling point to wait for the regimental transport. Whilst on our way met the divisional general and staff eye-glasses, beautiful brown boots and red tabs. Gave them a quivering hand

[1] An expression used by ladies when they dropped crumbs behind their brooches.
[2] Most of the principal roads in the Pas-de-Calais were cobbled.
[3] Most of the place names were omitted for security reasons, and have been added later.

salute, that produced a look of greeting from the general who recognised the guardsman and remembered how the Grenadiers had once or twice turned his mistakes into a mention in despatches. Thank God—at last some Grenadiers under the quartermaster. The men pretty dirty and muddy as to clothes, but that unmistakable 'Tihun' from the sergeant, bang of the heels and immovability from the men. A good deal of talk from the qmr, a most excellent fellow who told us the regiment were in the trenches having gone there the night before and that the C.O. would be glad to see us as they were v. short of officers.

Then we walked with him along a straight, typical French road, very dirty. This was within three miles of the firing line, everything absolutely ordinary except for a good deal of transport going along. The thing that strikes you is the absolute stark, prosaic, ordinary look of everything.

We next waited for a bit at the transport headqrs. for the transport officer, a nice fellow, who came up to my knee about. 'Oh,' said he, 'we'll ride out about twelve so as to be in time for lunch.' So we got up on ponies about that time and set off down this famous road, absolutely straight with wrecked houses on both sides. 'They used to shell this a good bit,' he said, 'but when they did we shelled La Bassée, so they chucked it.' There is a lot of live and let live about it, you know, for if they chose to shell the road they would make it hell for our transport and for our troops relieving. We can also make La Bassée even worse for them, so neither side does anything.

Well, we dismounted at a clearing hospital and got into a communication trench (a good many bullets over our heads), and after walking down it for about three-quarters of a mile arrived at headquarters, which are in a cellar. They were pleased to see us, or tried to be, and we had lunch. Afterwards along a zig-zag trench for about half a mile going through some mined houses on the way and eventually we, i.e. the C.O., second-in-command, the adjutant, A., B. and self came to a square formed by some sandbagged farm buildings and the shattered farm house itself; in the middle of the square a green slime pond. In one of the lean-tos Captain Clive and John Craigie asleep on straw. Introduction. B. was for this company so we left him there and on down a trench labelled Oxford Street. At this juncture we heard boom-boom and the second-in-command, known as 'Ma' Jeffreys,[1] flattened himself down against the side of the trench. 'Big-uns', he said. Then a slight pause and boom-boom, they burst about 500 yards away on the

[1] Major George (afterwards General Lord) Jeffreys.

top of the road about two miles from the point where the clearing hospital is. So on to the famous keep, the centre of a great deal of fighting, a network of trenches with a most comfortable dugout about twelve by six, and five feet high, with a board outside, 'The Guards' Club'. There are four enormous brick stacks roughly like this

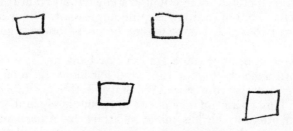

these are absolutely impervious to any kind of shell. The rear two were held by us, the front two by the Germans till the other day, when we rushed them. The line, known as 'the grave of reputation', is much better now as we have consolidated it. I spent the afternoon in reserve, i.e. in the Guards' Club, taking a walk round though of course to cover the whole of our position would take about two hours. The trenches are wonderfully deep and the first day were dry. This is their sort of plan [i.e. section].

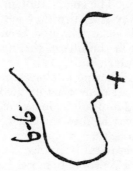

One man out of every twelve on the little step marked with a X on the lookout, the others sit on the steps or in little dugouts in the opposite bank. Sniping is pretty continuous on both sides especially at night. Bullets do not whistle, they sound just like the very sharp crack of a whip. No one shows himself on either side and the sniping is pretty innocuous, though we have a few casualties every time. One is not the least afraid, at least I wasn't, but of course things are quiet, a little shelling now and again, but not much. We lie v. low when it is on, right under the bank or in a dugout. All the men have little fires in this and keep decently warm whilst they sleep, which they do in amazing positions. 'Make way' is the commonest remark as we go along the lines, with elbows rubbing the sides. It is impossible to keep really warm, one is either hot and fuggy or else dankly cold. It is not a very active kind of cold but is quite unpleasant. I have taken a photo or two which I hope to send home by someone going on leave.

You see in front of you a greyish clay bank to about two feet above your head, to your right and left about six men before a traverse stops your view. We have, I think, established a certain kind of ascendancy over the enemy lately and any half hearted attempts he has made at attack have been repulsed without difficulty. At night the parapets are improved and men show themselves freely.

The night I was in, we completed a line of trenches gaining connection with the French (we are the extreme right of the British position) digging quite openly above ground without casualties except one engineer hit in the thigh. This, mark you, within 150 yards of the enemy on only a darkish night.

The R.E. are wonderful, they put up wire about 11.30 when the moon was quite bright, bang in front of a new sap trench, without loss. Amazing. The enemy though are chary of showing themselves and if they start fire they get a hottish reply. We buried a few of their dead who had been out for about three weeks, and who lay in the line of this new trench. There are 120 more about the place but we can't get to them.

This digging is ticklish work but losses are very small generally at it. However, it's all done now in the position from which advance is considered impossible, in face of a place known as the triangle on the railway held by the Germans which is impregnable. It will have to be turned elsewhere if it is ever to fall. The news you will be glad to hear is that we are to go back for a rest at once for at least a week, probably more. I am in rasping cue[1] in No. 4 Coy. with Ridley, a nice fellow who started his war on Aug. 10th, and E. C. Williams, a burly fellow (a famous oar), most delightful with a splendid sense of humour and a most cheerful pessimism, which he thinks is necessary for the campaigner. The rest of the regiment is marvellous. I don't suppose you could find better fellows. Most of them I know, they are

---

[1] Slang expression used by undergraduates at billiards.

superb, it is most awful fun, even in the trenches and in billets, where we have just come, even better. I will write more about billets and the others next time.

About supplies, Socks are always useful but food (tinned), potted meat, port and a few bottles of beer would be much appreciated. Port is the most pressing idea. All property is common.

The next letter describes going into the trenches.

[Received March 5th, 1915]

Billets. Béthune

We are resting now and very pleasant it is. No. 4 Coy are in comfortable billets and Oliver very popular with the proprietors on whom he airs a little French slang. The room in which I write is about the size of the upstair sitting room at Wittersham. Two large grey, plain cupboards on each side of the fire-place, which is filled in with a small black stove. Behind me, grey double doors with thick frosted glass panels. The wall opposite the fire-place plain white-washed. The only ornaments are a sewing-machine and a crucifix. It is very clean, and the furniture, a square deal table with a grey cloth on which is placed a sort of towel with a red border for feeding, and six chairs (plain), does not worry the eye. I have quite a chic though rather too elaborately pious bedroom, to which I mount by a flight of steep deal stairs. The servants are in the next room, the kitchen, and 'Tyson! Tyson!' (my servant, six foot six) is a frequent cry.

Our last two nights in the trenches were simply wonderful in point of weather, I say nights, because it rained in the daytime a little.

One night of our two, we are in reserve which is fairly comfortable (fairly comfortable is a phrase which does not convey very well the milder discomforts of the reserve) and really pretty safe, the other day and night we are actually in the fire trenches.

This is a little disjointed so I will describe going into the trenches, etc. more chronologically.

Beauvray. The square with the mayoral buildings at one end, and ugly cottages and houses on two sides, ugly though the roofs are all beautiful; the road bordered by a few pollarded willows; in what was once the green, about thirty horses belonging to the Transport,[1] tethered in the mud, and twelve or so wagons, grey and muddy. Towards the end near the official buildings, on

[1] i.e., Battalion First Line Transport.

a sort of *pavé* yard very uneven with piles of manure along the top side, a company of 250 men drawn up in column. They are clean, but every uniform shows unmistakable signs of active service, and three or four bearded faces and the canvas covers to every rifle show that appearances have gone a little, even in the 1st Guards. We move off, marching to attention until clear of the town, not a man out of step though they are all carrying an enormous amount of kit, wood, charcoal, etc., every rifle properly sloped, every man looking to his front. A sergeant shouts, 'Hold your 'ead up, Brown, you're not fit to be a blank highlander, put him in the report Idle Marching.' The time by the way is about six o'clock, the light rapidly going. Then out on to the famous high road Béthune–La Bassée. Absolutely straight with trees on both sides and *pavé* underfoot. About four miles of this and then we reach Brigade Headquarters, the beginning of the danger zone. The houses are shattered here on both sides of the road and a few bullets sigh over head and a few strike sparks from the *pavé*. A man is hit and the stretchers bear him away. Two shells then, not far off and most unpleasant as we are in column of fours. However no damages done. It is now moonlight and we turn off the main road, forming single file, the light showing up one side of the men very clearly and making their waterproof sheets glisten, and leaving the other in deep shadow. More bullets along this lane though all over our heads. These are all stray shots as we are out of sight of the enemy, as indeed we have been all along. Under the shadow of a building without a roof, but otherwise undamaged (used as a dressing station), a light: 'Is that you, Oliver?' 'Yes, Bill.' 'Tail of No. 4?' 'Yes.'

We turn into Hertford Street, the communication trench dug by the Hertford Territorials during the day, when there are only very occasional stray bullets about this area. Walking up a communication trench behind a lot of men is a beastly business. The trench is very muddy, and where the parapet is low and the bullets are coming two a minute (though high, mark you) you may bet the line is held up for a few seconds. This goes on for about three parts of a mile, and then we reach some farm buildings, the walls riddled with shell-holes, which make little irregular pools of moonlight on the floors as we file rapidly through; on again, skirting a big barn, without a tile on the roof, and the woodwork fined down by bullets and the moonlight, into a wonderful grey, gauze-like tracery. This barn has kept its dignity, unlike the other broken buildings that have all lost their self-respect. Next we come to Cuinchy church, a red brick tower that you might have passed by in a peace-time motor tour, but now worthy of notice from its sad decay, and its row of wooden crosses which it shelters from the crack, crack of the bullets, as if trying to keep some corner of peace for the dead. This church has seen, you feel, generations of saboted worshippers, and corpses laid to rest by the local undertaker, and now makes a special effort for those whom the war and their platoon sergeants have interred.

Well, Oliver, I'm afraid you're getting a bit too fanciful. Remember though, mother, that it is quite true, and is, whatever else, an undoctored, un-*Daily Mail*-ed, account of my impressions. I will give some more about the trenches themselves, which are much more prosaic, in a letter which I will post the day after tomorrow.

March 15th, 1915

I am afraid this is a very delayed one. We moved out of our decent billets at Béthune into the most frightfully cold and beastly billet. *Par conséquence* we could never sit in it at all, fed at the hotel (bad food of the Fontainebleau order[1]) and sat about in other people's billets, cafés etc. which makes letter writing of this kind impossible. I haven't in fact put pencil to paper since we left our first billets, nor did Soccer Williams, who is the most regular correspondent in the world. Last night I was exactly like the fellow in *Arms and the Man*. I just remember dinner (rather more about it in fact than the other two), then nothing more till I woke up still fully dressed; we had changed at 4.30. I found myself *on* my sleeping bag, not in it. I was, what they call, nearly through. This is what had produced it. Thursday at five, 5 a.m. I thank you, the battalion marched to a certain wood, about four-and-a-half miles. We pulled in again after some further marching at 8.30. Moved off on Friday at 4.55 a.m. and got in at six. Marched to trenches on Sat. at 12.30 and had the most terrific and critical work for forty-eight hours especially at night when we had no sleep at all. Well, more closely——

We had battalion orders on Wednesday night that a general advance from Givenchy to N. of Neuve Chapelle was to be made. That the bombardment of enemy positions would begin at 8.10, that the battalion would be ready to move at five. Excitement and some tension. Turned in for three-and-a-half hours. Then paraded. Pitch dark, every man with an extra bandolier: all our transport of course: three motor machine-gun sections attached

[1] I had studied French in a small house in Fontainebleau, where the food did not live up to French standards.

95

to us: haversack rations: O.L. yawning a bit: strong taste of tea and bacon in the mouth, no such feeling in the stomach: 'Have you got your field dressing Lyttelton?' from the doctor: all the same felt intensely exhilarated.

Sergt-major's voice, 'Are you present, No. 13?' Stentorian reply:[1] 'Present SIR.' So on down the company. We move off along the execrable *pavé*. The light began to grow about 5.45 and located a railway embankment with a few trucks and a ditch which we knew of already from another sense than sight. The C.O. and second-in-command came and talked to us, said we were in reserve. Chagrined relief. At 7.30 boom—boooom. We still were marching but we were thinking of fighting. Just then we turned into a dirty French village, the guns began firing like blazes, all the inhabitants turned out. 'La Bassée ce soir? compris Yes English.' We halted here and our cookers passed us along the left side of the road, smoking. The bombardment became simply terrific. People who have been out here all the time say they have never heard anything like it. We were told that there were 400 guns on a frontage of a few miles. The sensation of this sort of artillery fire is not that of sound. You feel it in your ears more than hear it unless it is only about 100 yards away. Well we moved on into a wood where we blobbed, i.e. artillery formation

$$\underline{1} \qquad\qquad\qquad \underline{2}$$
$$\underline{3} \qquad\qquad\qquad \underline{4}$$

the Nos. being coys, each company being blobbed in its turn by platoons. The whole formation then being

$$\underline{1} \quad \underline{2} \qquad\qquad \underline{5} \quad \underline{6}$$
$$\underline{3} \quad \underline{4} \qquad\qquad \underline{7} \quad \underline{8}$$
$$\underline{9} \quad \underline{10} \qquad\qquad \underline{13} \quad \underline{14}$$
$$\underline{11} \quad \underline{12} \qquad\qquad \underline{15} \quad \underline{16}$$

the Nos. being platoons. This is the best formation against shell fire (the intervals and distances are by the way considerable) and we here adopted it, fully thinking that we should see it put to the test. An hour's wait. Hungry. Then a printed order from Sir D. Haig,[2] extracts from same:

The enemy torn by internal strife, etc.
We are about to attack with forty-eight battalions a locality held by three German battalions. . . . Our airmen have driven the enemy from the air. . . .

[1] i.e. from the Platoon sergeant.
[2] Then commanding the 1st Army Corps.

Our magnificent troops, etc. Remember the heritage, etc. Fight for Old England.

Douglas Haig

I have left out 'example' and 'tradition' but they were used, I can assure you. Quick angry comment.

The only true sentence in the whole thing is that about the aviators. Well, there we were until 10.15 when we got our bulletin—Staffords taken trenches Givenchy.[1] Successful operations on left, etc. Twelve o'clock lunch with news that Staffords, 60th and Kings had completely failed to advance at Givenchy and had had terrific casualties. You bet your life it's our turn, was what we thought. Ordered to march. Got out of our wood on to the canal bank.

We were marching in half-platoons with a good distance between, so that the head of the battalion was about one-and-a-half to two miles in front. No explanation of our halt came back, indeed there was none. So we spent about four hours on that damned bank sitting on our packs and talking about supper at the Savoy.

Our field of view was this—on our right, the canal with a very muddy tow path and high bank opposite with telegraph poles and wires broken by shell-fire. All this against a grey sky giving an effect of sordid, beastly desolation. On our side a surprisingly clean little *estaminet* and a wonderfully dirty back yard. Behind that the feathery wood which we had just left. If you looked up the canal you could see a pontoon bridge and an armoured train on the rails firing like blazes with an enormous six-inch gun.

I saw Geoffrey[2] about six. He came riding down the bank: he confirmed the news that the attacks at Givenchy had failed and said that the losses of the three regiments were 800. I now know the position from which these attempts were launched. Our bombardment did not touch the enemy's barbed wire or *chevaux de frise*, chiefly because it was directed on the support trenches and not on the firing line. The Germans had heard of our intentions—indeed they were common talk in Béthune—and had packed their trenches. A lot of our fellows were killed as they swarmed up our own parapets and very few reached the enemy's wire. Murder.

Well, back we went to Béthune, six rather bad miles; followed by dinner (good), sleep for four hours and then back again to our wood. Felt sure we should not be called upon that day, so spent

---

[1] The usual battlefield rumour, and quite untrue.
[2] My first cousin, Major Geoffrey Lyttelton, Welch Regiment.

a most charming time with a novel, though it was too damp to sleep.

About 3.30, the battalion marched to billets at La Préol, a filthy little hole along the canal bank which, if I survive, I shall unquestionably visit and expectorate upon.

Next day we were for the trenches at Givenchy, so we marched soon after one. Two miles or so along the canal bank, then a sharp turn across the pontoon bridge which found us about half a mile from the village which stands up a little from the plain. We go along under the hill by a little red brick path.

I think I will send this off now as I shan't have time to go on till tonight when I swear I will finish off up to date.

The account is continued in the following letter, and describes going into the same trenches, but from a different angle.

March 25th, 1915

I was absolutely prevented from writing when I promised as I had to pay the company and then censor till we went to the trenches. Both these duties are terribly tedious, take hours and involve signing your name 600 or 700 times—I said I would give you some account of the * * * position[1] which is, in the words of the General, the pivot of all manoeuvres against * * * . (As you know it adjoins * * *, of which the same can be said.) Well—we march down the canal with 150 yards between half-platoons, and very unpleasant it is, for though we have only been shelled twice during the relief we always expect it, and of course the canal is a very easy place to range on by a map. After about two miles we cross a pontoon bridge and from here get almost our first view of Givenchy[2] village. It stands up from the plain on a gentle rise on the summit of which is, or rather was, the church. Beyond the church the hill falls away again towards the plain and the Germans. Having crossed the pontoon—a placard on which is stencilled 'Queen's Road'. Queen's Road is a little red brick path along a line of willows, which is the only break in the vast fields of mangles and desolation. Bullets come fast though they are rather high and, *absit omen*, we have never lost men along here. Next past a group of houses—one with a roof, under which a notice announces '4th Brigade Bombing Depot'. Just after this

1 One of the tasks of company officers was to censor the men's letters for security reasons. Officers were also, of course, responsible for their own letters. Here the names were omitted, but the 'position' referred to was 'Givenchy ridge and village'.
2 Some names have been subsequently added.

we set foot on the rise into the village, still on the brick path. On the right about 800 yards away, a factory with a chimney half standing, '*tout criblé de mitraille*'. We are now within 300 yards of the enemy, but the hill hides us from them. The whole ground here is pocked with shell-holes. Just as my platoon were getting into the village they started busting small shrapnel behind us— just too late fortunately. It makes a fairly loud bang and then you hear the bullets singing for about five seconds. There are 300 odd in each shell, but their penetration is small and almost anything is cover from them. We got into the village. It was the most extraordinary sight I have ever seen. A small winding street going up a hill. Every house riddled with shell-holes, what was left of them spitted with bullet marks, making yellowish spots—all over the red walls. As we came round the corner we met a company of the Irish coming out and the narrow way was thronged with men, machine-guns, servants with coals, officers, stretcher-bearers, gunners. The effect of all this life in that place was extraordinary. The village was peopled with a new race, but it had nothing left for them, except a few sleek cats, sleek as you shall learn afterwards. Well, as we came sweating—it was quite warm—and jostling along, they put three small shells into a house by our side. These are known as fizz-bangs as they give no warning. Their effect is very local but they are dangerous from their unheralded arrival.

Well, our men were for a place known as the keep, and I proceeded to get them there as quickly as possible. A barricade of bricks is across the road outside and you get into the keep by a small tunnel under the walls of a house. When you emerge the other side, you find yourself in a square courtyard formed by six houses. The middle was filled with old rifles, cans, and putrefaction. No house had a roof or top storey left, all the ground-floor rooms were holed by shells or loop-holes. I told off my men to these loop-holes, and then let them fall out into a sort of long barn which had some kind of ceiling to the first floor rooms. After which I looked round for company headquarters. They proved to be in the house nearest to the road. Quite a large room on the ground floor. The furniture three ordinary [chairs] and one very dusty red-plush chair. A large round marble-topped table. A bed and some sacking covering holes in the side nearest the road. Four sandbags nailed over the window looking on to the courtyard. The door screened by a bit of old and very ill-smelling carpet, which from its design and from the fact that it was hung by one nail only, gave the whole place a sort of raffish appearance. Next to the door a flight of curved stone steps leading to a cellar filled with straw. Out of the top room there is another where the telephone operator of the 17th Battery sits. The floor is covered with lath, plaster and bricks. My inspection over, I looked out to find the light going and so turned into the cellar. We were here 'in support'. The next day about three we went up into the firing line. To do this, it was then necessary to go along the street for about fifty yards past the church and then into a communication trench beginning by half of a brick wall, about three foot six high—all there is left of a row of houses. The church is an amazing sight. The only thing that is left standing is a sort of shiver of the tower, near the top of which an un-damaged crucifix is perilously hanging. The body of the church looks like a brick yard and a faint red mist hangs over it.

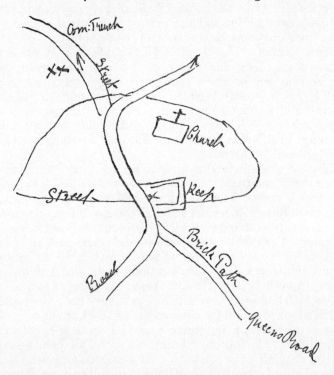

This will give you an idea of the geography of the 'village'. [The oval represents roughly the top of the contour.] X is company headquarters when we are in support, the two XXs, when we are in the line, are the place we turn into the communication trench. All the streets of course are full of shell-holes, bricks, bits of furniture, a cartwheel or two, and a lot of branches of trees. One more sketch map. This of the firing line as we took it over.

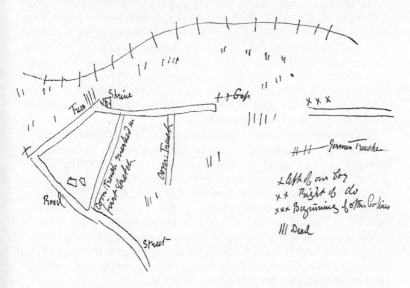

The distance between X and XX was about 300 yards. Of course I have only given you the principal trenches. I don't wish to be harrowing but all the area shown is surely the most ghastly spot—not that I complain or wish myself elsewhere—on this earth.

The village (you know, I expect) was held by the Indians,[1] then by the Germans and after a terrific fight recaptured by the Coldstream and the Camerons. Roughly 15,000 casualties have been incurred round this shattered village. You can hardly put a spade into any of the trenches without coming on the head or foot of some poor devil, and the stench ——

In front of the shrine, mingled with those of December and January, are those of the 1st and 10th March. Between the communication trenches there are a few. In the gap between the two lines, perhaps forty. In front perhaps 300. Amongst them the cats go howling all night—a most unearthly, unnatural sound. They are sleek —— most of the dead are phosphorescent. Enough. It is true, and not so ghastly to see as in the telling. I think it is worth saying and no picture of the place could of course be complete without it. That is my excuse. Well, the first

[1] Units of the Indian Army were fighting in France in the mud of 1915.

thing the brigadier wanted doing was to join up between XX and XXX, about eighty or a hundred yards.

As soon as it was dark, out we got with our working party, sixty men and dug like hell. Most exhilarating—as it was within 200 yards of the enemy. The men worked wonderfully, as indeed they always do when led by officers. A desultory fire was kept up but we had no casualties. It sounds impossible but it is marvellous how inaccurate rifle fire is at night. About every ten minutes, they sent up a rocket or turned a very powerful searchlight on us, whereat we prostrated ourselves, and lay quiet for a minute which makes you quite invisible.

Besides this operation—which is known as digging overland—I had a burying party at work and also every other man over the parapet of the trench we had taken over, making them bulletproof. The Line had been in these trenches for six weeks and at no place would the parapet stop a bullet and everywhere the parados was quite inadequate. These regiments showed the utmost gallantry in the attack but their ways are not ours at other times. When it comes to bayonet work they are as courageous as we are but they haven't got the method, the care or the discipline to make good their gains, or to show the same steadiness in success and reverse as the Brigade.

Well, all this was during our first forty-eight hours and of course we had no sleep but jolly hard work all night and day instead. Total result, that half of the line improved by about 80 per cent, the line joined up and one man in the report for grumbling when warned for duty. N.B. After eight-and-a-half hours' digging, five days confined to barracks was the sentence and 'Utterly unworthy of a Grenadier,' the C.O. remarked to the man. The next time we went in (I will not go into the work we did on the left, which I will describe next time), we were heavily shelled for twenty-six hours. Over my company alone between three o'clock on the 16th to 9.30 on the 17th when the bombardment proper began they burst 340 field-gun shells (about 20-pounders, i.e. quite small) besides a lot of shrapnel and fizz-bangs. At 9.30 they started with Jack Johnsons. By jove they are HELL. You hear them coming for about ten seconds and then the shell explodes. The concussion of the air is so great, if they are anywhere near, that you feel as if your hands and face were chapped. I can't describe the sound they make coming, it is not unlike a train coming up to you at high speed. Thank God, their shooting did not do much damage, except to the village which was already so humbled that no difference was apparent. One big one, however, hit the parapet about thirty yards from me and blew three men to pieces. One fellow we carried away and buried in five oil-sheets. Our total casualties were eleven in the battalion, seven in my company. The real enemy during a shelling is time. With these big ones coming about every one-and-a-half minutes, you feel as if a quarter of an hour would never end, much less a morning or day, and when you come back to billets everything, every cart rattling along the street, sounds like a shell coming for an hour or two. Our trenches now are magnificent; indeed they were then, as the casualties testify.

Am in superb spirits.

April 6th, 1915

There is nothing doing. We have got the line very strong now and expect to be moved back for a rest almost at once and then I suppose off somewhere else to do the same thing. It is wet now and the trenches are in an awful bad state, though of course not under water as they used to be. Things—*absit omen*—are amazingly quiet and the last time, from which we have just returned, the battalion had no casualties, which has never happened before. We are all anxious for our rest as we are getting stale and fed up. When once the line is made it is fearfully dull, you simply sit there praying they won't shell and hoping they will attack, occasionally watching an aeroplane. It is always fascinating to see them surrounded by the little white puffs of shrapnel. They never care a damn and the anti-aircraft gunners say it is like shooting snipe with a revolver. The enemy have been doing a bit more in the air lately, though not much.

I had a very amusing talk with Bobbety yesterday, we nearly always get a good crack now, and great fun it is. The more I see of him the more I like him.

A fellow called Stephenson has joined us, a brother of Guy of that ilk, and is posted to our company.

He is rather too old for our *ménage*, which is very young and knows itself inside out, but he'll learn, he'll learn.

About food. An excellent ham arrived and some fruit on my birthday, besides some other things all very good. Chocolate is rather wasted and matches we always have. Things like Devonshire cream from the Army and Navy, cheese cakes or pastry, *cigarettes* (none have come), a sparklet and the like are all very useful. You might drop a gentle hint to some of my friends and relations to send me food.

A patrol through No Man's Land near Givenchy, and the relief the next day.

I was in charge of an 'officers' patrol' the night before last. We had to crawl out in a mangle field which is planted along the top of * * * hill[1] and our object was to reconnoitre the German trenches which lie over the brow and which cannot be seen from anywhere in our lines. It is a most exciting business being out among the dead men with a revolver. The mangles, which of course have never been gathered, are very pulpy and feel to the touch like a man's head. But we can steer one's way by a sense other than sight. The great thing, and the most difficult thing, is patience. If you go slow enough and keep on your belly you cannot be heard or seen. Instinctively, though, you want to get on and get back quick, and it is hard to restrain the impulse. The Germans sent up several lights but they stood no chance of spotting us among the roots. We steered by a dead man (not by but for, I should say) on the brow and then waited under the parapet of the old German communication trench till one of their flares showed us what we wanted to see. Even then it is difficult to spot exactly how their trenches run, but I believe my *coup d'oeil* gave me the clue. We were about ten yards from the German wire and about twenty-five from their fire trenches, that was the most important thing and showed that their line was a salient and came right up under the brow of the hill. The C.O. and the brigadier were very pleased with the information. I only saw the former—of course if you dig a trench or pull down a house or reconnoitre you always get thanked by the Brigade though they are none of them operations of a really dangerous kind.

One of the really pleasant parts of fighting is coming back to billets after forty-eight wet hours in the trenches. We did it last night. Everyone was pretty muddy but I was worse owing to my crawl in the mangles, being simply caked half an inch deep all over. When it dries it goes quite hard and scaly and can only be washed off. If you attempt to scrape or brush it half the cloth comes away as well.

Just as we set our backs on the village and were coming down to the brick path, the rain stopped, the evening sun showed himself before setting red behind the woods where 'Mother', the big howitzer, is waiting and the poor old chess-board, shell-holed countryside looked almost pleasing. As you walk down you feel that there is a distinct pleasure in being above ground. You are very tired but as you pass two tall standards by the canal bank

[1] Givenchy.

(beyond which no one has yet been hit) you feel much refreshed. By now it is dark and Préol, with the splashes of light round the cookers, the strong smell of rum and tea, the chaff of the men to young 'Square Guts' (a French boy of five), the canal reflecting the lights of the cottages, looked warm and substantial. The smell of rum will always remain with me as one of the best and will rank with the smell of gas and tar which brings back the fives-court to every Etonian. Considering that the average Englishman bears no resentment to John Allyman,[1] I think Uncle Edward flicked the public rather unnecessarily on the raw.[2] If it comes to presenting the other cheek and Gibraltar, it's a little hard to know where you are to stop, and I only hope that Tedward loves Sir G. Craik and those who have criticized him whole-heartedly.

The next letter shows up our sort of humour, in and out of the trenches. I hope we may be forgiven by the *avant-garde* of today if it sounds a trifle puerile.

> *2nd Batt. Grenadier Guards,*
> *4th Guards Brigade, B.E. Force*

> *Monday April 12th, 1915*

(I have just been out to see a German aeroplane shelled, a sight which though common I can never quite resist.)

The talk is that we are to be relieved from here before the end of this week, though there is no confirmation of the rumour as yet. 'Things is quiet'—*absit omen*—and I think a little longer here, barring accidents, wouldn't be so bad.

Just now I saw a very typical looking Coldstream officer marching at the head of ten unarmed men. So, assuming the most carefully modulated voice, I said, 'Bin' practisin' bombin' wha'?' Said he, 'Yes, just finishin', marchin' home.' 'Good mornin'.' 'Mornin'.' The whole without a smile. He will go home and say, 'Who's that in the Grenadiers with the curly hair, what?' 'Oh, that's young Lyttelton'. 'Good fellah I thought, wha'?' Here are two true stories. A sergeant (of a Line regiment) had been hit through the ankle and could not get to the stretcher bearers during a little attack. So up comes an officer and says from his stomach, 'Here, get up on my back and I'll carry you

---

[1] Soldiers' name for a German.

[2] Edward Lyttelton, then headmaster of Eton, had preached a sermon suggesting that Gibraltar be handed to the Germans as a peace move.

in.' 'What!' said the sergeant, 'you get the V.C. and me get my behind full of bullets—not likely, sir!'

Another time a German was heard to shout, 'Anybody there from Birmingham?' No answer. 'Anyone there from Birmingham?' 'Yes, I am.' 'I've got a wife and two children there,' from the German. 'Well, you'll bloody soon have a widow and two orphans if you don't watch it.'

We had a capital day's bombing last time we were in. It really isn't bad fun as you have plenty of time to get out of the way provided there aren't too many men in the trench. You hear a very dull woolly explosion in the distance. Then a cry, 'Bomb left.' You look up and there is a thing like a large black candle sailing slowly over. You sprint round the next traverse, and then there is, after a pause, a terrific bang which half deafens you. For every bomb they give us we give them two, the whole operation being known as 'trench frightfulness'. In our company during three months, again *absit omen*, we have had only one man wounded by them. Now we have got a thing called a trench howitzer which the Germans loathe—it is pretty silent and throws quite a decent sized shell about 500 yards, so we hoist their parapet whenever they get offensive.

Oh, there was another casualty the other morning from bombing. We heard a bomb explode about 100 yards away, but took no notice, as we were lunching in our dugout, until we heard 'Stretcher bearers at the double' being passed down. '—— those —— Bosches, they've got someone I suppose,' said Soccer, wiping his mouth, and getting out into the trench followed by me. We soon saw the stretcher bearers carrying a fellow. 'Where's he hit?' 'Don't know sir, very bad sir, I think,' said the corporal with the unfailing optimism of the lower classes and of stretcher bearers. 'Got it in the stomach,' I said, 'as I can't see any blood, did he?' Another fellow came up, a gunner; said he, 'He was running to get out of the way of one of them bombs, and fell over hisself, he aint 'it', and spat apologetically but accurately into the water sump. The 'wounded man' was a gunner, one of the trench howitzer team and pretty new to the game. We cussed a bit and returned to our dessert. Talking of incidents though, I haven't laughed so much since the war began as I did three days ago. After being woken by Stephenson with the words 'Getting on towards 3.30' (for which he got cursed with 'What the devil do you mean, is it 3.30 or not?') and promptly going to sleep again, we were reawoken by a gurgling sound to be greeted by the sight of Stephenson drinking 'whiskey and water' and reading *The Card* by the light of one candle which threw his grotesque shadow all over the mud walls. He was immediately known as 'Whiskey Stephenson', and I didn't stop laughing till 4.15, which made me a bit unpopular though it was admitted I had had provocation.

We have got a first-rate dugout with two joists in the roof about twelve by six and some wheat on the floor. 'It does not drip' is pronounced 'Fizz-bang-proof!' Just below the joists you can see the young spring grass sprouting on the ground level. It is or rather was quite an unique feeling to be underground.

Try sending some kippers.

P.S. I was much chaffed the other morning, after I had been showing some Territorial officers round, as their faces were so long.

'Oliver, you properly old soldiered those fellows, they had the wind absolutely up them. I suppose you "cossacked"[1] about the 17th March (the worst day in most of our lives when we got the twenty-six hours' shelling).' 'Some,' said I, though as a fact I adopted the matter-of-fact swagger which I believe to be the chicest, e.g. when a new Terr. officer keeps himself very low, in a place where he could not possibly be hit if he stood up and semaphored, and his pal laughs at him. 'Don't you laugh, my friend,' I always say, 'take my advice and no risks.'

2nd Bn. Grenadier Gds. B.E.F.
21st April, 1915

Our 'rest' has begun. Only two days though, i.e. four in all, two days we should have had ordinarily and two extra, the whole spent in Béthune. No news much, except on subject of our future movements. We are to be permanently in the trenches, only going back to billets about 500 yards behind the firing line, where every damned shell or gun wakes you up at night. Still we are not grousing, for the strategy is this—the Territorial divisions 2nd London and Midland are, I believe, to occupy practically the whole line recently held by better troops. Givenchy, Cuinchy and Le Plantin are so vital that they will not trust them to the Territorials, consequently the 4th Gds. Brigade are to hold this line which would ordinarily be held by at least two brigades of regular troops and their reserves. The whole of the rest of the Army are going (we imagine) to make an enormous offensive movement. This would not be possible if the pivot was not absolutely safe. The pivot is Givenchy, Cuinchy and Le Plantin.

[1] 'To Cossack' is to pitch a horrible tale. An old buffer, in the course of a Crimean anecdote whilst on the King's Guard, said: 'And then the Cossacks came over the hill.'

So there we are. The brigadier is much pleased with the honour of holding with one brigade the most vital spot in the line, which would ordinarily be held by two or more. We perhaps don't feel quite so pleased, as three weeks in your boots isn't much fun.

If they are successful on the left the Brigade, supported by two divisions (notice the anomaly), will take La Bassée, the rest of the army will push away left into Lille if they can. There will be a lull for a week or two and then we shall do it again. There is no doubt that we can defeat the Germans 'where and when we like'; it is simply a matter of loss justifying gain. I hope you understand the geography. I will show you roughly. Of course

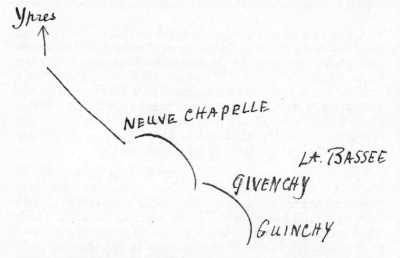

the proportions are wrong. The distance between Givenchy and Neuve Chapelle being only four miles roughly, between N.C. and Ypres about twenty-four.

Once the rest of the army gets through between N.C. and Y. the enemy will be turned and the time will be ripe for us to walk into La Bassée. I don't suppose the devils will go without a fight but we are all confident, i.e. the Brigade, that we shall do without severe losses anything that is asked of us, simply because nothing here is ever chanced. Cavan[1] refuses to move unless the thing is done his way. Perfect plans backed up by the best infantry in Europe and there you are.

'I know quite well,' he said, 'that I can do more with my brigade than anyone could ask an ordinary corps to do.'

[1] Brigadier-General (afterwards Field-Marshal) the Earl of Cavan.

The gist of the whole thing is this. Whatever we do will succeed, but what shall we lose?

Cavan will not move until the artillery preparation is perfectly complete, that is the answer. Speaking generally, I am sure that we could take the trenches in front of us *now* with a loss of 250 men and six officers to the Brigade. If and when the German is threatened from the rear, I expect we shall get in with a quarter of that.

My grandfather had sent out a hamper from Cadbury and Pratt, the best known cheese and delicacy merchants in Bond Street.

This is how I thanked him.

> *2nd Bn. Grenadier Gds. 4th Gds. Brigade, B.E.F.*
> *April 21st, 1915*

Scene, a road somewhere in France, I expect you know where. The wrecks of a few houses on one side. A very hot muggy afternoon. Across this road sixty sweating and swearing men putting up a barricade of sandbags (they are heavy things to handle) under a sweating and swearing officer. The officer is 2nd Lt O. Lyttelton, Grenadier Guards.

There are a few (very few) bullets hitting the houses crack, crack, or going swish over our heads. The danger is small but the task unpleasant. We have not been to sleep (except incidental dozes) for forty-eight hours and we are keeping an eye open for our relief (the Irish Guards).

Up comes the post-corporal, salutes and presents me with a letter addressed in a well-known hand. I devour it and feel much better. Towards the end, I notice references to Cadbury and Pratt, I feel still better, and my word, there are the Irish!

Off we go like schoolboys though *some* of us have twenty years' service and four medal ribbons. O.L. thinks of *foie gras* and finds on reaching billets that it has already arrived, and by jove, plovers' eggs and Port Salut!

This is a true tale and not faked, and I could have thanked you more gracefully on that road than I can on this paper.

Best love to Granny and Aunt Mary (who I hear has not got my letter so I am writing her another), Uncle Jack and Aunt Valerie.

Do write again.

The Germans had used gas in an attack in the Ypres salient.

We are all served out with masks improvised from field dressings and tubs of diluted bicarbonate of soda to soak them in, against this filthy trick of asphyxiating gases, which might have easily had a great effect on the campaign.

However, we have just heard on the telephone that the situation at Ypres is well in hand and that the Belgians tried wet handkerchiefs against a gas and infantry attack yesterday and suffered no ill effects, repulsing the Germans with considerable losses. Really it is the last word, even in this war. Fortunately, they have got to live in it to be able to attack and so there must be some remedy. I mean they can't employ fire-damp or some unassailable gas.

Here comes Derriman, a captain, second-in-command of the coy., who has just joined and has nothing to do. A nice little man with a stiff-leg who is always wanting to know where east is and always thinks it is in the direction due west when I tell him. A second captain is rather unnecessary as he cannot do a subaltern's work and one man can command a company better than two, at any rate in a trench. However.

I hope you realize that if I survive I shall become entitled to leave in a little more than a fortnight. That doesn't say I shall get it of course, but still the brigadier is very good about it. Gosh, if Bobbety and I could come home together!

This next letter describes the 'offensive spirit' in the trenches: it deals with shelling, noise and how the sense of hearing is developed and refined.

May 1st, 1915

There seems to be no prospect of leave, I fear, as things are rather in an uncertain state. Our lack of ammunition delayed our offensive and the Germans rather forestalled us, though purely locally. The gas of course is a very serious thing, and has caused us indirectly to lose a lot of men. However, no one thinks anything of the Ypres incident though the Canadians really have done well. This time it is not the newspapers who have trumped up routine gallantry into unprecedented heroism. They had to deal with a nasty incoherent situation, the one thing we dislike, and they coped with it of course with courage, but also with a large measure of efficiency which is a thing not usually expected.

Well, here we are with nothing behind us and making ourselves perfectly intolerable to the Huns. Bombing them, sniping them, shelling them, digging new bits of line so that they know by now that the dreaded brigade is opposite them! What I hope they don't know is that behind us there is Fatty Cavan and his orderlies and the first line transport. However, we are confident. This is a beastly life. We are never in one place for more than twenty-four hours and never far from the fighting line. Our guns have been at it the whole day. One big fellow in particular hardly ever leaves off, and he shakes our windows so that they nearly break every time he goes off. Our position is immediately left of the one we were last in; its details and the work we are doing on it are not very interesting and tonight finds me in rather an unpictorial mood. I am however sending you the nose cap of a medium-sized shrapnel which arrived between my orderly and me the other night whilst we were superintending the digging of a communication trench. The shell itself burst 300 yards away and we picked this bit up quite hot. It was so close that we found it even though the night was quite dark. I could send fifty like it but this one was interesting as it nearly had us.[1] Through the door at this moment I can see four 'wooleys' (composite shells, head shrapnel, tail, high explosive) bursting over the Coldstream, and a German aeroplane about 1,000 feet up, where incidentally it is quite useless for observation purposes.

The sense of hearing becomes extraordinarily developed at this game. Newcomers cannot distinguish between our own guns and the enemy's shells, much less say what type of shell was just burst. We hear a salvo perhaps two miles away and can say, 'French.' Again two or three shells burst together. 'Two wooleys and a fizzy-bang over the left.' 'There's one of our howitzer 4·7s back. A dud, too!'

Well, *au revoir*.

The next letter describes a battle as seen by a spectator.

[Received May 14th, 1915]   *2nd Batt. Grenadier Guards*
                              4th Guards Brigade. B.E.F.

There is some depression here, among officers at any rate, at the present features of the great offensive.

The day before yesterday I saw what was going to be the biggest battle in the history of the world—a combined attack by three English Army Corps N. of La Bassée and seven French, South of Cuinchy and N. of Arras. My appreciation of the strategy,

---
[1] This would have meant a nasty bruise or a broken arm.

III

which was more or less guesswork, proved to be remarkably near the truth.

In battalion orders of the 8th we read: 'The attack will commence at daybreak. All men must be in their "dugouts" by 3.45 a.m.'

Our company, I may say in explanation of above, was in support that day, resting in some roofless houses on the Pont Fixe road. So at 3.30 out we got, rather thick-eyed, into a fresh morning, with a N.W. wind blowing in sharply but not unpleasantly. Cloudless blue sky and except for the drone of three aeroplanes everything quiet. Hot cocoa at 3.45 and a visit to see if all the men were below ground, found they were. Returned to our little room and looked at our watches—3.54, six minutes more. A certain tension. Then out we go into the little windy street—more windy because of the shell-holes in the houses opposite, not feeling very human in spite of our hot cocoa. Then up some stairs into the roof which was filled with old clothes and a broken perambulator. I got quite a good place by smashing off a few tiles, and there saw the Plain of Flanders beneath me, stretching away hard and clear in the early light with little shadow to dapple it, but the freshly bursting poplars that mark the Rue de Marais and La Quinque Rue standing up clear and aristocratic above the bourgeois uniformity of the country. By craning my neck I could just see (through glasses) the Bois du Biez on my left, perhaps four miles away, and the sandbagged rows of trenches for about two miles before losing them among some buildings and small trees. These trenches were chiefly on the frontage of our own brigade, and the London Division of Territorials, that is to say trenches from which no attack was to be launched.

The *coup d'oeil* was not unlike that given to someone standing above Romney Marsh, except for the poplars and the fact that one's range of vision from our house was not more than four miles. Well, at four o'clcok the bombardment began—the greatest bombardment there has ever been. The whole countryside, except that just immediately to our left, was covered with bursting shells. You would see four of five angry little red flashes and then the white smoke about twenty feet above the ground. The pictures you see of shells bursting over battle fields give a wrong impression. Shrapnel never bursts or at any rate should not burst high in the air. About twenty feet up is the best place. Again it does not look like this [Here follow two primitive diagrams of shell-bursts] but the burst of the shell carries the smoke on with it, something like this. I can't draw it. I doubt if many better artists could! The big shells usually burst on percussion and they throw an enormous column of earth and black smoke into the air in this sort of shape [Here follows another diagram].

That morning the smaller artillery kept up a sort of jarring roar, but above it you could hear and feel the big ones crash. If you want the effect of an 8–5 bursting near you, stand on the edge of the platform when an express is coming through at sixty miles an hour, and imagine that it runs into a siding about twenty yards away.

It struck me looking at that shelling that it would be very unimpressive to a layman who hadn't been shelled himself, except for the shaking and trembling of the house. There is nothing in a flat, sparsely-wooded country to show the effect of shells. True, a poplar or two may have its top taken off, as clean as a carrot, or a cloud of red smoke show that half a house has gone; true that the 'wurrump' of the big ones is almost majestic in its power; but with a wind the smoke is gone in a few seconds and everything looks wonderfully ordinary. The fact that some barbed wire and a few sandbags have been swept away seems to give nature the same feelings as a man has who gets his back scratched or has a shampoo.

Two typical days in a battle.

May 24th, 1915

I have had little or no chance of writing for so long as we have been engaged in the last big battle and when we came out for a rest I was billeting officer, a job which is usually thankless but which I fulfilled this time without 'losing my name'. Chiefly I think because everyone was so pleased to find themselves out of the Valley of the Shadow of Death!

It was a close afternoon when we pulled out from Givenchy, and there was an oppressive promise of thunder as we sweated along the canal bank which has been our neighbour for five months. On the other bank, with their faces the other way, were the Black Watch and the London Scottish, fresh from their knock of the Sunday before, and as we passed Brigade Head-quarters—a cottage close to a boat-bridge—we could see the 1st Divisional red-hats and the attendant *jeunesse dorée*[1] taking over from our staff. I talked to one or two fellows I knew and learnt that we should bivouac that night in the open, that we were 'for it', that the 2nd and the 7th Divisions were to attack over the same ground as the other three corps had failed over on

[1] i.e., the A.D.C.s.

Sunday, that the machine-guns were in concrete, etc. Not reassuring. Pack very heavy, and brow very moist. We halt at Gorre and a little breeze springs up which turns the day greyer. Excellent coffee at a workman's cottage just off the street. Returned to find all our officers and the Prince of Wales and Claude Hamilton[1] halting by the side of the road. Wales, as he is called, said that all the genera l:at G.H.Q. spoke of the 1st and 2nd Divisions, the heavy guns, the 8th Division etc., etc. *and* the 4th (Guards) Brigade.

Soon after fell in, and marched a longish eight miles, the men shouting to every gunner we passed, 'Mind and cut the wire for us, darling.' About nine o'clock arrived at a place called La Casan, behind the Richebourg position, and left the men to rum and tea and a night in an orchard, and went ourselves into a very small billet owned by a charming *garde champêtre* and crowded by twelve offsprings. Soccer and I being a pair of pretty old soldiers immediately got into a large barn with two mattresses— a barn in which several people had died of infectious diseases, mark you; this is a favourite yarn and always *has* beginners who don't know the French peasant. The next day to our horror was wet and frightfully cold, and we had sent home all our thick things, and as the men had 'given in' their great coats it was most inopportune. However, we walked about in the mud most of the day, and spent the rest playing bridge in a smell of stew and children. A great deal of discussion went on as to how and when and where the Brigade were to push, and no conclusion was arrived at. A general feeling of tension showing itself in an unusual politeness and restlessness. That night we were told to be prepared to move at 10.30: at five, however all arrangements cancelled twenty-four hours. Next day also very wet, and spent in the same way, however no orders to move at 10.30 p.m. but went to bed in full kit with equipment: called at 3.15 and marched at 3.27. Tremendous artillery fire all round us as we turned into Zatoinal[2] in the half light. The roads were awful. The next thing was a motor ambulance, with an officer with a pretty fresh wound in the arm sitting on a box and about ten men inside chiefly with face and arm wounds. Soon after four Germans looking muddy but clean under escort. This last was a goodish sign as it meant we had at least got into a trench somewhere. Passed a dressing station—an old *estaminet* with about forty very bloody men standing outside, all slightly wounded however. A mutter of 'The Guards' and every face to

[1] Captain Lord Claude Hamilton, Grenadier Guards.
[2] An unidentified hamlet.

the windows to see our perfect swing and step. Still went on in a good deal of row and passed a continual stream of slightly wounded men. Order passed down to blob, i.e. artillery formation. Saw Bobbety for a minute before he marched off and heard that we had taken two miles of trenches, and that we were to go up immediately and pass through the Berkshires, take a line of trenches and try to reach the Quinque Rue. Everyone seemed pretty cheerful as it was clear we were in course of wiping the eye of the rest of the army and justifying the German name of 'the Iron Division'.

Well, left the road on to a grass track through some trees, the day reforming to heat and sunshine, the birds singing, and a terrific fire going on from our fellows. Passed two well-concealed batteries of field artillery (18-pounders) in action. 'Two minutes right 369 section fire,' or something like that, an officer was shouting through a megaphone. The gunners' orders are always quite incomprehensible. We began to feel that no battle should be begun till all troops engaged had had breakfast. Next passed over a wooden bridge with a printed board 'Guns and infantry in fours', and turned into a superb avenue of enormous trees, rustling dispassionately to the wind. All along the side under the trunks, batteries were firing fast and furious—making our empty stomachs feel emptier with their din. Some perfectly deafening remarks from another battery behind us firing straight over our heads. On again down the avenue and turn to the right along the edge of an orchard. Further blobbing—into sections this time, a pack animal breaks a footbridge. Halt. Hands held up and we lie down, oo-oo-oo-preeen-hum. Shrapnel from the enemy. Wisp-wisp-wisp-bullets. The company in front have taken their packs off, we'll do the same. 'Oh,' said I to Derriman, who is a beginner, 'my experience of modern battles is that we shall be here for the rest of the day much like this'—(here we were practically knocked over by the concussion of one of our batteries about 100 yards directly behind us)—'except for more shells from the enemy. I shall tell my fellows to dig themselves in.' Went up and found that they were already nearly out of sight. Went myself and lay in a ditch. Noise of the battery behind something perfectly inconceivable. Tried a hard-boiled egg and found it quite revolting. Why I wondered, and looked at my watch: 4.40 a.m. Took a look round. About 300 yards on our left front was a farmhouse—our headquarters, so I heard. Some wooleys seemed to be going rather too near it. Beyond that a line of trees bordering the Rue du Bois parallel with us, and beyond that again and all over the road what we call 'an enemy barrage'. A common practice of both sides is to make a wall of shrapnel behind the enemy's front troops, to render it difficult for him to reinforce. Known as barrage.

Here is a sketch of our position.

> Germans in their third trench
>
> British in second line. German Trench
>
> British in front line. German Trench
>
> British lines
>
> Shrapnel Barrage
>
> Rue du Bois
>
> Fields with tall regular avenue mentioned above
>
> Farm House
>
> No 1
>
> No 2
>
> O.L.
>
> Each of these squares
>
> No 4 subdivided into four

This is frightfully rough, of course. Well, for the next two hours we expected—particularly the new hands—the order to move up to support the 6th Brigade through the barrage. No orders however and O.L. pronounces it a certainty that we shall not move till night. Enemy shells begin to come amongst us about 8 a.m. A few casualties, all slight wounds as German shrapnel is very gentle, especially when burst at all high. The day wore on and our ditch was frightfully hot and the noise of our batteries behind us deafening. About ten, i.e. six hours after our arrival, artillery fire on both sides slackens. Ted[1] comes up and talks delightfully for about an hour. Says the casualties are nothing terrific. Not much news. We all mind our own gun-fire more than the enemies, which is, thank goodness, short of us for the most part. Twenty-five casualties in the battalion all day. Ted leaves at eleven with the very just remark that it is most unpleasant only

[1] Father Edward Talbot, my first cousin, son of the Bishop of Winchester.

having to face fire when you think fit; feel however that I wouldn't mind being a chaplain to get behind our own guns where the noise is nothing. We all failed to sleep in our ditch. In the afternoon the enemy's shelling rose to 'Intense' previous to the counter-attack, which was however broken up by two 'Mothers', whose observing officers saw it assembling. An argument started as to whether we should have to go and dig that night, stay where we were and attack the next morning, etc.

At 4.30, twelve hours and a half after our arrival, a lull. Went on to the road and had bread and jam and tea quite uninterrupted by two high shrapnel over our heads. We could see none of the bullets strike. Enemy shrapnel all day very bad and ineffective but then, 'H.E. (High Explosive) beautiful'—this was the gunner officer to me. Such percussion! A lovely burst, nearly perfect, beautiful. We did not agree. At six the quartermaster comes down the avenue with the news that the 7th Division have got the Quinque Rue (not quite true by the way) and that our 1st Battalion and the 2nd Scots Guards have had a fine kill and a lot of prisoners too. A letter from you arrives. A whisper: 'We are going back to billets.' Things are looking up. At 8.30, sixteen hours after our arrival, we march back and reach billets about 9.45, dinner, and then turned into our barn above the manure heaps merely cussing the news that we must be prepared to move anytime after 3.30 a.m. Some fairly old soldiers ordered breakfast at three but Soccer and I decided to risk having to move breakfastless and told our servants to call us when the order to march came through. A successful manoeuvre as we rose at eight and took an excellent breakfast at 8.30. No orders.

This ends the first period of our battle and though it doesn't sound much it was one of the worst days I have ever had. The noise fearful, anticipation of being 'for it' on an empty stomach, a very hot day, a lot of shells near us, boredom and danger. I can see every blade of grass in that cursed field now. My boots in front of me on the tip of the ditch, the orchard on my left and nothing to be seen near in front except lush grass and cowslips, the line of the Rue du Bois in front and the avenue behind, the white smoke of the barrage, and the black smoke of the H.E. further off by some farms are all indelibly photographed, not because they were remarkable but because they were immovable, and gradually wore into one's memory like the text of an interminable sermon when you are half-asleep.

May 28th, 1915

I hastily sent off my last letter as the post was just going out, and I hadn't time to finish it.

That afternoon as there was still no orders we sat down to bridge, the weather being grey and drizzly. We had only just begun when the order 'Fall In' came round and in four-and-a-half minutes the battalion was on the march. Reached Lacouture in a fine rain about 4.45 and the captains being interviewed by the commanding officer, we learnt as follows. The 7th Division had got on well: their left was on the Quinque Rue; the 6th Brigade, i.e. the right of the 2nd Division, had taken two or three lines of trenches and rested on point so and so: between the left of the 7th and the right of the 2nd, however, there was a gap or rather a wedge held by the Germans. The 4th Brigade were to drive the Germans out, and connect the two divisions. The Quinque Rue however did not run exactly parallel to us and the position may be drawn *à la Belloc* like this

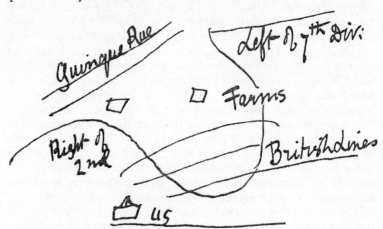

We were much pleased to hear that we were to attack at night, as among *regimental* soldiers this is considered the cheapest way of taking prepared positions, where your men can be launchd easily from a line of trenches, you take me I hope. What I mean is that in rushing one line of trenches from another you can easily deploy your men into their battle positions without much fear of their losing touch with one another, and again their objective is clearly defined. The advantage of night operations in short hold good for trenches, while many disadvantages are absent.

You must imagine us then moving through the village of Lacouture over very muddy roads, with strings of ammunition limbers and transport making the command 'Feel your right'[1]

---

[1] Military expression for inclining towards the right.

very frequent. At the end of the village we turned sharp to our left along the high road. Here there were ambulances, supply officers, staff, cavalry, all finding something to do, and on both sides of the road Indian troops at their ablutions with their hair done up into top-knots. Noticed enemy shrapnel bursting very high about 1,000 yards away. Greeted one or two friends but felt rather like gladiators, '*Morituri te salutant.*' So on to a grass track where we blobbed to 100 yards between platoons. Shrapnel about 200 yards to our right, but still high. Next along a very thick avenue of trees about ten feet high, where the trees had dripped and were still dripping on to the pathway, making it a sea of mud. Here the commanding officer and adjutant came up and told us to advance across the open and take up our position in a line of trenches, thought to have been the original British line. This we immediately carried out under a desultory shell-fire, a man in my platoon being slightly wounded close to me, and found ourselves in a shallow trench. Beyond us we could see a breastwork untenanted immediately to our front but seeming to contain some Highlanders further to the left. Headquarters were in this trench, their signallers using a Neats disc[1] and keeping communication with the two companies in front who had already reached the breastwork I have spoken of.

I had time to look round, though there was considerable shell-fire. To our front as I have said a breastwork of brownish-coloured sandbags, looking fairly substantial, separated from us by about 100 yards of open country and a couple of dykes. On our right front an orchard being heavily shelled, and behind some farmhouses looking pretty intact. In the trench my platoon—Crawley de Crespigny[2] next me—a wounded man having his head bandaged and trying to keep the blood out of his eyes with his left hand—the C.O. and adjutant—signallers working a disc. On the left of us, about 250 yards, a farmhouse surrounded very closely by some scraggy trees into which the Germans were putting 'coal boxes'[3] six at a time. The whole country is very flat, so flat indeed that we could see nothing beyond the breast-work immediately in front of us, in addition the light was uniformly grey, it was beginning to rain and it was decidedly cold. Up comes an officer, apparently a gunner, who asks, 'Is the 2nd Division feeling their left to make room for you?'—an ungrammatical and somewhat unintelligible question. It becomes obvious to Crawley and me that no one knows where

1 A simple piece of signalling apparatus.
2 Major C. R. Champion de Crespigny.
3 Soldiers' name for a form of shrapnel which produced a black cloud.

we are but our information as to where the others are is more than likely to be wrong.

However we get the order to move on to the breastwork in front. We do so without loss, though a few bullets seem to be coming from somewhere—but I judge them to be nowhere near us. Found ourselves very squashed in the breastwork, our left on the Gordon Highlanders, our right seemingly in the air. One or two of the Yorkshire regiments appear. All the troops hereabouts seem much shaken and exhausted. The breastwork certainly shows signs of having been shelled and I noticed what, I think, were four men and an officer half buried under the parapet, terribly mangled, two in halves, one lacking a leg, I judge the bodies to be twelve hours old. A new horizon is now apparent. Namely a German trench to our front which has evidently suffered terribly from shell-fire. It is made almost entirely of white sandbags. Get the order to occupy this. Do so advancing across the open. A few bullets. It was across here that I understand Arthur [Penn] was hit later on. There were two companies in front of us and one behind (Arthur's).

As we got into the trench I noticed a pile of English bodies (perhaps thirty) and one or two isolated corpses. Gained the German breastwork. It is just getting dark and the rain is now coming down steadily.

We are to feel our left. Do so and meet a platoon of our 1st Battalion, who say that they are in support of a company which occupies a line of hastily-dug trenches about 400 yards to the front, that they took the trench we now stand in twenty-four hours before, that they had lost four officers, only one killed, had caused the enemy heavy casualties and taken themselves 300 prisoners, lastly that they could have pushed on as far as Violaines but were kept back by orders.

When I speak of moving down a trench 'feeling our left', etc., you mustn't imagine that it is like walking down a road. We stumbled along treading on and in the dead, pushing past other troops, clambering over traverses, getting amongst wire, making way for wounded men, having to go outside to avoid places where the parapet had been blown in, losing touch in front and behind. All these are minor ills but give the brain a confused impression of horror, disorder, anger. Men, legs, dead, wounded, water, blood, sandbags, mud, the last the most dreaded of all obstacles except darkness which soon closed down upon us.

That trench was a shambles and muddy at that. You slipped back more than you went forward, fell amongst the dead, retched at the smells and just kept your temper. It was a night I shall never forget. Eventually I found a foul dugout, with two corpses across the door through which I crawled and found half a dozen candles. Got rid of my pack and put one of these candles into a German mess-tin and sallied out on the grizzly task of 'getting the trench clear'. It will not dilate upon it. I will only tell you that no horror could affect me in the least now and that those I encountered only turned me up for about ten minutes. After that you cease to feel that you are dealing with what were once men, and realise that you could easily make jokes like the grave-digger in Hamlet. We were trying to drag a body out—it had no head—and I found by flashing a light that one of my fellows was standing on its legs. So I said, 'Get off.' 'How can we get it out if you stand on it, show some sense.' Then I flashed my light behind me and found that I had both feet on a German's chest who had been nearly trodden right in. Enough. We cleared the trench and when the 'grey light of early dawn' showed us our abode we found it nearly clean. Beyond what had been the parados but was now our parapet however, the sight was appalling. Amongst a mass of filth, latrines, old food, wire, rifles, equipments, cast off greatcoats, shell-holes, ammunition, lay sprawling about 150 German dead in every position and every state of repair. Again I will not go into many details but perhaps one word in the list of debris will give you an inkling of the full ghastliness of the spectacle.

The parados was of course very knocked about. Where we could we repaired it and where we couldn't we moved the men away to where it was higher. About eight o'clock (five hours after dawn) shells began to burst and continued all day the firing rising to intense between eleven and one. We had been told to attack at nine, but about seven it was postponed for unknown reasons. The anticipation of this attack did not enhance the day. We were very lucky (and not a little skilful) during that shelling. They hit the parapet, they short-bracketed the trench, they put them short, over and in, but God and our dispositions prevented many casualties. You can usually tell what the 'line of shells' is going to be and you can move your men to the right and left of 'bracketed' trenches [or] pieces of trench up to a point, but of course the fact remains that 200 men have got 300 yards of trench and have to stay there.

Well, our pleasures consisted of a bad tin of bully (which made me sick subsequently) at five, and another good tin at eleven. We soon had telephonic communication with the rear and with the two companies in front. At three the news came through. The Grenadiers will attack P14 and 15 at 4.30 supported by the Irish

Guards on the left, and the Canadians on the right. Nos. 2 and 3 Coys were to be first followed by us (No. 4) and last No. 1. I can't go on just now as I have to pay the company, but more anon.

The battalion came out of the line, and I wrote:

June 1st, 1915

Just let me say that our rest is going on most unexpectedly for at least another week. We are now at a mining town called Noeux-les-Mines and are going to take over a new bit of line, in which British troops have never yet been, from the French. We hear that we are to be quiet for six weeks because of the lack of shells, which is not uncomforting.

However well 'offensives' look on paper, in fact they can only be described by impolite dissyllables. As four o'clock approached that day, we began to feel a bit excited in a horrible sort of way but were relieved by an excellent tea. This was the only decent food we had had for two days, and where the servants got the new loaf from is still a mystery. I think it was 'lifted' from a territorial mess in the background, that is in the very reserve trenches. However, at 4.20 we closed the company up on to the German communication trench. I may say first that our shelling had become intense at four, the shells were going over our heads at the rate of about forty a minute. A field-gun shell sounds as if it only just missed your head, whilst the heavy stuff goes over like the tearing of silk. At 4.25 bullets began to come fast from an unknown direction and began to strike the very low parapet (the German parados). This augured ill and showed that the artillery practice had failed to knock out the enemy machine-guns. Well, at 4.30 exactly, our leading platoon crossed the little piece of open and got into the old German trench. It was a nasty little bit in face of the fire and I got my braves across, a section at a time for fear that a jamb would occur in the trench in front, and some men be left in the open. I hope this is clear. In other words I did not move all my men in at once, but not until there was room for them! I was surprised to find myself thinking of this, I remember, and delighted to find my platoon sergeant (a very old hand, one of the original lot who came out on Aug. 10) was carrying out the scheme which I bawled in his ear with admirable calmness. I only mention this profoundly minor incident to show what small things may make a difference. I remember when telling Sergeant Gambrill to feed the trench in front, with only a section at a time, when I shouted, giving the order, rather to show him that I was still in possession of my senses than as a necessary piece of caution. It was in fact almost 'swank', like the continual order 'Keep closed up' that I kept passing down. A fluke, but afterwards I thought it unpleasant that perhaps ten men's lives might hang on such small things. Anyone of course who sent in a platoon all at once into a trench up which two others were already moving would be mad, but such things are terribly easily forgotten. Well I found myself with three sections of my own in the communication trench. This part of it was roofed in and well revetted on both sides with timber. I could see nothing but could hear shells beginning to fall near us. Beyond this sort of gallery I could see another short piece of open ground. Let me explain that these pieces of open were caused by the fact that our artillery had knocked the German communication trench about when it was in possession of the enemy. This little sketch will show you the sort of idea of the attack.

There we were in the gallery and the open bit in front of us. A jamb: one or two shells very near us. Then my orderly and I rushed the little open bit but couldn't get far as the men in front were still jambed: the rest of the platoon were then about ten yards behind me, and my orderly and myself and another man were immediately in rear of the platoon in front. About five minutes after the Germans plumped ten shells all exactly at the mouth of the gallery trench and wiped out two of my sergeants (one was not much good, he was wounded severely all down the left side but will recover, the other, the best junior sergeant I had, has since died) and the whole of one section. The men were all wounded and buried except two who dug the others out. One man is missing completely. A shell burst on him, I believe. After these ten perfectly-placed shells they switched off a little to our right where they did no damage. I kept asking myself whether the intense excitement was pleasurable or not and came to the conclusion that I could satisfactorily live without it. However, it was a debatable point. All this time I could see nothing of the progress of 2 and 3 Companies as the trench and a fold in the ground hid them from our view. Bullets continued to strike round us. The German trench hereabouts was made by bundles secured to poles and filled in with earth. I sat there smoking and fingering that hurdle and could see about ten men in front of me behind me a little open space with some old equipment—a black leather pouch and a haversack, and then the trench with my platoon sergeant smoking a pipe, his back against one side, his feet against the other. Suddenly they began to move forward in front. Up we scrambled along a piece where the breastworks were very low. I saw a man fall about twenty yards in front and soon after stepped over him. He was shot through the head, which was lying in a puddle of blood. Next, moving quickly, came on a German lying right in the trench. He pointed to his feet imploringly. They were wrapped and bandaged with sandbags and showed signs of having been trodden in to the mud. I just avoided them and shouted to the men to do the same. Here the trench branched off into a dugout with wallpaper and what looked like a gas apparatus outside. An unarmed German was limping about on one leg, smoking. The cigarettes I learned subsequently had been given him by our men. We jambed again. This time, however, by looking over the top which I did sparingly, I could see the attack. On the extreme left, perhaps 800 yards away, I could see British infantry pushing forward in rushes of about a platoon, extended to three or four paces. The Germans were bursting wooleys right on the parapet of the hastily thrown up trench: nearer to me I could see a platoon of Grenadiers doubling forward thirty yards at a time whilst two platoons kept up a hot fire from the trench to cover them. It was a stereotyped attack and as far as I could see perfectly executed. Another platoon followed the first. I don't think I saw any fall but some motionless forms were left behind each time. I could see very little more and so sat down in the trench and waited. An hour later heard: 'Attack is held up by machine-gun fire, the Irish are not getting on on the left, no sign of the Canadians on the right. One company (No. 3) has got forward 250 yards but have been badly cut up. Major Barrington-Kennet is killed, Mr Creed is wounded, Mr Carey is missing.' This was not gathered all at once but dribbled through in various messages sent to the C.O. Then the wounded began to come along. Perhaps a hundred of them. Mostly slight wounds, feet, thighs, shoulders, two with smashed wrists. Very pale like all wounded and mostly profane. One said that only eight men of his platoon were left for the last rush, and that two other platoons had suffered heavily. The wounded all gave remarkably accurate accounts of the attack as we pulled them or helped them along the very narrow trench. We waited on another hour and then another. It was intensely cold and beginning to get dark. Then 'Ma' Jeffreys appeared on the other side of the trench. 'Did you hear about the Commanding Officer?' he asked. 'No.' 'He is killed, I'm afraid: it is awful, shot through the head.' He passed on. He is one of the best soldiers you can imagine. Nine months of the most terrific fighting have left him completely unmoved. He is exceedingly careful of his own safety where precautions are possible, but where they are not, courageous. Any risk where necessary, none where not. He has vast experience and unerring judgment. He has of course been second-in-command all along. He is known sometimes as 'the Drill Sergeant' from his love of smartness and discipline. 'Shaving the upper lip' and 'Dirty boots' are anathema to him. They are never passed over, nothing is ever passed over. After seven months in the closest intimacy with a man whom he liked, you might have thought that that man's death by a bullet which passed through his own coat would have shaken him. Not at all. Even 'Copper' (Henry Seymour[1]), the bravest man you can imagine, was upset, but five minutes after the C.O. had been carried away 'Ma' wrote, 'If the attack is held up reinforce *once* and push on vigorously.' No one knew of course that this was not Wilfred Smith's[2] order till afterwards. A little later he sent, 'I do not hear enough covering fire. Please explain.'

Incidently I like 'Ma' Jeffreys more than the late C.O., who was a very nice fellow and devilish efficient, because he is cleverer, more human and more humorous.

[1] Major Lord Henry Seymour.
[2] Colonel Wilfred R. A. Smith.

This is a digression. Shortly after the rather staggering news about the C.O. a message from Crawley was passed down: 'To C.O. Can you send up my quartermaster sergeant as regret my s.-major has been killed.' This was another blow as the s.-major was most efficient and a very nice fellow. It was then dark and raining and we were told to go up and relieve Nos. 2 and 3. As we moved up saw Charles Creed on a stretcher with a smashed elbow. He shouted, 'Hullo Oliver, good luck', and seemed cheery.[1] Carey, I learnt, was slightly wounded but Barrington-Kennet killed, as we had heard. This was a great loss. An awfully nice fellow, with an ingenious and energetic mind: he was the pioneer of army flying and being bored with the job of adjutant to the R.F.C., which involved no flying, returned to the regiment. Very young and clever with ideas and knowledge of a lot of things.

Well, I think I will leave the account of how we got in our wounded and consolidated the line, how we joined up with the Canadians who were lost, and how breakfast involved more than a walk down the trench, till tomorrow as I am getting a bit stale. We look out on to a modern street here with a *pavé* road along which French and English transport, caissons and guns pass all day and make conversation difficult and thought impossible.

Best love. I am sending you a German forage cap which is a little more interesting, I think, than the hackneyed helmet. I could have had anything in the line of souvenirs, helmets, caps, rifles, gas machines, ammunition, equipment, watches, revolvers, maps, books, but I fear was rather idle about it. However, I am sending you my cigarette case which you will find interesting. A bullet went through my right pocket, smashed my revolver (which I have had repaired) and the case.

I did not find this out till twenty-four hours after. It was either lucky or unlucky! If the bullet would have gone through my thigh, I was unlucky in stopping it, if as I think more likely it would have smashed my hip bone at the leg joint I was lucky.

[Received June 21st, 1915]

2nd Bn. Gren. Gds. 4th Guards Brigade, B.E.F.
My first piece of news, and it is good, is what you should have heard by the time you get this by wire, namely that I am under orders to go to Wisques (?) near St Omer for a machine-gun course. This will last anything from a fortnight to a month—probably nearer a fortnight. A fellow in the Irish Guards is getting hold of their car and as Boulogne is only thirty miles away

[1] He died of wounds the next day.

it seems a clear case. I don't know the least how hard they work you at the course but I should hope that we get away about three or four in the afternoon.

The idea is precautionary; if the present machine-gun officer gets knocked out I should take his place, but I hope he won't be. I like him and, besides, being M.G.O. implies living at H.Q. where the atmosphere is a trifle too disciplinary for ensigns.[1]

Well, I promised to finish my account of the attack. It transpired that only one company left the trench, they advanced about 300 yards under a terrific machine-gun fire and when the only surviving officer looked round to find the men at his disposal he found about thirty in the front line and about forty in support. This being so it was determined not to commit any more to the attack. One of the errors made by the authorities was this. The Canadians reported that they had reached a point P8 or something, whereas in effect they were only at P7, about 500 yards to the rear. In addition their attack, which was supposed to have been simultaneous with ours, began half an hour or more late. The Irish Guards on our left were to have been supported by a regiment who shall be nameless, and who did not leave their trenches. The Irish who had rather further to go lost eighteen officers and 400 men and could not get on. Both our flanks, the Irish left and the Grenadier right, would have been, and indeed were in the air. It was therefore decided to try and join up with the Canadians on the right and to dig trenches where the attack left us. The two companies who had been in the front line were relieved by us when it got dark. We (4) moved up the old German trench and relieved the remnants of No. 3. It was pitch dark, raining and cold. There were many wounded in the scratched-up fire trenches and many others in front. John Craigie and Soccer Williams and I went out and brought in a few and Soccer continued at this all night. It was a bad job. Some of these fellows had crawled into shell-holes about twenty feet deep and getting them out was a critical business. One sergeant with both legs fractured, I remember particularly. I was in charge of the digging, which was difficult because in places the trench was up to our knees in water. We could not join them all up owing to a dyke with a bridge which was in the way. The whole place was a sea of mud, and the scene still remains incoherent in my memory. plunging about for overworked stretcher bearers, falling into shell-holes, losing our way, wet and tired, we felt all the time rather impotent. But the work was done. All the wounded,

[1] Ensigns: a term still used in the Brigade of Guards to denote second lieutenants.

including some of the Scots Guards who had lain out for forty-eight hours, were brought in and most of the dead buried. Some (I think it was three) died before we could get stretchers to take them back to the dressing station or on their way there. You see it takes four men to carry one wounded man and each journey to the dressing station could not be accomplished under four hours. This sounds rather incredible but no one realizes the difficulty of getting about, even for a man unhampered by anything. One mile an hour is good going in the mud for an officer, and you will always find yourself on the right when something has to be done on the left. No light can be shown, and you feel your way for about thirty yards as a rule before falling into a ditch or a shell-hole. You arrive to find you are only half-way.

The dawn showed us that we were entrenched in front of a wrecked farmhouse across a flat piece of terrain, bisected by the deep ditch I have mentioned before. Our right company had succeeded in getting into touch with the Canadians, who dug well, so the line was continuous. About 400 yards in front were the two farmhouses which had been our objective of the day before. During the morning 'Mother' put a shell into one of them and it disappeared. We felt that this ought to have been done before we attacked.

Crawley, Soccer and I looked over the parapet on that grey morning and realised that we were cut off, by the dyke, from our servants and our breakfast. We were not reassured by the fact that a sniper had already got one fellow crossing the bridge before it was properly light. However, it had to be done and we scuttled across safely. About ten we heard we had to attack again that afternoon and try and make some more ground. Soccer and I were not pleased by this as we were both pretty done. We crawled however into the remains of the cellar of the farm, and whilst I was saying, 'I think a little shut-eye', fell asleep for two hours. Meanwhile the snipers had got four fellows crossing that infernal gap. They were however all wounded.

After lunch Soccer and I repaired to a shell-hole which was No. 1's H.Q'rs and found Copper, Jack and others. Here under a desultory shell fire we spent two hours and then heard there was to be no attack but that we were to be relieved by the Coldstream. Immense relief. Soon afterwards: 'The 2nd Division are going back to refit.' Jack and I with one voice: 'Leave.' We immediately became very jumpy especially as the shell-fire increased. The interminable day wore on and at 9.30 the Coldstream arrived under severe wooleys. Off we went back along

128

the old German trench, with its dead, along the English wire out into the open. Everyone pretty beat but the quiet of the country and the lights of the main road were balm. A terrific march, the men singing a little. About 2.30 sighted an enormous group of chestnuts with a fire and horses in the middle. It was one of the most picturesque scenes, and might have been an old-fashioned bivouac of 100 years ago when war was more of a picnic. The night was still, we were tired, and far away you could hear the guns and see the rockets as we swung into the shadows of the trees. A long sleep—from which we woke to find a perfect day. I paid a visit to No. 2, who were in an enormous farmhouse. Their room looked out on to a courtyard, the buildings casting broad dark shadows, and the middle dappled and chequered by the light through the big chestnuts which whispered sedately to an air from the south. The effect of peace was scarcely less marked there than that of war which we had left a few hours before.

Best love and hoping to see your face before many days.

At this point, when I hope the reader will have already gained a more intimate insight into the nature of trench warfare in 1915, some interpolation on military operations and dispositions appears desirable.

In October 1914 both the Allies and the Germans had raced for the coast: the Allies to protect the Channel ports, the Germans to outflank the Allies and possibly even to restore the famous Von Schlieffen wheel on Paris. These movements led to the first battle of Ypres, won largely by the highly trained fire-power of the out-numbered British infantry. The line was stabilised: the war entered a new phase: trench systems, protected by several rows of barbed wire, were rapidly organised by both combatants, and soon stretched from the sea to the Swiss frontier. The defence became dominant.

By Christmas 1914, then, the military art was in complete abeyance. For example, the need to cut the wire by artillery fire precluded surprise. Movement, which is the expression of the military art, ceased. Napoleon could hardly have said at this moment, 'Aptitude for manoeuvre is the supreme skill in a general: it is the most useful and rarest of gifts by which genius is estimated' (quoted in *Campaigns of Napoleon*,[1] page 151), or

[1] *Campaigns of Napoleon*, by D. Chandler, Weidenfeld and Nicolson, 1967.

'Marches are War', (page 149). And what of '*la manoeuvre sur les derrières*', the key to so many of Napoleon's victories?

It is easy to write books like *The Donkeys*,[1] and to deride British and French generals, many of whom were admittedly not stars in their profession, but the authors who air these criticisms must attempt to answer the question, 'What would you have done?'

Certainly the first attempts on the British Front—the battles of Neuve Chapelle, Festubert and Loos, in two of which I took part —were pitiful and costly attempts to break the deadlock. I cannot escape the opinion that any dispassionate or truly professional summary of the chances of success on any scale by commanders and the General Staff would have concluded that our resources at that time were not adequate to the task. In both wars the German General Staff at times coldly calculated either that the resources available to them at a given moment were not adequate, and the operation was not launched, or at another that a limited victory, tactical rather than strategical, was all that could be expected. Their summaries were cold, professional documents.

Under Sir John French these 'appreciations' were founded either on wrong data, unwarranted optimism, or upon failure to understand the changes which machine-guns and wire had imposed upon the encounter battle.

My own experience as a junior officer early convinced me and others of my age and rank that it would be some years before the offensive initiative could be regained effectively by either side in the West.

The dilemma facing the High Command was baffling. What should be done next? In the Brigade of Guards we used to discuss these matters—professionally—for hours at a time. Our conclusions were that if, tactically, movement or '*la manoeuvre sur les derrières*' was impracticable in France for the present, our leaders should try a strategy which would weaken and unbalance the enemy by attacking a distant flank.

These conclusions rejected the idea—the lethal idea—of a war of attrition, but would admittedly have condemned us to a defensive role in the West. Tactically, that defensive would have to be directed to pinning down the enemy in the main theatre:

[1] *The Donkeys: A Study of the B.E.F. in 1915*, Alan Clark, Hutchinson.

no more. We thought that this pinning down should be effected by a number of small operations with limited objectives, not to be exploited beyond the initial success, and above all not to be renewed or persisted in after initial failure.

This pattern of battle became known later in the war as a Plumer battle. Plumer[1] commanded the 2nd Army: his chief of staff was Sir Archibald Montgomery. So comprehensive was the planning and mounting of his battles that local successes were gained with comparatively small losses and with comparatively little confusion.

The limited nature of the objectives—and consequently the limited time necessary to gain them—largely overcame the inherent defects of these set-pieces. The element of surprise had, of course, to be surrendered for two main reasons. First, the construction of corduroy roads through the mud, the piling up of ammunition dumps, the movement of large bodies of troops, the field hospitals thrust forward, and so forth, could not be concealed. Secondly, the massing and registration of a huge number of guns would inevitably be discovered by the enemy. All these taken together announced the threat, and roughly defined the lateral limits of the impending attack.

On the other hand, taking this type of operation as a model, preparations for two or three of these limited offensives could have been undertaken simultaneously at widely separated points in the Front. Provided the objectives were modest, and on no account any idea entertained of a deep or decisive penetration, the enemy would be obliged to keep a central reserve. By the time this reserve reached the battlefield the battle would be over, the limited objectives would have been gained.

Moreover, if the tactics were not to press on when the set objectives had been reached, the line could be consolidated very quickly, and counter-attacks by the enemy would be faced in a few hours by a dominant defensive.

So much for the pinning-down operations in France, which would become the holding theatre. What else should be done?

Most soldiers believe that what Liddell-Hart calls the 'indirect approach' is one of the roots of military wisdom. This concept was seen in vigour in the last war by our reinforcement

[1] General Sir Herbert (afterwards Field-Marshal Viscount) Plumer, commanding the 2nd Army.

of the Middle Eastern theatre and by our subsequent landings on the Mediterranean littoral. I believe it to be indisputable that the elimination of the German divisions in Africa, followed by the successful invasion of Sicily and Italy, so weakened the enemy that then, and then only, the landings in Normandy became a practical operation of war.

If the 'indirect approach' became the agreed policy, the obvious flank to attack was the Dardanelles and we, the fighting soldiers in the Brigade of Guards, whole-heartedly favoured Mr Churchill's strategy, and even hoped that we might be the spearhead chosen to carry it out. We recognised that the enemy held interior lines of communication, but thought that our supremacy at sea outbalanced this advantage.

Unfortunately the Higher Command, both in London and France, became obsessed with the dictum that final victory could only be gained by defeating the main enemy forces. This is a truism, but it was soon translated into the military fallacy or sophism that the only way to victory lies in attacking the enemy where he is strongest. The path of a truism to a fallacy is shorter than the path of the sublime to the ridiculous.

Tragically, this misapplication of a principle led to the Dardanelles strategy being regarded as a heresy, and support for it was half-hearted both in the Navy and the Army. Pursued with determination by one or two tactical commanders of drive and initiative, it would have succeeded with little loss. Unfortunately, the chance was missed, and failure must be attributed partly to hesitance at home and partly to the incompetence and dilatory conduct of certain subordinates. The war of attrition in the West was the result.

When Sir Douglas Haig succeeded to the command of the British Expeditionary Force, a much more professional outlook was apparent. He was an intellectual soldier, and versed in his profession. Unfortunately, he too was indoctrinated with the belief that the West was first and last. On the German side, Falkenhayn's insistance on the Verdun offensive, which Von Hoffmann so acidly derided, matched the Allied mistakes.

Sir Douglas Haig is an underrated commander, partly because to regain the initiative was virtually impossible when he succeeded to the command, partly because the subordinate generals, his instruments, were not, with few exceptions, of high professional calibre, partly because the citizen army had little battle experience until 1916.

My own criticism of the High Command would not be sweeping, but would be confined to three faults.

The first was that an obsession for ground, as such, grew up, and permeated the minds of all the junior formations. Capture a pig-sty at the bottom of a hill, overlooked from three sides by the enemy, the sump for the local drainage, and hold it we must and did. Any local commander who wished to withdraw 500 yards to the ridge behind him would have been in danger of being relieved of his command. Even to suggest it provoked questions about his competence and his courage. The large-scale example was, of course, the holding of the Ypres salient: a military folly of the first order. 'Ah, public opinion in France, Belgium and Great Britain would not have stood the shock of a withdrawal,' would have been the argument. Yet that same public opinion remained steadfast and unshaken when we had to evacuate the Dardanelles.

If this was a mistake on a large scale, the mistake was repeated in innumerable small instances: positions of no tactical importance whatever were tenaciously held, unnecessary casualties, unnecessary discomfort, hardship and sickness were incurred. These obsessions should and could have been eliminated in a few weeks by sensible readjustment in the line.

History shows how readily the great captains of war abandoned positions or cities despite their sentimental or prestige value. One example will suffice. Wellington, in 1812, after a number of victories, judged that the balance of force had swung against him. He retreated from Madrid, Burgos and Salamanca, and marched back in November to positions which he had held in May. These movements, if translated into the terms of 1915, would have been contrary to the military tenets of the High Command.

Secondly, it must be confessed that many of the subordinate generals, at least as high as corps commanders, had little or no experience of handling large bodies of troops and had not, by their past or training, been able to replace experience by professional or theoretical knowledge of their art.

There were, too, some long-standing causes of this lack of talent. In my youth, the father of a large family did not choose

133

his most but his least intelligent son for the Army: he may have destined him for the family living, but if the boy had greater inclination towards (say) shooting or hunting, had a better leg for a boot than a brain for a sermon, the Army was to be his career. 'Harry seems to be a bit stoopid, and not over good at his books, so he's for the Army class and—let's hope—Sandhurst.'

Unfortunately, the profession of arms requires in its higher commanders great intellectual powers, as well as those of courage and personal magnetism. The great captains of history, Alexander, Caesar, Marlborough, Napoleon, left ineffaceable marks far from the battlefield on the history and politics of whole continents. Napoleon, when he turned from strategy and tactics, remodelled not only the whole political but the whole legal system of France. Who could imagine that it was a general who wrote the famous words on the foundation of the Helvetian Confederation?

It might be said that, once master the military art, and even politics will appear within a man's intellectual grasp. This is not, of course, to say that a Marlborough or Napoleon would often be thrown up: the argument is that if the military career had been regarded as a fit career for those of high intellectual capacity, we should not have suffered from so many bad generals.

It would have been wiser to cut out the dead wood, as General Marshall did in the United States Army in the last war, and to have boldly experimented with much younger commanders, even if they had not been soldiers in 1914. Some of them had become veterans not in years but in experience on the battlefield and some, from superior intellectual parts, might have added theoretical knowledge from study of the 'campaigns of the great captains'. Yet the only high-up commander, as far as I can remember, who had been a civilian in 1914 was Sir John Monash, and a very much admired and respected corps commander he became.

Lastly, arrangements and dispositions were made which tended to increase the disabilities under which many corps and divisional commanders suffered. For example, the system which often made the H.Q. of an Army Corps a static H.Q., through which passed different divisions as they relieved others, was a fundamental mistake. Administratively it had many advantages: tactically, psychologically and from the military standpoint it had none. Corps commanders settled into their châteaux like freeholders, not temporary tenants: their staff with them: the paper work grew comfortably under the military version of Parkinson's Law. No *esprit de corps* could be built up: none of the troops knew to which corps they belonged. Furthermore, this static bureaucracy got out of touch with the troops and the conditions under which they lived, fought and died. In all my time I only saw one corps commander further up than Brigade H.Q.: he was Sir Julian Byng.

Once troops are given orders that they know cannot be carried out because they arise from ignorance of the local tactical position, they soon begin to doubt orders that can be. Of course many of these failings can be traced to the huge expansion of the Army, many others to the crippling casualties amongst regular, trained officers in 1914, but much more could and should have been done to rectify them.

Having said all this, do not let us ever forget that it was the Scottish tenacity of our Commander-in-Chief, coupled with a profound and theoretical knowledge of the military art that, in face of much contrary advice and political pressures, brought about the black day of the German Army—8th August 1918—then victory in November 1918, and led to the famous dictum, attributed to Foch: 'The French were exhausted, the Americans were disappointing, and the British were invincible.'

*   *   *

In July 1915 Lord Cavan, who was a Grenadier, was given the command of a Line division, the 50th. He asked the 2nd Battalion to release me from regimental duties to be one of his A.D.C.s.

Lord Cavan had retired from the Army before the war, and I am sure had never aspired to a higher post than that of Lieutenant-Colonel, Grenadier Guards. War and casualties had, however, given him command of the 4th (Guards) Brigade, and he had gained a glittering reputation for his handling of troops in the field, particularly in the First Battle of Ypres. He was typical of the best type of regimental officer, was not versed in staff duties, and I should guess had never studied the profession of arms from a theoretical or historical standpoint.

He often said that his reputation was chiefly due to the superb quality of the troops which he commanded. This was only partially true and unduly modest, because he exhibited one of the most outstanding virtues in a fighting soldier: he remained calm at all times, and in all circumstances. He told me that during the most critical phases of the First Battle of Ypres, when we were outnumbered several times over, and hard pressed, he never came to a decision until he had lit a small cigar. He found this simple device worth all the volumes of Hamley's *Operations of War* and *Infantry Training* put together.

Be that as it may, his decisions were right, and he deployed at every crisis an imperturbable common sense.

I reported a little reluctantly to H.Q., 50th Division, for duty. The general was not the Ouida type of guardsman to look at. He was not much taller than many jockeys, and had a round-about figure. He was not as smartly turned out as most guardsmen. That about sums up his defects. He had a delightful character: never sought or spoke for effect, and was impervious to praise or medals. I think he quite enjoyed the promotion which afterwards took him from brigadier to divisional to corps commander, and may even have relished being made C.-in-C. in Italy of the British forces diverted there after Caporetto.

I feel sure that apart from the salary—and he was far from rich —he did not care about being C.I.G.S. after the war, a post for which his experience and training did not particularly fit him. He wanted very much to get back to hunting his hounds in Hertford-shire, and generally found excuses, including a sore throat or two, for not delivering judgment or speeches on staff rides and schemes at the staff college.

He was kind to a fault to his A.D.C.s: in fact being at his H.Q. was rather like staying in the not very well found house of a peer who was much preoccupied with managing his estate.

I was happy in my job, but soon began to be restless. I felt in a back-water, *embusqué* if you like, and anyway it is irksome for a man of twenty-two to live entirely in the company of those much older than himself.

I was just about to apply to return to regimental duty when the Guards Division was formed and Lord Cavan was desig-nated its commander. There was thus no point, for the moment, in making my application. The Guards battalions, which were serving in different divisions or brigades, were to be withdrawn into the back areas and formed into a division. For a few weeks, therefore, they would not be in any fighting and, moreover, I should soon be in the company of a host of my brother officers, whom I keenly missed when banished to a Line division.

The formation of a Guards Division was much debated and criticised at the time. Many considered that the example and standards set by the Brigade of Guards should be spread as widely as possible by brigading battalions with other troops. Moreover, since the Army had lost the great majority of its trained professional officers in 1914, it was felt that to form a Guards Division, in which there were still a large number of professionals, might be to repeat the same mistake. If the division was used as intended, namely for special tactical roles, whether in attack or to restore stability where tactical disasters had occurred, we should lose too many of those whom the Army could ill spare.

However, the decision had been made, and my general rode over to his A.D.C.s to supervise the formation of the division. I found that the Prince of Wales was a supernumary officer on his staff. He was a Grenadier through and through, and had a passionate desire to serve with a battalion. His wishes were never met: fear that he would be killed or captured was the reason: he thought himself that it would not matter if he was killed, and scornfully repudiated the slightest chance of being captured if he served in a Grenadier battalion. I have described elsewhere how I fell under his charm. In a letter to my mother I described his great attention to keeping physically fit, against the day when he could serve as a regimental officer. 'The prince,' I wrote, 'eats little and walks much: we eat much and walk little.'

These were quiet and golden days, while the division was forming, but as soon as we were destined for the battle I became increasingly restless, and was again about to put in my application to return to duty with the battalion.

One day I was told the general wanted to see me urgently in his office. 'Lord,' I thought, 'one of those damned horses is lame again, probably that old skin of his which I was riding yesterday.'

Imagine my surprise when he told me that the regiment had asked for me back, to be adjutant of the 3rd Battalion, Grenadiers.

This is what I wrote to my mother:

[Received October 25th, 1915]

H.Q. 3rd Battalion Grenadier Guards. B.E.F.

This is a mere scribble. I am fearfully busy. I am afraid I have a blow for you but not nearly such a blow as you think. They offered me the adjutancy of this battalion and as I should anyway have *had* to return to duty to the Grenadiers as their losses have been so severe as to amount almost to irreparable, I accepted.

It is rather a big thing for me and as the battalion owing to losses and an incompetent C.O. has got into rather a bad state it is a great compliment.

I am absorbed in my job. I have such a terrific lot to tell you about and, other things pressing, I will delay till we get properly out. At present we are about 4,000 yards back and quite safe. We have had a spell in the trenches proper and are going to get a rest right back on the 26th.

Mother, I am afraid you will mind rather, and be anxious, but an adjutant is *far* safer (*absit omen*) than a company officer. At any rate I know the fact that it is a great chance for me will weigh greatly with you.

I have had a dewdrop or two already.

3rd Btt. Grenadier Guards, 2nd Guards Brigade, B.E.F.

October 27th, 1915

At last I have a moment. We are out twelve miles back for about three weeks starting from yesterday.

I have got an enormous lot to say but the first thing is that I don't think I have ever come nearer to enjoying the war than I have during the last fortnight or so.

The adjutant of this battalion, a very nice fellow called Guy Nugent,[1] went sick with varicose veins in the middle of the battle and on the 15th the general said to me, 'I have a chance for you if you like to take it, Porkie (Corry[2]) has applied for you to be adjutant of the 3rd Battalion. Would you care to go?' So I said, 'Yes', then, 'I will send in your name in the morning.' Fatty[3] seemed quite surprised at my taking his offer but was very pleased that I did. That day I heard that they wanted me at once, so I had a fearful rush handing over to Claude Hamilton, and the next day off I went in the prince's car to join.

It was rather unpleasant leaving our comfortable château, especially as I knew that we were for the trenches and probably for a 'push'. Freddy Blackwood, Basil's brother and very like him, turned up to join just as I was leaving, so we went off

[1] Captain Guy Nugent, afterwards Sir Guy Nugent, Bart.

[2] Colonel N. A. L. Corry.

[3] Nickname of Lord Cavan.

together. We met the battalion as they were on the march, so got rid of our kits somehow on to the baggage wagons and I was given a pony and the battalion message book and found myself adjutant. The commanding officer had gone on to the trenches, and a very nice fellow Montgomerie was in command at the moment. He is about forty-two I should say, and a dugout.[1] I got the hang of the battalion from him in about twenty minutes, and it was not cheering. All the old hands had been knocked out, there were only six company officers who had started with them on the 25th. I knew some of these but was not writing home about them. The commanding officer was very difficult to get on with. They had lost all their best N.C.O.s and 400 men, so there was a large proportion of new drafts. These six officers knew only what they had gleaned in the course of three weeks' fighting, and were all rather in the state of 'Isn't it awful?' and doing very little to make it less so.

Well, we rode on talking and halted in the grounds of the château which holds the divisional staff. The evening was turning to a bleary grey and a few wraiths of mist were just beginning to cling round the top of the great pyramid slag heap of Annequin. I could almost smell the hot tea and scones that I knew were just being put on the table inside. Well, on we moved along a road that is more than familiar to me, past the slag heap through the outskirts of Annequin down a long straight road into Vermelles. It was dark when we arrived there, and our guns which are now hidden among the ruins of the town were firing intermittently, and far away on the horizon you could just see the flicker of their shells bursting. Then up came Porkie rather like a monkey on hot bricks. Where was everything? Why hadn't he been told? We were to take over a line from K1 to K3; why weren't they marked on the map?, etc.

However, we saw each company get ten boxes of Mills bombs, and a reserve of forty boxes, sent a party off for some sandbags and moved up a trench out of the town.

Eventually we reached a hedge running along the railway, and there waited while Porkie fussed about sandbags. It was so simple. Send a party for sandbags with an officer, and let them follow us up the trench. Meanwhile let us go on. But he would have it that the whole battalion should go off, get the sandbags, eight per man or whatever it was, come back and then go on. However, I prevailed upon him to send a party, though the delay in discussion had already amounted to half an hour, and two wounded. Eventually off we went down the communication

[1] An officer on the reserve, not serving when the war broke out.

trench for about two hours with the usual 'Lost touch in rear' coming up, and so on till the C.O. and I and our headquarters— i.e. servants, signallers (telegraphists chiefly not flag-waggers you know), orderlies, etc.—arrived in or near the front line. Just as we arrived a bomb attack started about two hundred yards off. An extraordinary sight at night. A thick cloud of smoke made red by the bombs bursting underneath bang, bang, bang, bang in quick succession and red and green and yellow rockets being sent up over the cloud the whole time. Also the dug-dug-dug of machine-guns. Well, as soon as this attack started the Germans of course started to shell the communication trench, in which we were. This is always done in bomb attacks. the idea being to embarrass the attackers' supply of bombs and men from the rear. However this bit of shelling put the wind up Porkie and incidentally buried three men, and cut off our communications with the rear. We found no officers in the front trench except one second lieutenant, and he knew very little about it, and men from two units the 5th and 6th Sherwood Foresters. Well, after a very long delay we got our men in—it was about one in the morning—and the other fellows got out.

I will send this off as an instalment or I shall miss the post.

Do send me my top boots, some thick soft unshrinkable vests *s'il y en a*, and a Shetland waistcoat.

More to-morrow but we are off to practise being reviewed by the King!

Your letters are arriving anything but chronologically, but from something you say about Bobbety I gather you got my first letter.

[Received November 2nd, 1915]
3rd Btt. Grenadier Guards. 2nd Guards Brigade. B.E.F.
I am rather at a loss to know whether you got my first letter, for although you seem to refer to it you still address me H.Q. Guards Division, which probably accounts for the fact that your letters arrive irregularly.

Today we were to have been reviewed by H.M. but it was so wet it was put off, though not till we had marched out five miles. I am writing this having changed and had a bath in our very comfortable and warm sitting room. It is however rather like a Scotch dentist's waiting room.

The trouble that night was that there was no commanding officer to take over from, no headquarters, and not nearly room for the battalion in the trenches. However, the C.O. and I got into a little hole under the parapet, perhaps six feet by four, and got out some orders about digging a new sap.

The difficulty of soldiering lies in having to think in places where civilians would swear; it is damnable when your map won't unfold, and you can only spread it out over the boots of the commanding officer. The trench outside is so packed you can't get out of your dugout, much less get along; the situation becomes: 'If the orderly would come back to say that he had found my servant it would be something, if my servant turned up with my knife, I should be able to sharpen my pencil, and write the orders, and then I could probably find someone to find the captain of the company who ought to be in K2 by now but who hasn't reported accordingly, yet.' This is only imaginary, but it is that kind of worry which makes clear and definite statements difficult to make, and not any intrinsic complexity in the tactical situation.

However that night, as Montgomerie was in rear, it became apparent that if anything was to be done I should have to command the battalion and the two companies myself.

I therefore asked the C.O. to stay in our scraping 'in case anything came through' (which, as there was no wire yet laid, was quite impossible) and sallied out myself. I found the night dark and the trench packed, and our orders to bomb down a sap.

However, meeting the brigade major by the mercy of heaven, I discovered that the sap was said to be untenanted, so I prevailed upon a fellow to get a party out to occupy it, as far as he could, and dig out the shallow bits. This was done successfully and without loss, and work went on till daybreak.

The C.O., Montgomerie who had by then turned up, and I next established our H.Q. in another and more capacious dugout.[1] It was then about 5.15 a.m. and we all had that peculiar feeling in the stomach accompanied by acute depression, which is the inevitable feature of a long night and a cold morning. Found Tyson and some bacon however, got the primus going and announced breakfast in a quarter of an hour. Before that time had elapsed, however, the jolly Hun opened a terrific shell-fire, buried our breakfast, and bust about fifteen shells within five yards of our dugout, completely rattled the commanding officer, and made me think a bit about the divisional staff. However, after an hour they lifted, except for one shell which covered our second breakfast with dirt.

Went round the battalion lines and got them all sorted out. Temper shortish and language not suitable for Penshurst[2] but

1 Dugout in this case a wider section of the track with a sheet of galvanised iron as a roof.
2 Where a prudish relation of mine was living.

not very shocking. Could see that there was no method particularly in anything, and no uniformity, but that the men who didn't seem very confident in their officers were rubbing along like good 'uns. Was sent for to Brigade H.Q.s in the afternoon, and told roughly the plans for an attack that evening. This was the position

expressed roughly. Where I have written 'Germans' the trench is known as Big Willie, a part of the Hohenzollern Redoubt.

We, the Grenadiers, had to join up with the Coldstream by digging through and cleaning out any parties that might be in our way. Having joined up we were to bomb down Big Willie till we met the Scots Guards, who were to start bombing from the other end. Now these bombing attacks are matters requiring the minutest organization. You can easily throw 500 bombs in about two hours, and your supply of bombs to the bombers, who number three and who can each carry about twelve bombs, is not an easy matter. It is held by most people now that two trenches are necessary and that you cannot supply over the open. Whether I agree or not, is immaterial, but the brigade ordered us to dig through that bit and assure our supply that way, and not rely solely on bombs being passed down from the Coldstream. Well, I saw the gap and put it at seventy-five yards, the captain of the company promised to have sapped it by 9 p.m. and I considered that he could work over-ground at night if it wasn't finished and so I told the C.O. I thought we could promise it by midnight. The bombing attack was therefore to begin at 5 a.m.

The brigadier came up in the evening about 6.30 and we had a conference, in which he repeated his views and gave us the written orders.

The conference was interrupted by a bombing attack from the Germans which we easily repulsed.

I then wrote the operation orders as I was the only person who

knew the ropes of these attacks. I confess to being very proud of
them at the time, and I was enjoying myself beyond measure
seeing as how I was virtually commanding the battalion. When
the orders were written, the C.O. sent for the captains and made
me read them to them. There we were seven of us in a tiny
dugout. There was a tremendous fug and in the candlelight every
head was bent over the map, which had been made from an
aeroplane photograph.

About 11 p.m. I went out down to the sap and found they
were not getting on well and advised the C.O. to make them dig
in the open. Both the Coldstream and the Grenadier captain
reported that it was impossible to do so in view of fire from the
German sap head. I still thought it possible but these two officers'
opinion outweighed mine and the C.O. decided to go on sapping.
These two captains did not really know the game, and did not
know how high fire is at night. My point was proved by them
digging in the open the next night and joining up without loss.
Well, to cut a long story short, in spite of my barging along
through men and over men to that sap about three times they
finally reported they couldn't get through. This was at 3 a.m.
I told the brigade. Then: Your colonel has got his orders and if
he doesn't get through the consequences will be that he will not be
able to make the attack. This was awful, because he has got a
poorish reputation for ability and is supposed to be likely to cart
you. However there was nothing for it and I said it was
impossible.

I could have cried with chagrin and disappointment over our
attack not coming off and all our arrangements being made to
no purpose.

When the Coldstream started to attack at five where we
should have been, it was worse than ever, and I have never
been so bitterly despondent as I was that morning. However,
our bomb supply system was reversed, and was of great use to
them. Nevertheless their attack, being hastily organised, was
not a success, though it did not matter as the Scots Guards could
get no further than thirty yards down their side.

The C.O. meanwhile was in pretty hot water with the brigade
owing really to the captain who was digging the sap having
carted him. He looked grey and hopelessly rattled and walked up
and down swearing, accusing, excusing, and asking me questions
which no one could answer, like a child. 'Do you think the
brigadier thinks. . . . ?' etc. 'It's the fault of the Coldstream, they
didn't help . . .' etc., etc.

I may say that as soon as the bombing attack began the

Germans opened a shell-fire upon us which I suppose has rarely, if ever, been equalled for intensity. It did not reach its height till about 11 a.m., at which time I discovered an enormous dugout tunnelled out of the chalk fifteen feet down with two large rooms. Into this we got with our telephones, etc., and soon the brigadier came up. One of the nicest men in the world, John Ponsonby. He evidently did not mind much about the sap, which restored Porkie's morale at once. He asked me what made me think we could get through, so I said, 'Because I consider that it could have been dug overground.' 'Yes,' said he, 'I think so too, and as we are the oldest hands it shall be done tonight overground.' (As a matter of fact they got through without a casualty.) So the matter passed off and nothing mattered.

That day we lost one hundred men from shell-fire, heavier casualties than I have ever heard of from shells alone, and that night we dug through to the Coldstream (Montgomerie taking out a company himself). During that day two officers were buried in a dugout and both went off their heads. One poor fellow came and raved in our H.Q., which was rather dreadful. The night before Freddy Blackwood was blown up and badly concussed. He had joined up that morning.

[*Posted December 22nd, 1915*]
We come out for ten days' rest on the 24th and after that go into a very quiet part of the line. Not bad, do you think?

I have been very hard worked indeed lately, as my orderly room sergeant has proved terribly incompetent and until a new one arrives I have to do all his work besides my own. I got a cake yesterday from you and a very good one too. About food—could you send me a parcel about twice a week, do you think? A dozen kippers say, a pound of fresh butter and a cake or a cooked bird alternatively. Send them off if you will on Mondays and Thursdays.

The great thing is to know when to expect them and for the parcels to come pretty regularly!

I must give some description of our times now.

We ride out through a dreary fen-country, flat and featureless, occasionally one of our own guns making a flash near us and the shelling singing over one's head.

Thus for two or three miles when we strike the La Bassée road running as straight as a die as far as you can see. We ride through a desolated little village with a large crucifix and on past two muddy little forts to a barricade known as Euston Post. There we leave our horses, steaming and muddy in the reek, and walk on a few hundred yards and then to our left down a lane. The dug-dug-dug of a machine-gun can be heard and perhaps you will see a long file of soldiers with packs and bags of coal and trench waders slung on them, splashing and cursing along. Soon we come to Ebenezer farm, the farm itself wrecked and the moonlight showing through the roof and the walls. We turn into a little courtyard with a sentry, pass through it—there is a scurry of rats, and we stand in the doorway of the dugout. Inside two oilstoves make it wonderfully warm. Round the walls hang a few maps and files of messages.

Until the relief is complete we are very crowded, but when the Kiddies[1] get out and we get to work there is enough room.

The next morning, perhaps about six, we splash off up the willow-lined road to the trenches and round we go, the C.O. wasting time looking at the Aubers range through a periscope and saying that he can see Germans everywhere. He never makes a suggestion which to my mind is worth a damn, and instead of looking at our lines which is the place which wants attention he peers through a periscope. It maddens me at times. If he goes up alone, which is rare, he always comes back having had the narrowest shave and having behaved with the utmost coolness. _C'est pour rire_. It is now 3.15 in the afternoon and he is drinking a stiff whiskey and soda.

However it doesn't matter, as all his work is done for him by Mark Maitland[2] and me.

By the way who is Jessie Lawrence,[3] who sent me a Christmas present? Do let me know at once because I must write and thank her. _Au revoir_.

[1] Brigade slang for Scots Guards.
[2] Major Makgill-Crighton-Maitland, second-in-command.
[3] Lady Lawrence, afterwards Lady Trevethin, mother of Lord Oaksey.

2

At this point there is an unexplained gap in my file of letters covering nearly three months. I have not reproduced a letter of the 8th January: it describes too many personalities.

During this time my commanding officer was superseded, and Lieutenant-Colonel G. D. Jeffreys temporarily[1] commanded the battalion until Sergison-Brooke, who was to be the next commanding officer, arrived.

As his adjutant I saw 'Ma' Jeffreys, one of the greatest regimental soldiers, at work: I learnt, in a week or two, more about the art of command, more about the interior economy, more about the thousand and one details that are necessary for the efficiency of a battalion, than I could have learnt in six months in an Officers Training Corps.

'Before we inspect dinners,' he might say, 'let me look at the corporals' mess fund.' 'Here it is, Sir.' '. . . Yes, all right. Thank you. Let's check the cash with the quartermaster: get him here.' The quartermaster arrives: the cash is, of course, correct. The C.O. to the quartermaster: 'I don't think you should keep quite so many francs.'

Now to dinners. Out we go to the cookers.[2] To the sergeant: 'Take the lid off that. Hm, looks too greasy. Sergeant, the stew is not up to standard. Take the cook's name. I will not have good rations spoilt by careless cooking. I shall come again the day after tomorrow, and unless there is a marked improvement the cook concerned will be returned to duty.' 'Sir.' 'Let me look at your biscuits. Hm, rather soft: they must be kept in as airtight tins as possible.' 'Sir.'

Return to the orderly room. 'Oliver, check the battalion's

---

[1] The Order of Battle does not show this, since Colonel Sergison-Brooke's appointment was antedated.
[2] Horse-drawn field kitchens.

handcuffs.' 'Sir.' They are in order. And so on, until every detail had been checked.

He paid the most careful attention to the orders which I had drafted for the commanding officer about the issue of the rum ration, and which were a first and hurried attempt to remember and imitate those of the 2nd Battalion, in which I had served. One of the salient points is that the rum ration must be served out under the supervision of an officer accompanied by a sergeant, and in the trenches when a man refuses the ration (and there are always a few teetotallers) it has to be poured out on the ground.

His inspection took about a week, and he pronounced the battalion to be in good shape. The adjutant was not returned to company duty and was nearly, but not quite, commended.

Then 'Boy' Brooke arrived: as good a soldier as 'Ma' Jeffreys. I was his adjutant until he was wounded in September 1916, and his brigade major at the end of the war. This relationship in war is one of the closest in human affairs, and I admired and liked 'Boy' Brooke without reservation, unless it be that I wished that he spoke more often before luncheon. He was to me the example of a soldier, a commander and a friend: strict but humorous; highly trained, he knew as much about the theory of war as about its practical application. He inspired love in his subordinates and something near fear in his superiors. The battalion under him became one of the very best in the Guards Division, and that would put it pretty high in the Army.

I could, of course, tell countless anecdotes about him and his methods. Here is one.

We had a rather unpopular temporary officer in the battalion who, we thought, should not have found his way into the regiment. He was at once rather over-refined and a fearful snob. One day he was sent on as the officer in charge of a billeting party. We had marched twelve miles behind the Somme battlefield on a hot, dusty day, and the dust is chalky in that part of France. The C.O.'s jaw was set, and he was obviously as thirsty as I was. No word was spoken during this five-hour march.

We reached the cross-roads outside the village in which we were to be billeted and at which the billeting party, with details of the billets allocated to each company, and the guides were to meet us. No billeting party was in sight. Through clenched teeth: 'Where are the orders?' I produced them from the battalion pouch. It was all right: the orders were clear and precise.

We had to march into the small square of the village and halt. 'Find him, and bloody quick,' he said to me. I cantered off, but no trace. Just as I had got back from my fruitless search, the officer in question emerged from an *estaminet*, and gave some impression of wiping drops of beer from his moustache. He came up and saluted, and not a Grenadier salute at that. His jacket was flecked with white at the back: he had probably been sitting against a white-washed wall in the pub.

'Ay regret to inform you, Sir, that the accommodation in this village is quaite inadequate.' The C.O.: 'Is that any reason that you should be covered with bird-shit?' He was shortly afterwards made the chief commandant of a muddy camp, but I do not remember an ill-brushed jacket behind the lines from that day forth.

After two or three months of routine in the trenches, chiefly in the area Richebourg-Neuve Chapelle-Laventie, where the mud was the chief enemy and where the billets behind the line were poor though watertight, we were sent to Calais for drill and rest.

March 5th, 1916

This on arrival at Calais. But first let me tell you about our other camp and our departure and Morton.[1]

Eventually we got the officers' mess very reasonably warm, which made the whole difference. Nobody minds getting vilely cold all day as long as there is a prospect of coming into something warm at the end of it.

I think I told you about the day of our arrival there. Cold simply fearful. Canvas huts. Heavy snow. Wind from the N.E. Officers' mess with a gold beater skin roof. No hot food. Rather tiresome work. Men mostly in tents. Crimea a joke to it.

I am just going to send this off by John Hopley,[2] who has got leave because his wife is very ill (but he has just had better news).

You will be pleased to hear that I am now going to write to you every day beginning tomorrow.

Oh, Mother, I want a pair of ordinary boots. Would you get hold of a pair of mine and get some artist to make me a pair of thick brown ones, not too square in the toe and with those tongues that overlap at the bottom and let the water out?

[1] Morton Stephenson, a friend and neighbour in the country, not in the Guards.
[2] Captain John Hopley, Grenadier Guards, slightly wounded in the knee.

3rd Bn Grenadier Gds.
March 14th, 1916

Thank Goodness, it is now warm and beautiful but we were really under quite severe hardships on our arrival here. The second day we arrived we sallied from under our canvas to meet a snoring N.E. flecked with snow. At about 8.30 the wind dropped a little and the snow came streaming down. Nothing but canvas to get under. Cold intense. Answering official correspondence with the pencil in one's fist, washing, shaving were all loathsome. It lasted about four days.

Nearly every evening we dine in Calais to escape the chill at a good second-rate restaurant where you use the fork for everything, don't you know. And so to bed—via a drive in a *fiacre*—about 11.15 p.m.

Sometimes, as we clank through the town on very well-groomed horses followed by mounted orderlies, we are almost Prussian in our '*splendeur militaire*'. Meanwhile this brigade goes into the line last, i.e. about 26th or 27th, which is an enormous pull as we get the benefit of the others' work. Already the other division (a regular one) has done a lot to make the line safer and by the time we get there we think it will be quite 'cushy'.

17th

At last, though I ought to be on parade, I am writing to you! Forgive the delay and remember that whenever I don't write there is nothing doing except hard routine work. It is much easier to write when we are in the trenches than not, when it is often impossible. The last three days, however, I admit that our organised pleasures have taken up a good deal of time.

Yesterday afternoon the ground round the camp was a marvellous sight. The sounds too were a wonderful mixture. In one corner the chaplain was holding a voluntary service. Within fifty yards a boxing match was going on, with the usual applause and exhortations between the rounds. Immediately beyond this the Coldstream were holding some quasi-comic sports. Sack races, fighting on the greasy pole. Oh I forgot, the band of the Scots Guards—full band—was playing at the voluntary service. Next to the sports we were playing an officers' cricket match on cocoanut matting. About 300 yards away our drums were playing and the men occasionally joining in the tunes or whooping. Overhead but some way off two German aeroplanes were getting a proper piece of shelling from our anti-aircraft guns. A shell or two could be heard crashing in about half a mile to the north of us—a favourite spot and regularly shelled.

149

'As it was in the beginning'—played by the band—'Kill him, Dusty,' from the boxing match, roars of laughter as a sack man fell, crack from our cricket match,

> The one that use ter
> Wake me up at 4 a.m.

fortissimo from the men. Dug-dug-dug-dug, from the anti-air-craft pom-pom. Crash, crash from the shell.

It was exactly like the work of a modern composer of the Strauss variety writing a descriptive piece. You would have smiled.

March 21st, 1916

I try very hard to write every day but we have been trekking about such a lot and getting in about three in the afternoon and then I have to fix up a hundred and one things and nearly always end by missing the post.

My only piece of news is that leave has reopened and that if all goes well I should get it in exactly a month (twenty-eight days), i.e. after one go of sixteen days (in front line and support) in the trenches.

I am writing this in the orderly room at Poperinghe. Our stay in Calais was very nice towards the end. We got up some horse races, in one of which my pony was second. I was delighted to see him gallop so well. This was on the sands on a glorious afternoon. All the officers of this brigade were there and all of us had our ponies in the races. The massed drums played and the day came under the heading of *splendeur militaire* and was very like the traditional race day.

Every evening we dined in Calais and came out cheerfully to our camp in a hackney carriage. It is true that dawn sometimes held a somewhat stark reality for you as the wind whistled round your pyjamas. But by eleven one was happy, warm and probably went for a gallop in the afternoon. Eventually we had to go and bid good-bye to our restaurant and the admirable claret, and the chance of giving your pony his head.

So off we started, breakfasting on a raw morning on eggs like the morning, at 5 a.m. and journeyed not without Bacchus to Cassel. The day had turned hot when we arrived and we sweated like heroes on the way up the steep hill. The road zigzags up it and you could see the serpentine battalion down to its tail. Cassel stands up very sharply from the plain and gives the most superb reward to any who have toiled up. The whole country lies at your feet and fair enough, with only the blot of one or two aeroplanes looking like midges flying over it.

Well, we swung away from the hill to Oudezeele, a charming little village almost Dutch in cleanliness. I lodged over an impractical shop full of blue and white china and felt a bed under me for the first time for twenty-five days. From there we moved this morning, breakfasting at 5.15 a.m., to Poperinghe into Divisional Reserve. The other two brigades are in and we relieve one of them in sixteen days.

Poperinghe is a foul town, really Belgian in dirt, but full of my friends. The *on dit* now is that there are to be no more big pushes and nothing except these little shows like the Bluff, preceded by terrific artillery fire. But nobody knows. Anyway we are not for it at present.

In March 1916 the Guards Division joined the XIV Corps, 2nd Army, holding the left of the British line and the Ypres salient. We remained in this sector until July. A few words about Poperinghe and the Ypres salient are therefore necessary.

Poperinghe is about eleven miles from Ypres, and gave what shelter it could from shells and the weather to the reserves behind the salient.

The troops, by the way, called Ypres 'Wipers'. It is intriguing to remember that the English soldiers of the Middle Ages—their forbears—used this insular mispronunciation.

The *coton d'Ypres* was a textile widely known in the civilised world in those ancient days. I was brought up to believe that, from elision, mispronunciation or false analogy, we got our homely English word 'diaper' from *coton d'Ypres*. The Oxford Dictionary pours some scholarly cold water on this agreeable fallacy, and icily remarks: 'A gratuitous guess that this word was perhaps derived from Ypres in Flanders has no etymological or historical basis.' I am always sad to see legends taught in youth die so ingloriously.

Ypres was utterly destroyed, a dead city. On the other hand a new life, which it had never seen before and was never likely to see again, had come to Poperinghe. No *ville de lumière*, its drab streets and dingy environs were thronged. Everywhere there was movement, young men, voices, laughter, horses, guns, wagons, all the back-stage view of war: truly a strange contrast to the silent, deserted shard of the city of Ypres.

Though I must have spent many days there, I remember strangely little of Poperinghe itself except its concert party—

all male—which had modelled itself on the Co-optimists.[1] By contrast, I can see very clearly in my mind's eye the railway that led from Poperinghe to Ypres. Fear and its milder brothers, dread and anticipation, first soften the tablets of memory, so that the impressions which they bring are clearly and deeply cut, and when time cools them off the impressions are fixed like the grooves of a gramophone record, and remain with you as long as your faculties. I have been surprised how accurate my memory has proved about times and places where I was frightened, and how faded are the memories of gaiety and pleasure.

The Germans had a tactless habit of shelling Poperinghe railway station with a high-velocity naval gun: its shells gave no notice of their arrival. One day Aubrey Fletcher and I were returning from leave. We were in one of the front carriages in our train, and as we pulled into the station a shell whistled in and apparently hit the train a few carriages behind us. The enemy usually followed the first with a few more before tea, so 'Flick' Fletcher ordered the engine driver to pull a hundred yards or two out of the station before the troops detrained. He obeyed with alacrity, and while we were all detraining sure enough the second shell hit the place where the train had been.

Five or six officers who were reinforcements, and who we were told were coming into the theatre of war for the first time, were killed by the first shell. Aubrey Fletcher had been at the Front from 1914 and I from February 1915. We were untouched. Such are the fortunes of war.

When we relieved troops in the front line we used to go by train from Poperinghe to the base of the salient. We got into our carriages in a field in the pitch darkness, and got out of them in another field ten miles further on just west of Ypres. Getting the guardsmen into the carriages was like trying to put a swollen cork back into the bottle. While this slow insertion was going on, our ears were pricked for shells. As far as I remember, none ever came. Perhaps the Germans did not believe that anyone could have the effrontery to go to Ypres by train. Anyway it is not in the book, or their book.

March 24th, 1916

Well we are now at it and have been for four days. I will tell you.

[1] A well-known concert party, dressed as pierrots, of which Pélissier was one of the most popular stars.

We left our billets and got into the train on a pitchy dark night. The men were carrying gum boots, a blanket and steel helmets, they looked like Christmas trees and it was with the utmost difficulty that we pushed them into the train. Often they got stuck completely in the doorway and it wanted two men to help them in from behind.

We bumped along for half an hour, and then got out just beyond the town.[1] I was to go on with our H.Q. behind the leading company. So off I went along the railway for a short distance, then turning into the town.

Anyone who has been there will know the meaning of the abomination of desolation. When he hears it a definite picture will be recalled to his mind.

Of course I have seen villages and little towns laid flatter, and very desolate they are. But a big city empty and ruined is an unnatural crime. You have been through the City on Sunday and how depressing it is, but add to that the half light and the shattered houses and the voracious scream of shells followed by their roar of anger as they only make desolation more desolate, and you have a picture of it.

Well, we went down a narrow street, then across the square and then into some dugouts on the canal bank, dug well into the sides with roofs of iron girders and ten feet of earth above them. These were to be our quarters for four days. From here we do four days in front, then back for four more, than up again for four, then back to reserve billets miles away for eight. The canal bank is a good enough place as far as shells are concerned but you can get no exercise as very little movement is possible in the day. So it means one gets no exercise for sixteen days practically. You live like a rat. Of course the horrors of the place are grossly exaggerated and the real trouble has been the appalling idleness and incompetence of the troops who have been holding the line. Nothing whatever has been done, they have simply sat there and a lot of their casualties have been due to the bad state of repair of their lines.

The birthday cake was a terrific success. I am in the middle of Mary's[2] novel and think it awfully good. Of this more anon when I write to her. Books are essential here.

[Received April 5th, 1916]

By the greatest piece of luck, instead of spending four days in Ypres, this tour we have got four days in a camp right back and

1 i.e., a little south of Ypres, not east of it.
2 My sister, Mary Lyttelton, afterwards Lady Craik.

153

we shall always have this when we are in this sector. After our next sixteen days, which I hope to spend in Gt College Street, we shall be in this same place and we shall get four days in and four days out in the camp.

We got rather snuff our first night, some very intense shelling from all directions which laid most of the trenches flat.

I went on with the signal section to take over a little earlier than the battalion and as I passed through the city of dreadful night there was absolute quiet except for the occasional crash of a tile.

Our headquarters were well back in a deep dugout in a wood about three hundred yards from the road.

As you come up this road you see the Verey lights all round you.

That night the situation became very critical, all our trenches were flat, the shelling was intense and we anticipated an attack which unfortunately never came. However most of the night we at H.Q. could not get communication with the Front and only got news from an officer who came down from the Front trenches. He had been twice buried on the way down and was a bit rattled. His account was very lurid but Mark Maitland (the C.O. was on leave and Mark felt the responsibility rather acutely) and I, being pretty old hands, divided his story by six and this estimate turned out to be about right. It was true that the trenches were flat but all the same in the morning the men had got some kind of cover and all their ammunition cleaned and laid out ready.

We had an artillery barrage set up most of the night to stop any rot.

I won't deny that it was a wearing night and the noise was hideous, everything shaking and throbbing and crashing with sound. But continuous noise in a way is not worse than those stabs of sound at five-minute intervals which is one's ordinary lot.

The next four days were dead quiet.

Post going.

April 19th, 1916

It was rather a crusher about leave.[1] However it is confidently stated by everyone that it reopens on the 25th or 27th. If all goes well and it isn't stopped again I shall be back on the evening of 27th or 28th. We are now going into billets in support for four days. I hear that it was stopped entirely because of the Easter traffic in England. Scandalous, I call it.

[1] It had been postponed.

Well, since I last wrote we have had a quiet, but very busy time trying to get our mud-hole into something like order. The trenches are in a very bad state, knocked about by shell-fire and very fairly wet. You have to be careful about showing yourself in daylight so that all work has got to be done at night which makes it slower.

The attack mentioned in the papers was just on our left but did no earthly good even though the bombardment preceding it was terrific.

It is a poor spot up here and very uncomfortable. You never get a bed or any furniture in your room even when you are in Divisional Reserve. In the trenches, of course, you live like a rat and come out at night. Our dugout looks back down the road on to the town about a mile away and the landscape consists of two cemeteries, one latrine and four ruined houses into which the Hun daily plants salvoes of 5·9s, much to our satisfaction as they are 400 yards from us. After four days in which one gets no sleep and a great deal of what the French call *cafard*, I believe, we trek down into the town and board the train. In this place you never arrive anywhere or leave anywhere except between 2 and 4 a.m.

On the way back last time it was a perfect moonlight night that made the ruins ivory and every line of desolation stood out sharp. I went into the cloth hall, which looked superb with the moonlight streaming through the shell-holes and windows leaving thick mysterious shadows. If you go through the town late there is absolute quiet except for a few shells homing it like ducks. But the town beats them every time and wraps them in silence and all you know is that it is silent, silent, silent.

[Received June 3, 1916]
I cannot understand why you have not got my letter. I wrote and sent it home by Eddy Ward[1] at least a week ago. Can he have forgotten to post it? This is a short scrawl sent home by my servant to ease your mind.

I am sitting under a large tree outside in quite a nice garden. Rather tired however, having marched sixteen miles and ridden a few round our scattered billets already today. But they were miles in the right direction—away from the Front.

We shall have, I hope, a fairly peaceful time, although to-morrow at 6 a.m. we are off on another march of ten or twelve miles.

[1] Captain Edward Ward, Grenadier Guards.

Personally I have been very busy indeed and have kept hard at it—not without enjoyment—the last three weeks except for one day.

I looked forward to it like anything and sprang off my air bed at about 8 a.m. to look at the weather like a schoolboy on the day of the Eton and Harrow.

It was calm and blue and a faint haze gave promise to heat. The bugle sounded very neat and sharp. Breakfast, Devonshire cream: excellent. Commanding officer almost talkative—and as this was breakfast it augured well for his 'form' later on. Three-quarters of an hour in the orderly room. Horses at 9.30 a.m. Very well turned out and fresh. White head rope, sparkling harness, wash leather gloves, very smart gaiters and spurs. An hour and a half's ride through the wood. Conversation—super-tax, grouse shooting, dinner parties, women at the same, etc.—a pleasant feeling of pleasure to come.

So back to our camp: the commanding officer and I. Found Morton and Hollins drinking Vermouth in the mess with Sloper Mackenzie, a particularly delightful fellow who commands a company. A large motor was waiting. To be continued in our next.

The next letter describes a day's leave, for which we got a lift in the staff car mentioned above.

Well, we got into the motor and drove along a rather pretty road, with the usual avenue, through uninteresting country. Very good the change, though. Arrived at Dunkerque about 1.30 and repaired to a little hotel. Morton had ordered the lunch, in fact he insisted on giving it. It was quite admirably cooked. This was the menu (of course there was a little too much: it would have been perfect without the tournedos, for instance):

> Hors d'Oeuvres.
>
> Soles à la Princesse.
>
> Tournedos.
>
> Asparagus.
>
> Poulet rôti.
>
> Salade.
>
> Strawberries.

The whole washed down by Château Yquem. A terrible orgy.

156

So on to Calais. Walked about on the sands. Everyone incredibly dowdy in black. Back again. Antoinette[1] *en vacance*. Damn. Cinema. Charlie Chaplin at a music hall. Quite admirably funny. Dinner. Moderate, but a good bottle of Perrier Jouet, and so home sleeping most of the way.

We shifted on the following Thursday and got a message: 'You will only stay in the new area one night.' Great excitement. Vimy, Verdun and, by some very young officers, Egypt, Baghdad. However, it only turned out to be that there were no training grounds available.

Marched at 7.30. This means getting up punc. at 5 a.m., you know. Very hot and dusty march. Arrived about 1.15 p.m. Blanket lorry in ditch. Rode about three miles for it. Back again: lunch: new defence scheme to work out. A lorry to arrange for. Cajoled one out of the 6th Division. Took two hours' intrigue. Back again by 7.30 p.m. Orders for new move arrived 7.45. Worked them out and got out a new defence scheme by 9.15. Dinner. Bed. Dead.

Marched again at 7.30, getting up at 4.30. Reviewed by the generals *en route*. Battalion looked fine. Arrived here 1 p.m. Verrry rrrustic, consequently not very comfortable. Sheets, however. Hard work on fatigue scheme, etc. New defence scheme. Dinner about 9 p.m. Bed. Dead.

Up the next morning at 5.30 to dig. Back at 11 a.m. Two hours' complete peace.

Specimen of three days in the life of an adjutant. Rather fun all the same.

Have you seen the Cinderella menu thing? I think it charming. I want to hear, you know: the exact takings and expenses and all that.[2]

June 17th, 1916

We are in the line again, having been rushed up by lorries to a place I expect you know of,[3] where there has been a good bit of fighting. By the time you get this we ought to be out again, as we are only stopping the gap for a bit. Things are not so bad as they are painted, but the troops we have relieved were very rattled and demoralised, perhaps not entirely without justification but largely from their own fault. Our training was very strenuous, as we had night operations and all sorts of horrors and during

[1] The very pretty and charming milliner's assistant, with whom we all joked and flirted.

[2] Apparently it referred to some function in aid of the National Theatre.

[3] The Ypres salient, in the neighbourhood of the Menin road.

the last part of the time it rained like anything. Then we suddenly got the order to move and off we were rushed, up into the line in no time.

I am afraid I can't tell you any more at the moment because of course these sort of movements are very secret and even a description of this place would be unwise.

I will write you a fuller account later.

Am very well and looking forward to leave in three weeks, which is only a week! A rotten letter I fear.

———

This is from a dugout—a pretty good one though.

I was very interested by the article in the U.S. magazine but did not think it extraordinarily good. Some the the things were worth saying, others were calling in different names what everyone knows. To say that the Germans in their original advance on Paris sacrificed the principle of concentration to the principle of movement is truistic.

But perhaps to a civilian who imagines that you can whisk divisions, say, from the Trentino to Cernovitz in thirty-six hours it is more instructive than to someone who has seen an ammunition column trying to detrain on its arrival out here.

The writer when he gets off strategy and comes on to tactics is obviously and patently at sea. All the principles he enunciates might conceivably be known even to the press. That to break thro' successfully you must create one defensive flank before operating on the other is known to the proverbial schoolboy of Macaulay. And to talk to us about what an infantry soldier should carry in the attack smacks of the grandparental eggs.

Do we not all know that to be successful the soldier must carry: one rifle, one bayonet, one entrenching tool, 170 rounds of ammunition, six bombs, one pair of wire cutters, two days' rations, six sandbags, one coil of French wire, five pickets, one roman candle, one red parasol and a toothpick? Weight 840 lbs.

June 26th, 1916

We are having a very peaceful time at this moment. Raymond [Asquith] and I are sitting outside the officers' mess. It wants about half an hour to dinner. We are in huts in a wood and very safe. Nor do I think we are going to do anything very violent for some time, but only the ordinary routine.

It was really very interesting our last six days. We were dug in in a wood, which had been shaved and cut to pieces by shell-fire. The whole ground was like a Gruyère cheese, only worse, because the shell-holes overlapped everywhere. However, shelling was not very effective there as, owing to the thick undergrowth, made even thicker by fallen trees, boughs and debris, we were difficult to locate. It is rather a relief feeling that perhaps the Hun does not know exactly where you are, after you have become accustomed to facing him about a hundred yards away on the flat.

Damn, here is an orderly with a whole packet of stuff, which completely tears me for any more tonight. I will try and send this by someone going on leave and will finish it tomorrow.

You must really try and restrain people from talking in London about things of which they know nothing. John Buchan may know everything but he hasn't been within a hundred yards of the truth yet. George West's[1] only piece of information was at any rate correct, but both the above are the sort of people who lose us a good 10,000 lives simply because of curiosity.

More tomorrow. Gt. haste.

August 3rd, 1916

Phew! It is hot. One's throat gets filled with chalk in this country and these hillsides are sweltering.

At this moment we are in a camp on top of an exceeding high hill and moderately comfortable.

We are very much in reserve and in the background and it is a case of 'If so and so and so get there and if such and such gain the line about ten miles off you will be required to assist them in entering Berlin.' We are very much the Emperor's prize gladiators.

We are doing some pretty severe fatigues, but they don't 'take' me, as they say, and so I am comparatively idle.

Marching the other night—a close and thickly scented night —I have never heard the men in such form. They sang for at least three hours on end and never the same song for more than three mins.

It is not wholly unpleasant at night, this marching to the sounds of 'Op along Sister Mary, op along', and 'I'm a married man so for Gawd's sake don't take me home', and 'Les Cloches de Corneville' appearing incongruously between 'Michigan' and 'The Sunsheeine of thy Smeeiles'.

I really have never seen men in such trim as these. They are wonderfully cleaner than anything else you see and with their bronzed faces and enormous physique make the ladies of France look out of their windows, I can tell you.

[1] George Cornwallis West, husband of Mrs Patrick Campbell.

I am writing a long and fairly comprehensive account of some of our doings, which must remain at present secret.[1]

Well, more soon. There will be nothing to excite or make you nervous for a fortnight.

[Date indecipherable, presumably about 6th August, 1916]
I think we are in the worst billets out of the line that I have ever struck.

The filth left behind by the troops is inconceivable and would make the Germans buck up if they could see it.

However we are gradually getting it clean, but the flies we shall never master quite, I fear.

At present sleep after 4 a.m. or during the day is out of the question. Yesterday morning I woke up and, gradually opening an eye, counted seventy-two flies on the arm of my pyjamas between my shoulder and my wrist.

There were thirty-two dead ones in my shaving water, so that will give you an idea. *Mon Dieu.*

My bedroom, twelve feet by six, opens on to the kitchen and looks out on to the midden. However, I have left it, and Guy Rasch[2] and I have had a most luxurious bivouac put up in an orchard. We can sleep now and until the sun gets right up the flies leave us alone.

I rode up[3] a little way yesterday. The whole place behind on the rolling country is one vast camp. There was a storm coming up black behind us, near us a few men were playing cricket in the middle of some horse lines and in front of us you could see 'history'.

Every detail shows up, and no wonder Mr Beach Thomas[4] can give some fairly comprehensive *coup d'oeil* of the trouble. It was a very impressive sight as you had all the mechanical inventions of war at your feet, lorries, trains, guns, above you streams of aeroplanes, and in addition all the solemnity of a wide and sombre view with the rolling smoke of shells bursting along the skyline and the stabs of light from the guns. Behind, the storm, and nature taking a hand.

Well, more anon. We have a most tiresome dinner with the A.S.C. tonight. But where the cars are, there one must dine.

August 17th, 1916
I am writing this in a tent, on my back on the air mattress, rather

[1] It is now untraceable.
[2] Major (afterwards Lieutenant-Colonel) G. E. C. Rasch.
[3] i.e., towards the front trenches.
[4] The well-known war correspondent.

tired after three days of continual movement. They never leave us alone for long; we shift apparently without reason about every twenty-four hours.

However we have had practically no trenches, in consequence it is not so bad. But shifting means hard work and not very much time to oneself.

The civilian world does not realize perhaps that a thousand men moving with everything means a certain amount of packing up and a certain amount of general discomfort.

Oh, by the way, this silver pencil and chain are the absolute blessing of my life. It is not so much when I am in the orderly room and have sat down to it, as when I have just to sign my name or something like that [that] it is so invaluable.

We have I think moved eleven times this month.

Yesterday the *Hun* made us shift.

We were perched rather uncomfortably in a camp in the middle of a little village. The commanding officer and I were feeling most anxious for lunch as we had breakfasted at 6 a.m. and were making our way down the street when we heard that most bloody of all sounds—the approach of a salvo of 5·9s. The first one or two which were unpleasantly close to him and me did not get anyone, but we lost two men getting the troops out of the town. There is nothing more unpleasant than being shelled when you are very tightly packed in a village and when there are no trenches or dugouts or anything to get into. One shell, you see, bursting right may get fifty men—that is one thing—the other is that there is usually only one way out of a village, sometimes two, and that is down the road. All the approaches are of course marked and duly shelled, so that evacuating a village is highly critical.

Well, when all was over we returned in an absolute torrent of rain which made the main street simply one torrent of muddy water and which was pouring through the roof of our mess room, but not keeping down the flies which rose like starlings from the downs, off the [cold] tongue.

This was about 3 p.m. Then the sun came out and the rain stopped and all was well.

I sat down to write a few things when I'm damned if a battery of 60-pounders[1] about forty yards away and only just off our direct line started firing. They are the noisiest guns there are, and the concussion of the report is terrific. That night every time one of them went off it blew out all the candles in the mess, so that will

---

[1] i.e., our own guns.

give you an idea of what a resting battalion gets sometimes. Well they loused off regularly every three mins. till about 6.30 p.m. when I started this letter. I am afraid I fell asleep after writing a few words till 7.45. Then I had just taken off my field boots and was in bare feet when sssew,[1] they began again.

The commanding officer and all the officers had gone out to the trenches. I was the only one in camp except a capital fellow called Jackson.

So we proceeded to get the men out again. This time the shelling was worse—I think the Hun was looking for our friends the 60-pounders—and four or five shells fell plum in the middle of the camp—by the mercy of heaven just as we were leading off with the rear company and this time no one was got except fifteen of another Territorial battalion who were in dugouts at the other end of the village.

After this we stayed in the fields for about an hour and then back again—the men much amused by the operation and singing 'Here we are, here we are, here we are again.' Then the commanding officer arrived and the others with news that the brigade wanted us to shift, which some of us were not sorry to do. Now we are twice as comfortable and quite safe and listened yesterday morning and this morning to our late billets being shelled, oddly enough, or rather according to frequent German practice, at exactly the same time.

I have got a large hut with a big table which I share with that most delightful of men, Guy Rasch. In the morning, I represent 'Intelligence' and he represents 'Operations'. I ascertain by a careful system of espionage at what time the commanding officer will be called and I keep 'Operations' informed in the morning of how far the C.O. has got with his dressing. We generally succeed in either defeating the opposition and being at our eggs and bacon first or at any rate in tying with him.

Well I must stop now.

September 9th, 1916

I have just got your letter with the picture of Wittersham.[2] The mails you will see are most irregular. Do send me some photographs of the other side of the house. Looking at this one I could absolutely feel my finger in the peculiar catch on the front door and hear it open and see the visitors' book and Doll Liddell's barometer, the smoking room door and the view of oneself in the glass over the little gold infant.

[1] i.e., the enemy 5·9s.
[2] The family house near Rye.

But I should like the view from the rose (or Italian) garden.

By the way, the fly sprayer was a tremendous success. So much so that the muslin was hardly needed for two days. The flies are no trouble at all now in the mess room. There are a few it is true round the sideboard, but they cannot get at the food because we have got the little covers over all the butter, etc.

But the Heppel solution was wonderful. We are trying to get some as an 'issue' and if you could send out say a couple of bottles we might get it from H.M. Gov. by the time that runs out. It is very expensive, isn't it? No fly can live under it.

By the way, I don't think they can keep us out of the trouble for very much longer, do you? Things are going well, though very steadily. The Hun I don't think cares about waiting much just now. A lot of people have been shot in the back by him coming out of deep dugouts, so naturally assaulting troops who have to cross a line don't leave much to chance or collecting parties behind them.

The enemy's losses have been really heavy, some of the sunk roads being breast high in dead. We saw the Somme films the other night in a field. It certainly does give some idea of it. It was not very well attended out here though everyone should see parts of it. All the last part, German prisoners and troops on the march and so on, are better looked at out of the window.

I have been very busy lately.

September 21st, 1916

At last I can write to you. I hope you went and saw Streaty[1] as I told you and have heard all the news first.

The 15th[2] was the most wonderful day of my life. I drank every emotion to the dregs and I was drunk. It was superbly exhilarating.

The show as a whole was not a complete success. We did not, I mean, gain our last objective but that was because our right flank was in the air—the division on our right did not come on. But we forced our way across 1,200 yards of ground and captured two trench systems and 500 prisoners. Our casualties have been frightful but that was a matter for the next day—that day we had joy in battle and felt the passions of hate and fear and grief and anger and pain and fatigue—it can be a passion to wish to sleep—and gratitude and prayer and peace.

But I will tell you.

[1] Colonel Sir Henry Streatfield, i.e. 'the Lieutenant-Colonel' commanding the regiment. Headquarters Birdcage Walk, London.

[2] The Guards Division attacked the Flers line on 15th September 1916, as part of the battle of the Somme.

The 14th was dreadful. We were right back and were due to relieve at night. It was like going back to school or to the front, only worse. Some of us knew what it would be like and that we couldn't get out under twelve officers and two hundred and fifty men. Some of the young fellows were looking forward to it but I think on everyone else there was that aching load of anticipation. Then I had to write to you; then people asked me to write to their relations if they were knocked out and so on. And the chaplain—whose profession says that the life hereafter is a better thing—had the longest face of all. Well, that day dawdled away. Ovid and his mistress would not have addressed the gods that day: *O lente, lente currite noctis equi.*

And all the day when one had forgotten, the great 9·2s stabbed home their crash into your very brain and said, 'We are preparing for the punies to make their rush tomorrow.' Crash. Brigade orderly. Routine orders. 'Officers proceeding on leave will carry their written authority for such leave with them.' CRASH. 'We are preparing for the punies to make their rush tomorrow.' 'Kits of deceased officers will be returned to railhead packed in canvas and labelled Cox's Shipping Agency.' Thanks. No, nothing to send back. Opened *Country Life*. Nothing there but pictures of tom tits sitting in unbelievably wholesome woods. Tried *Buried Alive* by A. Bennett. Amusing. *The Grand Babylon Hotel*, ha! ha!, capital, and seeing his own funeral at Westminster Abbey. CRASH. 'We are preparing for the punies to make their rush tomorrow.'

Yes: a horrible day and blowing through our bivouacs enough to make us keep stirring like uneasy crows from stook to stook. Action. Changed into thick clothes, filled everything with cigarettes. Put on webbing equipment. Drank a good whack of port. Looked to the revolver ammunition. Crash. We are ready for our rush tomorrow. The leading company is marching off. The commanding officer and I are standing about, as they say. Suddenly the Huns, as if to say, 'You have begun it now', put half a dozen shells along the top of our camp. And so we marched off in the dark, along the road through the village we captured on the 1st July towards the fight. But thank God it was action and movement.

Well, we crossed the wood, not a shell near us, and then out into the moonlight beyond into the most extraordinary desolation you can imagine. The ground is like a rough sea, there is not a blade of grass, not a feature left on that diseased face. Just the rubble of two villages and the black smoke of shells above them to show that the enemy did not like losing them. On we went, the men in file, stretching into the future [as] it seemed to us behind.

'Hullo, Acraman'—the q.mr. of our 2nd Battalion—'Good night.' 'Good night, Sir, good luck to you.' A check. On again. On our right a tank fussing away and making a noise like ten aeroplanes. More checks. The guide has lost the way. He is an Irish Guardsman, who says 'I do not know, Sir' to all questions. We reach the first village however and steer after that by the compass. I wish I could give you some idea of the ground. There is not one square foot without a shell-hole, they all overlap and stretch drearily away into the half-darkness.

We cross the last village, it is 1 a.m. and fairly bright. The attack is to start at 6.20 a.m. Five hours and twenty minutes. We 'form up' in the open. This means that we join up shell-holes as best we can and get into them. By about 4 a.m. everything is ready. It is rather cold. Sleep a little and eat a ham sandwich and drink some rum and water about 5 a.m. The steely light of the dawn is just beginning to show at 5.30. 'I wish we were going now,' says the commanding officer. 'It is very quiet and they will probably spot us on this bank.'

Well, I will send this off now. I can't finish it, being about the busiest man alive just now. If, as is possible, we are to attack, once more I am to be left behind with the transport. We always have a proportion of officers there and I am to be one.

Good night. It is 1 a.m.

The light was growing and at 6 a.m.—twenty minutes—the pearly outlines of Ginchy could be distinguished. It was a chilly hard light and at 6 a.m. precisely our heavy guns sent over a continuous stream of big shells for five minutes sounding like a monstrous flight of ducks homing it at dawn. It seemed to us to be an announcement of our intentions and certainly the Germans took it as such for they set down their barrage on to Ginchy.

But we were not there and so escaped. At 6.10—ten minutes— I destroyed all the orders, papers, etc. except one map. 6.15 I announced to the commanding officer—five minutes to go. Not an anxious five minutes: the fight was for those five minutes beyond our control: nothing could be altered, no more orders given. Four mins. I hope sincerely the barrage if it does not come down at the right time will be late and not early. Three mins. Silence complete except for the faint stir of nature at dawn. Two mins. A flash of one or two bayonets. One min. . . .

'The front line is off,' I said. The commanding officer smiled as if to say, 'I am well aware that it was likely to happen at 6.20.' And so up we got, yelling to the men to watch the dressing.

I could see men falling more on our left but we appeared to be escaping. Our 'creeping barrage'[1] did not seem to me to be very clearly defined. The smoke was terrific but one could see (and indeed feel) the whole brigade pressing on. We were met by considerable machine-gun fire. Then we caught sight, just below the hill, of Germans along a line of shell-holes. Three got up and ran back. A hundred men stopped and fired on them. They all fell. I heard the commanding officer shout, 'Why in God's name don't they rush it?' He did not have to shout for long. We were in the front line by then and on they came. I saw Luss[2] who gave several terrific whoops—we all yelled but it was not a great sound. The commanding officer and I flushed two or three Huns from a shell-hole, who ran back. They did not get far.

Then we killed. I have only a blurred image of slaughter. I saw about ten Germans writhing like trout in a creel at the bottom of a shell-hole and our fellows firing at them from the hip. One or two red bayonets.

There seemed to be a check. What had happened? There appeared to be lots of men but they were not going on. I thought that they were not 'for it'. Then I realised that a lot of men thought the trench we had just passed was the first objective and had accordingly halted beyond to let the barrage get on. I last saw my colonel about here. I kept shouting or heard myself shouting like a man in a novel, 'Come on boys, it's all right', and I remember thinking how particularly I disliked the phrase 'boys' when applied to men. And on we went.

By that time it was impossible to distinguish 'waves', and I saw Scots Guards, Coldstreamers, Irish Guards and our own fellows all mixed up. But no one cared. We were getting a fair number of shells among us and not a few bullets. The dust and smoke hid everything.

The left flank seemed exposed so I collected about a hundred men and felt my left to close the hole. The brigade swung away right-handed from me. I saw an aeroplane smashed on the ground. I halted to form a line. A Coldstream sergeant came up to me whilst I was halted and showed some inclination to bayonet me and one or two men near. The brigade had swung right rather and he thought we were malingering. When he saw me he said, 'Oh, I beg pardon, Sir, but oughtn't we to be going there?' pointing to the rest of the brigade.

We set the map by the sun and saw our direction roughly. The brigade was going about right. Then it was that a flash of sun

[1] An artillery barrage, the range lengthening in stages.
[2] Sir Iain Colquhoun, Bart., of Luss, Scots Guards.

showed us British troops advancing about three hundred yards to our left.

The left flank was no longer in danger so we too swung a bit right and went on. Mylne of the Irish Guards, a most gallant fellow, had joined me. We struck the German trench and saw the wire in front of us: it was much beaten down: so up we went with a yell, and in and over the trench. We thought that at the time we were the leading troops, but some of the 1st Brigade were crossing simultaneously on our left.

We all fairly had our tails up and the men simply itching to be going on.

'We must reorganise,' Mylne kept shouting, as if he was quoting the book.

I begged him not to worry and that that was what I proposed to do, but I told him we would push on beyond this German line and make a line in the open. Other troops seemed to be crossing on our left. So on we went. After going about a hundred yards I heard behind me the unmistakable sound of a hunting horn. John Campbell,[1] thought I, and looking round saw that it was indeed he, blowing his horn and yelling 'Stop!' and using some pretty expressive language to give it 'tone'. So we stopped and I went back to talk to him.

'This is great fun I must say,' was all the report I could give. 'Fun be damned,' he said. 'We have taken everything in sight but, you blasted idiot, if you go on you will be in to our own barrage. Don't you know this is the second objective? Dig! Where's my map? Where's my adjutant? Damn, he's been killed. Sharpe, where are those pigeons?' 'Here they are, Sir.' 'Oliver, give me your map.' I expressed the opinion that it was the first objective, owing to the contours. He and Longueville[2] laughed at this and wagged their fingers at Ginchy, which did certainly look the hell of a way off. Anyway a pigeon message was sent off by J.C. to say that he had reached the second objective.

We dug. Soon we discovered that we were not in touch with anyone on our right and that the Germans had a trench running at right angles to the one we were in and on slightly higher ground. From this position they could enfilade us with machine-gun fire. We could all see about forty of them in this place and so Col. Campbell sent out one of his companies and faced them right to attack this trench which, as I have said, ran at rt. angles to our position. But they could not get on in spite of the covering fire

---

[1] Lieutenant-Colonel (afterwards Brigadier-General) J. V. Campbell, V.C., Coldstream Guards.

[2] Afterwards Lieutenant-Colonel D. F. Longueville, Coldstream Guards.

which I was able to give with three Lewis guns, which I took out on his right flank. As soon as any of that company moved, the bullets came flicking along the top of the grass like anything.

Col. Campbell sent for me then and told me to bomb the Hun out. This was not easy to organise as we have very few bombs. However, with the aid of Mylne I slowly got together something like a party and after receiving an order from Rocke[1] to start at 11.10 a.m. all was ready. We proposed to cover our bombing party with a few rifle grenades. Meanwhile our situation in the trench was becoming most precarious. A lot of men had been knocked out—nearly all shot through the head—and in addition to this enfilade rifle fire we were also getting shelled from both flanks by field artillery.

The day had become bright and warm but we were not enjoying it. Behind us was the rough sea of ground stretching down the slope and then up again to Ginchy. We could see bearer sections at work and also men of the 3rd Brigade digging a trench to form a defensive flank to our left. In front of us scrubby long grass and the ground flat for about 300 yards and then rolling down towards Gueudecourt and on our right front we could see the tower of Lesboeufs church. But, as I have said, our situation was precarious. Just at this time I saw what I took to be Germans bombing down from the far side of the gap:[2] at any rate the bombers were using German bombs. Almost at the same time we started bombing ourselves but had hardly begun when Germans began to pour back towards us down the trench. There were perhaps thirty or forty of them and they were all taken prisoner. We pressed on and soon had touch with a bombing party—evidently that which I have mentioned above—which was composed of all regiments. I recognised Sergeant Thomas of our 2nd Battalion.

The trench into which we had gained admission was a kind of redoubt or possibly a headquarters organised in some kind for defence. There were several excellent dugouts, an artillery O.P., a first aid post (containing several wounded and a medical officer who talked English).

The contrast to our previous situation was extraordinary. All resistance seemed to have snapped. We had just been getting it in the neck and had been looking back on the sea of desolation. Now we were complete masters of the position and were looking forward towards as perfect a bit of 'partridge country' as you could wish to see.

[1] Afterwards Lieutenant-Colonel C. E. A. S. Rocke, D.S.O.
[2] The gap that opened between 3rd Battalion and 1st Battalion Grenadiers.

Germans were retreating towards Bapaume and field guns were withdrawing from the neighbourhood of Flers. All the shells were passing over our heads. Here I met Luss of the bloody club,[1] and Hugh Ross[2] wounded over the eye and seeming weak and shaken. We all looked at the map and decided to push on towards Lesboeufs.

To our left a C.T.[3] ran away down a gentle slope out of sight towards the N. end of Lesboeufs. Luss therefore took out a patrol of perhaps twenty men and I myself took fifteen and cleaned up one or two dugouts and bombed down the C.T. for about 300 yards meeting with no resistance. This C.T. had a trail of blood down it, showing that walking wounded had been evacuated down it. I established a block 300 yards down it and returned. Rocke had come up with a good few men and had just gone on to join Luss. I collected a few more and followed. We carried on for about 600–800 yards and then found ourselves in a fairly good unoccupied trench running along the bottom of a little gully with standing crops in front of us.

We decided not to push on further, though we deemed it likely that we could actually get into Lesboeufs, so demoralised did the enemy appear to be. But in view of our small numbers—perhaps 120—and of the fact that both our flanks were completely in the air such an advance would have been madness. So we sat down and reported our position by runner, heading all messages, which were of course addressed to the brigade, 'To be read by all officers on the way.'

The merits of our position were that we were safe, or as nearly as possible, from artillery fire owing to the enemy being unable to get observation on us, but the defects of it were (in addition to our small numbers and the 'draughtiness' of our flanks):

(1) Our small field of fire to the front.
(2) The standing crops.
(3) The scratch nature of the party.

We pushed out patrols and organised our trench for fire.

Rocke of course was in command and the time would be about 1 p.m.

The patrols reported us about 150 yards from a well-wired line (the blue line running through T.s.a. and d) and 500 yards from the outskirts of Lesboeufs.

[1] He had fought some Germans with a club.
[2] Captain Hugh Ross, Scots Guards.
[3] Communication trench.

We got rather sniped from the standing crops in front and had to watch how we moved about.

We refused both our flanks as far as possible and posted Lewis guns, one on each flank and one to fire down the sunken road.

While this was being done, Mylne was severely wounded and one or two men hit slightly.

Well we sat there and suffered rather from lack of water. We had a fine view of all the country to the N. of us as far as Bapaume. About 4 p.m. a company or two of the enemy skirted the south end of Gueudecourt and apparently made towards Flers. A considerable number however appeared along a crest line on our left flank and were caught by our Lewis guns in enfilade, which seemed to confuse them. At about 5 p.m. we had the chagrin of seeing a whole battalion debouch from Bapaume and slowly make their way across the intervening ground towards our left flank. We had been promised support but it was clear to us that if it was not soon forthcoming we should be enveloped.

This did in fact occur. Both our flanks were turned by small parties armed with machine-guns and we were subjected to fire from all sides. About 7 p.m., after we had had several casualties by bullets fired from the rear a strong company, 200–250 men,[1] jumped up from the front and made for us with the bayonet.

We were thus completely surrounded and had to retire, endeavouring to delay the enemy by fire from our refused flanks. However, the Hun was so close on top of us being considerably hidden by the standing crops that personally I shared the trench with them for a moment and was obliged to throw my empty revolver at a gentleman who evidently wished me dead. Fortunately he thought it was a Mills bomb and ducked, which allowed me time to scramble up the parados and get away. The Huns lost their heads and instead of sitting down and shooting us, came on after us firing from the shoulder with an occasional man kneeling. Consequently we regained the main position with astonishingly light losses and once there such a terrific fire was opened on our friends that they took no further part in the battle that evening.

We passed (John Hopley in particular) an uncomfortable night being bombed from the right flank. Personally I did not see much of that part of the show as the worst was over by the time I got to John, but we had to have men standing back to back in the trench and firing both ways. About 2 a.m., the 16th, I was sent for to Brigade H.Q. to report on the situation.

---

[1] Part of an even larger body.

Unfortunately the orderly lost his way—very naturally, it being as black as your hat—and did not get there until about 4.30 or 5. I was given a whiskey and soda and went to sleep on my feet. The brigadier kept me at his H.Q. until the relief so I do not know much more.

September 26, 1916

I can only scribble you a line.

Alas! we were in reserve, I mean this battalion,[1] for we have had a wonderful show. Masses of prisoners and all the objectives right up to schedule time. The Boche is beat to the world and I hope we will be after him soon.

I am quite all right but frightfully busy, rather tired and a little sad, now that all my friends have gone from the battalion. I like my new commanding officer, 'Bulgey' Thorne,[2] who I knew before, but one gets into rather a habit of mind and it is rather depressing when it is broken into.

Tuesday October 7th, 1916

Christmas! What weather. We shall have the muddiest time on record when we go into the line, which we shall probably do soon. The rumour is that we are going to do about two months and then no more this winter. Quite enough I think, anyhow.

Horses have been drowned in the mud going to water and that kind of thing. The cold world outside this billet looks singularly uninviting. How about my 'coat warm British', has it started do you know and has it gone by ordinary post? I expect I shall want it before long, as we are beginning to think of frost and the winter proper. And the Germans will be a mere picnic to the Somme climatically at any rate.

I got a whole batch of letters from you yesterday and spent a most enjoyable hour over them but I fear this is the most moderate effort. I have got nothing whatever to tell you about.

We are leading a fine open-air, hard-working, hard-riding, hard-drinking life with a good deal of bridge.

Books. An etna[3] (with Tommy's cookers). Would you order some tea from the Army and Navy and send it out weekly? Also some big white peppermints.

November 19th, 1916

We are fairly in the mud but not the blood. We are going into

---

[1] The Guards Division attacked again on 25th September and gained all their objectives.

[2] Lieutenant-Colonel (now General Sir) A. F. A. N. Thorne.

[3] Small portable spirit lamp with refills.

the trenches in the ordinary way about the beginning of December.

The winter is setting in rigorously. The cold for the last five days in this canvas camp has been inconceivable. How I longed for my fur coat. Everything froze as hard as nails, including one's toothbrush and sponge. The thaw came last night and has taken the form of a strong wind and thirty-six hours' rain, which has changed the whole place into a sea of mud. Now however we have got a couple of stoves and have lined the canvas hut with two false linings and put tarred felt on the outside, so that we have at any rate one warm place. For the men however it is very hard, especially at night. But we grease them and give them a rum ration and there is very little sickness.

This last show has been very good. Of course as we have not advanced in that region before they have had the advantage of being on their old communications and had a very reasonable 'back area', which of course we haven't got as we are living in what was once German territory.

The mails are ghastly; it takes about ten days for letters to get out so all one's supplies are disorganised. It doesn't matter so much that the letters are old as long as they come more or less regularly, but it is annoying when butter is stale and so on.

However, we are all very cheerful and play a great deal of bridge. We are gradually getting, too, more or less even with the mud by making chalk roads. It is marvellous what 600 men can do in a morning. I wish we could have a battalion on fatigue at Wittersham for three weeks. Everything would be finished. Walls, roads, lawn tennis court—*tous*.

My name was sent in yesterday for staff captain but it doesn't mean much yet as there are others recommended and not many vacancies at present. It is a step, however. I think I should quite like a change when I wake up in the morning and see a vignette of the Somme battle communications through the bellying flaps of my tent and mud, mud, mud. Mud between your bed and your shaving brush, and your tent and your breakfast. The roads are filled with traffic which never stops day or night, and consequently they are churned into porridge.

Mother, will you do one or two things for me?

(1) Go to Johns & Pegg and find out when (or if) they have sent my coat. I am *simply furious* that it hasn't come. Threaten them with anything.

(2) Order a pair of *corduroy* breeches as thick as possible with 'self' strappings from Tautz (at corner of Grafton Street and

Bond Street) and tell 'em to send them out *by post* as soon as possible.

(3) A book or two?

December 12th, 1916

The coat has arrived and is the most enormous success. In this sort of camp where one sits—I have sat for six-and-a-half hours in the orderly room today—in a hut with the temperature well below zero holding the pencil in your fist, it saves one's life.

Really the campaign is more uncomfortable than I have ever known it. You see one is really never warm. One's boots never get time to get properly dry. The usual routine is to wake up about 4 a.m. with very cold feet (I am going to use that hot water bottle even if I can only get half a pint of water) and rise to a whistlingly draughty wash, put on wet boots, slosh across to an icy mess hut and swallow some *oeufs frappés à la Nansen*[1] and so to the day's work. And yet one doesn't give a damn for it. After all warm feet is only a habit and a cold in the nose is rare.

It is pretty strenuous otherwise—the distances are long and the arrangements consequently highly complicated.

Our winter though, thank Goodness, is to end in going.

No more news at present about the staff job.

Well, I must to bed. This is a most moderate letter, but it is one of a rather hard-worked man who among other things is giving a series of lectures on interior economy to the young officers. You must have some stimulant I think to react on paper and I feel it is rather lacking. The mess has become a trifle full.

December 25th, 1916

The very best Christmas to you. Here we have the eternal mud and a snoring wind and rain blowing through our cantonments like the devil. But one little week and we shall be resting.

There is a frightful congestion in the post so nothing but an excellent cake has arrived so far. Nevertheless as we are keeping our Christmas festivities for when we are out, it does not matter. As to leave, I hope, if all goes well, to get it about the 15th of January but I don't know.

There have been some developments with regard to the staff job as some of the staff in the division have been promoted, etc., which has worked off some of the people above me on the list.

However, the one job I really would like, which is staff captain of one of the three Guards brigades, seems very remote. That is what I should really like and perhaps John Ponsonby's good offices would do something if he is coming back all right.

[1] i.e., eggs only agreeable to an Arctic explorer.

I expect Grigg[1] will get some other job in the course of the next three months, then the staff captain would get his job and I should like his. However there it is.

Oh, I must tell you rather a typical instance. I shouted to my servant, 'Where is my book, Bean?'[2] 'Is that *The Passionate Elopement*, Sir?' 'Yes.' 'I haven't seen it since you last used it.' Used it, forsooth.

[1] Lieutenant-Colonel E. W. M. Grigg, afterwards Lord Altrincham.
[2] Tyson's successor.

3

The Guards division did routine duties in the trenches in November and December and relieved the French at Sailly-Saillisel on 1st January 1917. The trenches were in an appalling condition and men had sometimes to be dug out of the mud. I had ten days' leave in December, and wrote the next letter on my return to the Front.

January 9th, 1917

What a pig I am not having written before, but you have no idea of the amount of work about just now. Terrific. What nurses call 'morning, noon and night'. It really has increased enormously lately. I think it possible that we are over-Qd, if you understand that. The Q. department has got rather too much the upper hand. The French for instance subordinate all the Q. part entirely to their G. which is responsible for both sides.[1] However as a whole our staff is better than theirs I think, being much more highly organised and much more painstaking.

I cannot understand the French at all but I have come to the conclusion that offensively they are better though not very much than we are, but that defensively they are worse. They chance things which we ceased to chance two years ago. I don't think the French take any interest in soldiering unless they are pushing, whilst we rather over-elaborate the detail of defence. However there is very little that we haven't learnt.

I hear that people in England are talking about the depression of the enemy troops and so on. Of course it is the greatest nonsense. Everyone is struck when they go home with the appearance of 'perhaps' with regard to the war. Nobody ever dreams here that the Boche is anything but stiff. On the other hand put a fellow up to his waist in water and tell him to write a cheerful

[1] The British army staff is divided into two main sections: 'G.' and 'A. & Q.'. G. is the general staff dealing with military operations in the field, tactics, movement, etc. A. & Q. is the administration branch, A. dealing with men, discipline, promotion, etc., and Q. with supplies, food, ammunition, etc.

letter and he will talk about his discomfort and will probably say
—as a *façon de parler*—peace at any price. At the same time he
knows and will tell you when standing on a trench board that the
Hun when we have a few young Somme offensives going in the
spring hasn't an earthly.

I had a most delightful dinner in a café last night with Grigg
and a fellow called Gren. We talked 'shop'. We agreed that
whatever peace terms were offered now was no good. Say the
German offers us a *status quo ante* and chucks in a colony or two
and Alsace-Lorraine. No good. Until the actual population have
seen Khaki, the Hun will be entitled to say that the army is
unbeaten and they will merely prepare for a more favourable
opportunity, when say Russia or ourselves will not be involved,
in the next forty years to have another shot. Everybody in
Germany dislikes militarism even when successful, but when it
is unsuccessful demonstrably and patently and obviously, then
and not till then they will chuck it.

How remarkably prosy I am getting; [on the other hand]
despondency in England if allowed to get going will quite counter-
act say 10,000 prisoners and a couple of miles of ground.

We are having quite a good time but we shall be going back
to the line early.

I have more than a chance of one month's leave and should get
it about the 28th. I hardly dare hope.

The Christmas parcels arrived today. The Shetland blanket
is a colossal success. I cannot yet tell you about the puddings and
so on: they are still uneaten. The gloves I fear are too small but I
have an excellent pair of ration ones and shall send you back the
new ones.

Well, I now have to 'read reports', a most tiresome and mechanical business, so I must stop but I promise to write again soon.

January 26th, 1917

We are coming out at once, we are coming out. Out of this
damnable ice field to comparative comfort and extreme safety.
I really am very hopeful about a month's leave, chiefly because
lots of people who have got less service in the country than I have
have got it. But in my case I have ordinary leave in prospect.

Now about this staff business the commanding officer tells me
he has recommended me strongly for staff Captain of the 2nd
Brigade when a vacancy occurs which is of course *the* job I
should like, though what chances I have got I don't know or

when the vacancy will happen. If I get home I shall try and get J.P.[1] to say a word and if I don't get it I think I shall have to go off as G.S.O. 3 somewhere. . . . It is not really that I am tired, but I think too long at every job (I have been eighteen months at this) is a mistake especially if one wants to get on. I suppose I should be a more eligible business man as a reputable member of the staff than a regimental officer. And I don't see if I pop the parapet how I can avoid a bit of lead somewhere again, and you can't rely on them through the arm.

Nearly two years since I came out.

The prospect from the mouth of this dugout is a world of snow and ice so thick that you could march a regiment across any stream in the place. The frost is so hard that picks will not break the ground. Below us is the usual sort of village and in front of us a road with sticks of the avenue left. The village you can distinctly detect in good weather.

Oh, now please let me know what hospital at Rouen Hermione and Rachel[2] are nursing at, by return. I should love to look them up and ought with luck to be going through that charming town about the 3rd or 4th. On the other hand these special leaves sometimes go by another route.

Au revoir.

In the event the leave train did not go through Rouen. I got leave at the end of February and after ten days in London, I returned to the front.

March 4th, 1917

We really had quite a good journey as we had two nights in hotel beds on the way, and fetched up on the 1st getting a lift out of Neville Lytton[3] to the very door.

I have decided to go on with the course for a month or so but am keeping my eye pretty well fixed on what is doing in the battalions. There is an off-chance for 2nd-in-C. in four to six months, I think. However.

At present moment I have got a job training scouts, which is extremely difficult as only very little time is available, but not wholly uninteresting.

My only item of news or rather a piece of public opinion here is that if the Hun goes back far it will lengthen the war a little by

[1] Brigadier-General John Ponsonby.
[2] Rachel and Hermione Lyttelton, daughters of Lord Cobham and General Sir Neville Lyttelton respectively.
[3] The Hon. Neville Lytton, the painter.

delaying the offensive. But I suppose this is self-evident and at any rate we 'make' troops just as much as he does by the shortening of the line, and we take back a good chunk of France. On the other hand our 'billeting' area becomes even worse as the zone of the fighting gets deeper but in the summer it won't matter much.

I am very anxious to hear how you are putting glamour into the land schemes.[1] Obviously the best way is 'breeches' for all, or perhaps uniform of which they form a part.

I will write again soon.

P.S. Dyer[2] seems immovable, not that I wish him to move unless he is promoted. He is a very nice fellow.

March 11th, 1917

I have been having quite a strenuous week tramping the country with my scouts, teaching them how to stalk, use the compass, the stars, and the map. Owing to the very short time at my disposal I don't think they will do me very much credit but they are as keen as mustard, and are coming on.

But I must say that I am not enjoying life very much at present, and this idleness is revolting. I am trying to bring matters to a head some time soon, and unless they put me out of my pain quick with some job or promise of one I shall go back[3] and be happy. I hear 'Boy' Brooke will be fit in a month, and you bet he won't be long getting back here. I wonder if he will be coming out as a commanding officer or a brigadier. There are possibilities then of course.

With regard to what you say about the retirement[4] I don't think any one need be pessimistic. I don't think it will materially lengthen the war. I dare say however the Boche may make a despairing effort somewhere, but I really believe all will be over this year.

This from the H.Q. dugout, a long sort of cabin lit by acetylene and really quite comfortable.

The weather is mild, and everyone is doing a lot of flying.

The Germans duly shortened their line by withdrawing from the large salient (Péronne—Le Transloy—Hébuterne—E. of Arras) to the Hindenburg Line (just E. of Arras—Cruisiles—

---

[1] This was a scheme to recruit women, 'land girls', on farms. My mother was one of the promoters.

[2] Captain Sir John Dyer, Bart., Scots Guards.

[3] I.e., to the battalion.

[4] The Germans began to withdraw on 13th March.

just W. of Hermies). The withdrawal was covered by very heavy shell-fire on all our front areas, which made the life of brigade staff officers rather dangerous. A zone of 'scorched earth' was effectively carried through: booby traps of all kinds abounded: mined footbridges and dugouts, grenades in old helmets, poisoned wells and the rest imposed caution but did not inflict more than a few scattered casualties. I acted as one of two or three staff officers to a brigade group of all arms temporarily organised to handle the advance.

March 21st, 1917

Just a line from one of the busiest men in the B.E.F. John Dyer the staff captain has gone temporarily to be brigade major, 1st Guards Brigade, and I am acting as staff captain—during the advance. At the beginning of the advance I was adjutant of the 'Situation Centre', i.e. of the leading troops. We had terrific work but great fun and now we are out for the moment.

The war for the moment has changed completely and has become like Aldershot with an occasional shell to give the local colour.

We are through the destroyed belt and although the villages are burnt the country is to all intents untouched.

I don't think however that beyond bucking our fellows up no end the Hun retreat is going to have any effect on the war one way or the other.

It was rather exciting when they started to go and our patrols kept getting into line after line of German trenches and the shell-fire grew less and less and then died away. Our H.Q. were soon well behind the German line and open warfare began, but of a South African or child's play quality. Most amusing.

Well I must, must stop.

N.B. There is just a faint, very faint chance of my getting this job.

March 28th, 1917

We are out of the line making roads, etc., and are coming out for a good rest afterwards.

Meanwhile I applied to go back to the battalion but the brigadier refused it. So that's that. I am very disappointed at not being allowed, and wish I had never started this game.

However I have been doing staff captain while Dyer has been away and now the brigade major is off for a month's leave so I shall go on doing it till he comes back—another month.

Something I trust will come along in the meanwhile, and I might even get this job. It is a toss-up. However I can't get away, which I hope will be a comfort to you.

I have got the book, and think it awfully good. Of this more anon, but at present I must be off.

April 15th, 1917

I have just had Paris leave for two days. I was there with John Ponsonby for two days and with another fellow for one. Of course it was rather good fun with John who is too perfect when he is '*en permission*'. We went to Versailles during our only bit of sun and had an entertaining time there. But one's surrender to the luxuries of the Ritz and excellent food is extremely refreshing.

What do you think of the old war just now?

I really cannot see how it is going to stick it much longer. The important thing is not at all what we take in the way of ground or even of prisoners, but it is that they allow them to be taken. The truth is that they are so bad in 'morale' (the only thing which matters in war) that they cannot go on. I am sure that if in two months the submarine campaign is no better for them, they will chuck it. You cannot deceive yourself now that you have a completely new and limitless belligerent in against you.

Well, being very *affairé* and up to my neck after my two days' leave I must stop. Send me *The Newcomes*.

April 21st, 1917

We have got a delightful headquarters; for the moment it is a little uncomfortable but we are getting on with it.

From the windows of the office which is an Armstrong hut we look out upon Loch Nabo[1] or something very like it. We are completely cut off from everyone except by telephone.

Yesterday we felt the first natural warmth in the year and spent the morning smoking on the bank below the mess. Delightful.

John Dyer and I are very good friends and whenever the In box begins to dwindle he says, 'Come out, Cut-em-Down (my nick-name) and let's talk of love and likes.' And we do. We really have quite a good time as at the moment there is enough but not too much to do. When there are movements of troops and the like my work is severe and only by dint of long hours and great rapidity can one keep level with the correspondence, telegrams, telephone messages, etc. But now there is not too much. I have come to the conclusion that I will brush up my French—this after some

[1] A loch on the estate of Frank Tennant, my father's brother-in-law, where there was a shooting lodge in which I had stayed.

not wholly unsuccessful brushes with the head waiters of Paris—have sent for a grammar. By the time it arrives perhaps the inclination will have left but I find that I am more constant about the 'pursuit of knowledge' than I was!!—if possible.

I have just got *The Shadow Line* from you but have not turned the page yet. I am looking forward to beginning it on tomorrow, Sunday.

We embarked on a colossal discussion last night which was started by the signal officer saying that he preferred Whistler to Turner in whom he could see little! A sufficiently raw statement to begin an argument. The issue eventually became: Which is the truest conception of art, that which takes the commonplace and idealises it, that which merely presents an ideal or that which presents first the ideal and then brings it into focus with reality?

The first is my own view. You should present your ideal in its relation to the commonplace, and not the commonplace in relation to the ideal. The first is art, the second is political economy. This I'm afraid reads a little like hair-splitting but I give you merely the discussion condensed by Horlick.[1]

Will you please send me one or two French novels, a pair of new brown shoes I bought when I was last home, and will you buy send one of those clockwork 'Crasnow' oil lamps from Harrods Stores? Could you send the novels and the shoes out at once?

April 23rd, 1917

Just a line because I forgot it in my last letter. The Madonna[2] I bought at an old curiosity shop in Amiens. I am awfully glad you like it.

There are slight signs of the staff of the division beginning to move about a bit. I am most anxious about it. Two changes may happen quickly which might let me in but one never knows.

It is a lovely day with diamonds on our loch and black and blue ruffles. The wind is strong enough to make it very chilly out of the sun but our new mess is nearly done with a real fireplace.

We had a tremendous evening last night quoting and reading Shakespeare.

Great fun and the brigadier in immense form.

He made me repeat 'Tomorrow and tomorrow and tomorrow, etc.' three times, with special emphasis on

> And all our yesterdays have lighted fools
> The way to dusty death.

[1] As in malted milk.
[2] A French medieval Madonna carved in wood, now on my writing-table.

May 3rd, 1917

At the moment I am at Brigade Headquarters and acting as staff captain, which I have been doing all the time. I don't think things look very healthy with regard to my getting the job. There is an infernal fellow who has finished his 'course' which I have not had a chance of doing as I have been acting as staff captain who I think will get in in front of me.

However there it is.

Before many days I shall be at the division, I expect. I have no news: it is delicious weather and we are in camp in an orchard full of shell-holes in one of the destroyed villages. The work is fairly easy for the time being. We read a good deal and quite enjoy life. I think we shall go on like this for a long time.

Yesterday I attended a garden party within 500 yards of the very spot we reached with an advanced party on the 15th September.

The Irish Guards pipers—a new institution—with saffron kilts and green streamers, very jaunty, performed.

But this country stinks of corruption. As far as the eye can reach is that brown and torn sea of desolation and every yard there is a grave, some marked with rifles others with crosses, some with white skulls, some with beckoning hands. But everything is dead: the trees, the fields, the corn, the church, even the prayers of those that went there in their Sunday clothes with their sweaty pennies for the plate: it is all dead and God has utterly forsaken it.

'O prosper thou the work of our hands upon us', forsooth. But the pipes and the saffron kilts brought us back to life and the warm red blood of youth and laughter, and we walked among the dead and thought only of the spring and its awakening.

Rather an unusual vein for
Your loving Oliver

May 28th, 1917

I have just come back from Paris, and had an excellent time. Paris was full of incidents. The *midinettes* were on strike, and paraded about the streets singing, and so on. When they caught sight of the proprietors of the Louvre[1] who were looking out of the top windows they set up the most good-natured and humorous booing, at which the proprietor waved his hand and they waved their hands, and every one laughed and the police looked on, and they laughed, it was wonderfully good-tempered. One evening

[1] Magasin du Louvre!

Bill Bailey,[1] an enormous fellow in the regiment, and I after discussing a bock at the Café de la Paix were walking along the boulevards, towering over the people who all stopped to look at us, when suddenly a party, I should think about fifty strong, of the class which had just been called up, and who were wearing civilian clothes with military caps caught sight of us. They immediately began to chant to the air of some popular tune, '*Oh chic, les Anglais*', and formed a sort of circle round us and gave us a rousing reception in which a number of drinkers at the Café joined.

Oh damn, here's the general to take me off to see some sports. I will go on later but will miss the post.

Good night. Best love.

May 30th, 1917

Pour recommencer after that vulgar interruption. The brigadier and I sallied forth to the Australian sports. Not a very entertaining show, and accompanied by an extremely strong and rather warm whiskey and water, never a drink I very much like, especially at 4.30 in the afternoon. The brigadier however was in remarkably good form, and we saw one or two nicish looking horses, though all of the rather ugly Australian short-necked, badly hogged type.

I have forgotten where I got to or what I have already told you about Paris. Oh yes, about Bill Bailey and our reception in front of the Café de la Paix. The difficulties of escaping promiscuous introductions to dinners, dances, tennis, and even lunch or golf with the worst type of Anglo-American-Parisian Ritz type of society are very great. 'I am the Comte de Beaux-yeux and have just been lunching with Bunny Binks in your regiment. He told me you were in Paris. I hope you will forgive my introducing myself but I do hope you won't mind. I am giving (in a hushed whisper) a little dance at my house tomorrow night. I do hope you will come, everyone you know will be there including Elinor Glyn and Mrs Hwfa' or some such (Elinor Glyn was a fact— rather a good-looking large woman but I understand with a propensity for recounting her experience in pursuit of local colour amongst the Brigade of Guards).

However I escaped even the lure of being asked by the most appalling bounder in the Coldstream to go to a dinner party with him, and in a house where he himself had sat between two duchesses, or was it one duchess and a countess, he was damned

---

[1] Lieutenant-Colonel the Hon. W. R. Bailey, afterwards Lord Glanusk.

if he could remember. A fellow I had never seen, but met in the barber's that morning.

The massed bands of the Brigade were in Paris and created a profound sensation in which we participated. The scenes were, however, more or less as described in the *Daily Mail* but I don't think are piquant enough to write down. Thousands of Grenadier officers. There is no doubt that we are very popular just now with the French, and all the turns at the music halls are English or American, and the English song sung in English quite vilely by a gentleman named Chevalier brought the house down. Enough. I will tell you some more later about Gilot and the white wine and the clergyman at the Café de Paris. I have a thousand anecdotes which I am polishing up and propose dining out on when in London.

Not a particularly good letter but with the *potins*.

June 7th, 1917

Just a line. I have gone to the division.

Address me H.Q. Gds Division in future.

I am pleased by the change, and hope to learn a lot.

June 8th, 1917

Rather a dull letter. There is nothing doing at all. I am extremely short of work and very bored and there is no vacancy for the moment. I think I stand fairly well for the next.

We had quite an amusing Etonian dinner on the 4th of June, and quite a good dinner party yesterday.

I find it difficult out here to cut oneself off from soldiering. I mean as a soldier for the moment I have nothing to do and I can't make myself into an undergraduate, and frankly study something quite different. However these sort of impasses don't as a rule last long and very often break up surprisingly quickly. I really am very cheerful, and not at all depressed although this letter sounds like it.

I am absolutely mahogany-coloured from the sun and in addition am getting fat, which has brought me to the unprecedented resort of taking a two and-a-half mile run every morning before breakfast, and wrestling in the afternoon.

Give my love to Mary.

By jove there was a good deal I might have told you about my dinner with Neville Lytton, when I made rather friends with John Masefield. I liked him awfully.

June 16th, 1917

Some developments have taken place in the situation about this job. Jack Dyer is probably moving up in the world at once, and the A.A. and Q.M.G.[1] has told me in confidence that I am to succeed him. In the meanwhile I have gone back to the brigade staff, where I have for the moment nothing to do. But I am awfully pleased about it because it was the one thing I wanted and even if Jack does not leave at any rate I am marked down for the first vacancy. But that vacancy I was assured would probably take place in the course of the next week. *Voilà.* I think you know exactly what a staff captain is and does. He is the administrative staff officer of a brigade. It is not particularly thrilling work and it is a difficult and extremely strenuous job. But I shall be delighted if I get it in this division as there is a good deal more competition and it means a good bit more here than elsewhere.

I have no other news to tell you. I have become considerably more optimistic about the war since the Messines show,[2] as I cannot see how they can go on getting these knocks. After all war is more or less a business proposition. If the submarines are a failure, as they appear to be, if we can keep on taking nearly 10,000 prisoners and a lot of ground whenever we like as we appear to be able to do, if a lengthening of the war merely means that more Americans are going to turn up, and more artillery surely the Hun will chuck it. Every day the war goes on the worse his peace terms look likely to be.

I was much amused by your American news both about the mission and also about Viviani and Joffre: the Prince who I happened to meet who knows the two last, nearly cried himself when I decanted the story to him.

Really the gossip in London is a scandal. Every idiotic woman who talks about military operations and even hands on a rumour ought to be imprisoned. The leakage is awful. Whenever you hear anyone begin you ought to shut them up quick. Never ask anyone for information about movements or offensives. By doing so you are not only lengthening the war you are also killing men as surely as if you turned a machine-gun on them. If only people realized what they are doing and what they have done they would be horrified. There.

June 25th, 1917
I am practically a certainty now for the job. I am awfully pleased but over my neck in work just now. Which I don't mind a bit.

[1] Assistant Adjutant and Quartermaster General.
[2] The successful attack by the 2nd Army on the Messines ridge.

I am awfully pleased about Jack Dyer getting D.A.Q.M.G.[1] of the divisions. He is such a very charming fellow and has had pretty poor luck up to date but he must be one of the youngest D.A.Q.M.G.s in the Army now.

I miss him rather, there is less talk of 'love and likes' now that he has gone, which is a great pity.

All the same socially we are very good and unshoppy, whereas in some H.Q. there is a continual strain and talk about the war and small arms ammunition at dinner which makes life nearly intolerable.

Well, I must stop; the post is going.

I was duly promoted staff captain of the 2nd Guards Brigade, and my days as a regimental officer were over.

My brigadier, John Ponsonby, was a well-known and well-beloved character. He was brave and popular, but was not a highly educated or theoretical soldier: rather a regimental officer unexpectedly finding himself in command of a brigade. Budget Loyd was the brigade major, and in fact exercised nearly all the functions of command except the personal appearances. Once the brigadier, who kept a personal diary, came into the brigade office in our dugout and said, 'By the way, Budget, what *were* my orders?' He was referring to a small battle in which we had just taken part.

Budget was a highly-trained soldier, a master of the profession, humorous, imperturbable, and kept the brigadier under a strictly disciplinary eye. 'The old flamer wants to do so and so,' he would say, 'but I told him that he's wrong, and the staff work would show it up as impossible. Don't give me away.' In spite of some professional irritation we were devoted to John, because his sense of humour was unequalled.

He had a cleft palate, and, except to his staff or his intimates, he was incomprehensible. I knew his language pretty well, and his likely thoughts even better. On one occasion, however, I failed on both counts.

The central figure in the Carlton Hotel robbery, where some jewels had been stolen, was one Theophilus Metcalf, said by the newspapers to have been at one time an officer in the Coldstream (John was a Coldstreamer). It may easily be imagined that the

[1] Deputy Assistant Quartermaster General.

Grenadiers lost no opportunity of chaffing their Coldstream friends on the subject.

One day, when we were out of the line, I was sitting in our mess in a little *estaminet*, reading a newspaper which had just arrived by mail. Enter the brigadier. 'Well, Oliver, what's happened to Theophilus Metcalf?' Being, of course a model of keenness as a staff captain, and caught a little unawares, I thought he had said, 'What's happened to the officers' mess cart?' (a single-horse transport vehicle at that time on the establishment of Brigade H.Q.). 'Oh, Sir, it has gone into the village to try to get some green vegetables.' His reply sounded to me like this: 'I didn't say the officers' mess cart, I said the officers' mess cart, you bloody fool.' 'I know, Sir, it will be back soon, and if that idiotic corporal hasn't found. . . .' A bellow of rage, and then at last I caught on. I was within an ace of losing my commission. This was the only incident which I can recall of hard words being spoken.

On official occasions he often reduced Budget, the Signals officer and me to near collapse from suppressed giggles.

One day we had been ordered to attend a service to be conducted by the Primate of All Ireland in a shunting shed on the railway a mile or two behind the line. We were waiting for the appearance of this ecclesiastic. John: 'I am offering 7/4 to a monkey' (£500) 'that he's a man with a beard.' At that very moment up popped the primate with a beard like Abraham straight from the Sistine Chapel, and from a range of one yard gave out the hymn number: the wrong one. Half the drums[1] of the Irish Guards struck up the hymn on the paper, the other half the primate's choice. The banshee noise was indescribable, and Budget and I heard the familiar prelude to trouble, a suppressed guffaw from our brigadier. We did our best (I sweated through my Sam Browne belt for the first time in the war), but there is no denying that it was an unseemly performance, tears streaming down John's cheeks, his staff red in the face and shaking, and the troops in gusts of laughter—suppressed by the N.C.O.s—behind us.

We returned that evening to the trenches shaken men, and after our meal the brigadier preached his own sermon, a perfect parody.

[1] A drum and fife band is called 'the Drums' in the Brigade of Guards.

On the 31st July the Guards Division attacked on the left of the British Army, in what is now known as the battle of Passchendaele. We had been allotted one of the most difficult tasks, because in our sector the enemy front line ran along the eastern bank and our front line along the western bank of the Boesinghe (Yser) Canal. It looked a very ugly obstacle.

I have already described my part in the battle in my autobiography. The attack was a complete success. The weather then broke, and heavy rain soon turned the battlefield into a marsh. Even the artillery ammunition had to be carried up on pack animals. The discomfort of the troops generally was indescribable, but the high training, discipline and efficiency of the Guards Division made our sector tolerable compared with conditions further to the south.

This battle underlined the dilemma that faced the Higher Command. If the enemy wire was not cut the infantry would be slaughtered, and even if success crowned their sacrifice the cost would be too high. On the other hand, cutting the wire involved a huge expenditure of ammunition. In a terrain like the Ypres salient this intensive shelling broke up the drainage system of peacetime, little streams or becques flooded their banks and the country became as impassable to infantry as the sea.

Historians, almost to a man, condemn the battle of Passchendaele, but they have seldom attempted—indeed it is not their role—to answer the question, 'What would you have done?' The French were in a bad way. An attack had to be mounted by us to relieve the pressure, and should be directed towards one of the tender spots of the enemy front. I am inclined to the view that the wrong sector was chosen, and that drier, hillier country should have been selected, even if the immediate tactical threat to the enemy was less. There is an element of hindsight in this, because even we could hardly believe that the northern sector could be so much churned into porridge, and that in August.

September 2nd, 1917
I am just now acting as brigade major as Budget Loyd's on leave, and enjoy a change from 'Q.' to 'G.' especially when 'Boy' is about.

It really makes the whole difference to life. I easily can imagine that a year has not passed. The same silently malignant breakfasts, followed by the dawn of hope about 9.30 a.m. and then a morning of intense efficiency. No fuss, no worry, no sudden appearances in the office: merely, 'I noticed this, so I want that. Get it.' Gradually increasing benignancy towards the evening and finally no shop at dinner or after. What is so amusing about him, which I shall never have, is his restraint. He has hardly given the horse the faintest touch of the spur, but the horse has an instinctive feeling about it. Battalion breakfast hours get earlier for no apparent reason, and so on. Most refreshing.

I think that a month's leave looks all right a bit later on if all goes well and no surprising moves take place.

We were given a real rest soon after this and were billeted in some huts in a wood a few miles behind the line.

I was soon sent on a staff course at Cambridge, and took no part in the later stages of the battle for the Pilkem Ridge, battles which were part of the Passchendaele offensive.

The Guards Division attacked on the 9th and again on the 12th October. Their objectives were gained once the line consolidated.

November 25th, 1917

I have never seen anything like the beauty of tonight. It thawed yesterday and this morning but tonight the quiet snow has fallen again: there is a clear moon with a blue and white sky and our huts with their red lights look unbelievably comfortable and permanent in the little wood.

I got back after a terribly cold motor journey to find everything as I expected and prospects of a very far from uncomfortable winter.

We are really very happy. I think one feels that one is getting on with it here and that England is an interlude and that its pleasures are a little unlawful.

The only bore is that the brigadier has to go and command the division for a month while the major-general is on leave, which will be most annoying as we shall have good opportunities for 'getting at'[1] the troops for a bit.

Budget has after all gone to Cambridge for two-and-a-half months and I reign in his stead. What will happen after that *n'pas dire* but I think I have a good chance.

Our cast, i.e. our *dramatis personae*, will never be quite as good again because the learner is not either socially or at his work

---

[1] i.e., training.

above mediocre. There is the orderly: 'An officer of the Scots Gds. to speak to the staff.'

More tomorrow—really.

[Received December 11th, 1917]
Yes, I liked the extracts from Georgian poetry most awfully. Do send me the book.

> We who are left, how shall we look again
> Happily on the sun, or feel the rain ... ?

is unquestionably the best I think, and the same idea as

> What a small thing
> To remember for years.

What about

> Was there love once? I have forgotten her.

The other book I would like is *The English Sonnet* (Crosland) if only from irritation at being unable to fix the author of

> Now folds the lily all her sweetness up,
> And slips into the bosom of the lake:
> So fold thyself, my dearest, thou, and slip
> Into my bosom and be lost in me.

(not by any means perfect). Don't like slip.

Oh, do send me the paper copy of Alice Meynell's last book.

We are faring well and I am enjoying life. The family party tradition is living. Conversation after dinner is never about soldiering.

The fur sleeping bag is a success. We have good fuel. The lamp is excellent and really sometimes the room is not too bad.

The learners give me a lot of amusement: they are two 'chaps' of eighteen to twenty.

(1) Freddy Gamble.[1] Very good value. Six foot. Pink and white: engaging smile. Always untidy. Educated. Sense of humour. Contributes laughter and charming manners. Etonian.

(2) A. N. Other. Carthusian. Brushed back hair. Knows Lee White[2] 'at home'. Has not heard of Botticelli. Works hard. Love and wine not unknown to him. A good all-round type of stupid well-washed Englishman who never would do a thing like that.

So it goes on. With youth the war is tolerable even enjoyable: introduce an element of age or idleness, it is impossible.

As it is we don't care if it snows ink. *V. busy.*

---

[1] Afterwards killed in action.   [2] The well-known revue and cabaret artiste.

4

At the beginning of 1918 the shortage of British manpower was causing anxiety. It was manifestly impossible to maintain the same number of divisions at full strength and, wisely, brigades were reduced to three battalions instead of four. One battalion from each brigade of the Guards Division was thus 'surplus to establishment', and these three battalions were accordingly formed into an extra brigade, namely the 4th Guards Brigade. The battalions were:

4th Battalion Grenadier Guards (Lt.-Col. W. S. Pilcher)
3rd Battalion Coldstream Guards (Lt.-Col. F. Longueville)
2nd Battalion Irish Guards (Lt.-Col. the Hon H. R. L. G. Alexander)

I wrote on the 10th February:

Many events since I wrote. I have been appointed brigade major 4th Gds Bde (and incidentally am the second hardest worked man in France, the other being my chief clerk for the moment).

Very sad to be leaving the old brigade but professionally this new job is a tremendous compliment. I find it very piquant, too, starting off with a new show. I fear I cannot tell you all the details as they are hush but my address in future will therefore be H.Q. 4th Gds Bde. The brigadier is the Lord Ardee,[1] late of Grenadier, now of Irish Guards. Very nice man who was wounded—age about forty-six—early in the war and who hasn't had much experience of it since. Eric Mackenzie[2] is my staff captain. Other appointments are not yet made.

I think if you want more details Streaty[3] would give you some.

I am rather excited and amused by my responsibilities. I dare say it will wear off.

[1] Afterwards the Earl of Meath.
[2] Captain E. D. MacKenzie, Scots Guards.
[3] Colonel Streatfield, commanding the regiment at Wellington Barracks.

The work at present is terrific but will ease. We are very comfortable.

Do send me some postcards and I will try and send you a more frequent situation report.

You really must forgive this last lapse and also the disjointed letter among the telephone rings.

After some routine duty in the trenches the 4th Guards Brigade fought in the battles of March 1918, when they formed the hinge between the 3rd Army and the defeated 5th Army, which had recoiled across the old battlefield of the Somme.

A few days later, on 11th April, we were thrust into a different sector, into the most anxious and critical battle of our lives in the Lys salient, and in defence of the great rail and road centre of Hazebrouck.

I have already described these battles in my autobiography, drawing upon accounts that I wrote in hospital immediately after the events. There were no letters to my mother at this time, there being no chance to write while the battle was joined, and shortly afterwards, when the line was stabilised, I was unlucky enough to be wounded by a gas shell. I had several small skin-deep wounds of no importance, but the shell had burst very near me, and my service dress jacket had been sprayed with liquid mustard. It vaporises very quickly and I was severely burned. Some of the blisters on the infected wounds were a foot long. I was blind for a few days, and in great pain.

However, after a journey which was torture, I found myself in hospital in Boulogne, where I was successfully treated by a new French treatment which may even have saved my life.

I was soon in hospital in London, and three months later fit enough to return to the regiment and train a company.

I was not, however, passed by the Medical Board as fit for active service until mid-September, and was consumed, for some strange reason, by impatience to be back in the war. Moreover, I hoped that my old commanding officer, whose adjutant I had been—Sergison-Brooke ('Boy'), who was now commanding the 2nd Guards Brigade—would ask for me as his brigade major. There were rumours that the officer holding the appointment was about to be promoted and return to regimental duty. Should I be fit in time? I was. I was asked for by the brigadier and at the beginning of October got the job. I was overjoyed, as well for personal as for professional reasons, for I knew his mind and methods: a few words would suffice to enable me to write the orders: with still fewer I should know whether they were approved before issue.

When I was posted to France I had a bad time catching up with the troops. The trains were too slow, and crammed with reinforcements. I jumped staff cars and lorries, and cut down the journey to hours instead of days.

October 13th, 1918

Well, here we are again, but we are only birds of passage and are going forward pretty fast. It is great fun and the shooting is excellent.

I had a perfectly damnable journey in spite of everything and had some difficulty in catching up the division, but really didn't do badly. The Boche seems to be very weak and near the end of his tether. He has retreated so quick here as to leave the villages intact: a great boon to everyone. We all have the feeling of men let out of prison into the open. It is great rolling open country with numerous villages, and the warfare as open as the country.

Excellent food and drink. *Que voulez-vous de plus?*

Can say very little anyway, and am getting busy.

The reference to shooting is not to war, but to the fact that we had a few sporting guns and some cartridges, and added to our table by bagging a few partridges when we were not fighting.

We did not get many chances, for out of the last eighty-one days, from 21st August to 11th November, the Guards Division had spent fifty-four in the line, and twenty-nine of these had been days of hard fighting against a stubborn defence. We used to think that we had done a good deal more than our fair share, compared with other divisions in the Corps.

October 22, 1918

We have had a couple of battles since I last wrote and very successful too. Of course the villages are mostly untouched so that war is not very uncomfortable, though tiring for the troops and the staff.

The change is wonderful in my job compared with what it used to be in the other division. Here there is no fuss or worry and all the troops are what we call handy. They take a village at four o'clock. By five the outposts are a mile beyond and everyone in billets, cookers going, pianos tinkling, guards turning out, drill sergeants shouting, 'Come 'ere, that man', and Brigade Headquarters with the dividers out planning the next advance. It is just the same in the open. An extraordinarily good line is dug in no time, visual signalling is going, the cable cart brings the telephone wire, the Brigade O.P. keeps us warned of the exact situation. Breakfast is always at eight, luncheon at one, tea at five o'clock, dinner at 8 p.m. Our troubles are M.G.s and gas. This rolling country is well suited to M.G. rearguards and you cannot of course make set-piece attacks on their positions without very heavy loss. So we don't. We adopt a policy of infiltration, especially at night. Work up to the M.G.s, work round them, always pushing on with small detachments and using the darkness.

Our last battle began at two in the morning. Of course it was raining like hell and we had to bridge a river and I don't know what. We had very few casualties indeed but it was an anxious show even though we reached our first objective in no time and had the news back. You can ride almost anywhere, there is little or no wire and just a few shell-holes.

We have had, as I said, our fair share of gas, chiefly the sneezing variety which is quite harmless but extraordinarily unpleasant. You get a sore throat and a streaming nose for about an hour and it takes all the fun out of life for that time. They have a habit of shelling us out of our sleep with it about two, which is preposterous.

Strategically the Boche is in a little easier condition. He is in touch, as we say, along the whole line and for the moment there are no very dangerous salients for him. He will escape individual disaster but cumulatively he is hammered terribly. Every day almost we take from 4–6,000 prisoners on the 200-mile battle front. That cannot go on for ever, though I think it will last longer than people think. His new class, 400,000 men about, are not yet engaged I believe, but I don't know.

I should appreciate the situation like this. He will get back somewhere, Meuse say, and find himself about as strong as when he started, i.e. his retreat will not have benefited him materially while morally it may crack his nation. And after all Napoleon says the moral factor outweighs the material in the proportion of two to one. We have won but it will take six months to crush.

I wrote after the armistice:

194

Well, I will try and give a short account of our doings since the
3rd. On the 3rd we got the first warnings that the Kaiser battle
was to begin on the 4th. Four armies were to advance with the
object of gaining the general line Avesnes—Maubeuge—Mons.
Our line or rather our bit of it ran a mile W. of a town called
Villers Pol. We concentrated behind our lines on the 3rd, a day
of steady rain. We had the brigade billeted in depth, that is one
battalion in front, one in support under bivouac sheets (good
thing in the wet) and one in billets. The scheme of attack was to
attack successive objectives, one battalion leap-frogging through
the other. The depth of our advance the first day was to be about
8,000–10,000 yards.

There was only one road in our area and that of the division
on our right, running W. and E., so we had to lay on very
elaborate time-tables and traffic controls so that the troops could
flow forward without check. Zero hour was to be 6 a.m. on the
4th. The enemy on the afternoon of the 3rd retired about 1,000
yards and blew all the road bridges into Villers Pol. We pushed
on during the night of the 3rd/4th (as black as a hat and raining)
and secured the village. R.E. pontooned the river which runs
round the town. At six we attacked in a thick mist. Brigade H.Q.
at Zero was in a village. We breakfasted at Zero and started
forward to a ruined farm about two miles on at 6.30: Lyttelton
with attaché case, message pad, glasses and map. We had a
cable cart laying cable in front of us. We got to our farm
(absolutely ruined) at 7.30 and got our first reports. Things
seemed to be all right but a lot of machine-gun fire. Prisoners
coming in. So-and-so killed. Crawley de Crespigny commanding
the 1st Brigade was with us. We had a joint H.Q. About nine,
cable head having reached Villers Pol, we got on our horses and off
again. Meanwhile a brilliant sun had come out and the country
was sparkling. We rode along off the road along which a steady
stream of infantry and guns was moving. We arrived at the
pontoon just in time to see an artillery driver drive his pair of
horses and limber over the bridge into the stream. We cut them
adrift and got on.

Villers Pol, a little town cocked up on a hill with a thin
steeple. Rather pretty, with a meadow stretching down to a
wooded stream. Village still stinking of mustard gas. Headquarters opened at a ruined cottage on a cross-roads. Fine view
in front. A wooded country with lots of small orchards and
enclosures and the jug-jug of M.G.s everywhere. Further
reports. Grenadiers had passed through the Coldstream on to

the third objective. A few shells rather too close to our cottage for comfort. Went into the cellar with the brigade major 1st Bn. The brigadier went up to the line. Found the cellar occupied by two eviscerated Germans—stony—and one officer with shattered leg.

... [Details here too gruesome] Thomas Powell[1] said to the officer, 'How is your friend?' 'He's been dead these six hours,' said the Hun. 'Staff captain will arrange to remove.' Cold partridge luncheon at 11.30 above ground. Brigadier returned. My turn to go up forward. Sykes[2] and I set off on horseback. We had got about half-way when swish, bang, a shell burst a bit close and got Sykes' horse through the nose and put him down a bit stunned and shaken. I could see it was a bad day. However, sent Sykes back with the horses and went on with the orderly. Wherever we went we were unlucky that day. We reached the Grenadier H.Q. and got shelled and three men were killed about three yards off while we were there. The Boche had been holding quite an organised line and of course we had only a few field guns to deal with it. However the Grenadier got round the flanks and had them out with rather severe casualties. Saw front line and was sniped at a bit. Returned over a small stream. Boche shelled the bridge just as I was crossing, nearly got me and wounded two orderlies with me. Back to the support battalion. Talking to a platoon commander when, damn, the Boche started off with field guns on his platoon. Twenty minutes in a hole with shells all round one. Four men were killed and seven wounded. Had to get back with report of Grenadier position to brigadier. Worked my way through the shelling but just when clear, wang, one burst close, wounded my groom, who was on foot and hit me in the backside. Very painful and annoying but blood hardly drawn except on him. Back the Bde. H.Q. in a filthy farm in the middle of a wood. Very cheerful. We had gone 5–6,000 yards in face of very stiff opposition. Another bde to pass through us in the morning. Outpost orders for the night written and to bed, twelve of us in a small cellar. Whew! Next morning the other brigade passed through and we billeted in a village called Preux, where we were duly shelled all day. An old man owning our billet described how the Boche had commandeered everything. Poor old buffer. He burst into tears over his cows and the ruin of his livelihood. He cursed the Boche in the proper spirit. Many congratulations on our battle from the 'big noises'. We captured a good few prisoners (300?) and a lot of guns.

[1] Captain T. F. Powell, Coldstream Guards.
[2] Captain Claude Sykes.

Next day, i.e. 7th, it was our turn again. We had to make an approach march in the middle of a pitch black night and attack at dawn. The most difficult operation of war. Wrote the orders about 5 p.m. Alteration by the division about nine giving us a job to capture some of the objectives of the division on our left, who hadn't got on and who were two miles behind us. More orders. Started off with the brigadier at 1 a.m. Reached the 3rd Brigade through which we had to pass at three and talked with Arthur in a cellar. So forward to advanced Bde H.Q. (in small solicitor's house, quite untouched). Everything worked perfectly and all the battalions in their assembly positions up to time. A great triumph for everyone. Zero 6 a.m. All objectives captured by nine. Slight opposition only. Brigade H.Q. on again to a château—no furniture—but not shelled! Marvellous.

Brigadier and I went up the line. Still the same country, orchards and big woods. Rather pretty. No further advance to be made that day owing to division on our left not being up. Got back to H.Q. More orders. Final objective of 2nd Gds Bde tomorrow will be Maubeuge. Thanks: about nine miles. Orders. Zero to be 6.30. Off again at five to our advanced H.Q. in a farm on the main road. Reports. We had captured La Longueville. Very heavy M.G. fire holding us up on the left owing to chaps on the left not being up. What does Brigade H.Q. look like? Farmhouse room, telephone, message pad. Brigadier drinking a glass of Madeira. Red flag outside and a few shrapnel coming over.

Orderly. 'Message from Coldstream, Sir. "Following from right coy., timed 6.30: Have reached Les Mottes and hold line of wood in P.7 central—S.36.d. Heavy M.G. fire from houses in P.3.b. Enemy still holds Foignies to my left rear. Houses in P.3.b. contain civilians. Scots Guards on my left on road P.3.d. Civilians report station at La Longueville mined. Bad crater on main road P.3. central. Ends."'

'Shall we shell P.3.B., Sir, there are civilians.' 'Yes.' I ring the telephone. 'Are we through to right group?' 'Yes, Sir, line just laid.' 'Hullo, is that you, Sir?' 'Yes.' 'All available 18-pdrs., please, on to houses in P.3.B. What will that be?' 'Oh, about eight guns. I have three sections well up with the leading infantry. Right, 10–10.15. I doubt if we can get through to Coldstream in time, but F.O.O.s[1] will arrange direct all right. Good-bye.' 'Oh, what's that?' 'Good house for you in Maubeuge.' 'Oh, rather, Sir.' 'The next best, the brigadier says. No more have I,

[1] Forward Observation Officers.

197

they all seem a bit old and dirty. I expect you'll get kissed there all right. Good-bye.'

Well, we tried to get on all the morning but couldn't get far, still five miles from Maubeuge. Moved Bde H.Q. in the afternoon further up on the great main Maubeuge road, flanked with poplars and stretching to our last objective in front of us. Captured an orderly with all the enemy dispositions on him and ordering a retirement. Brigadier decided to be before the Germans. Grenadiers who were in reserve to pass through and march down the main road at night as an advanced guard. Daring operation which would make our advanced troops six to seven miles in front of the division on our left, who were held up. Grenadiers passed through at eleven; two a.m. no reports, though wireless had gone on with them. four a.m. no reports. People on our left level with Bde H.Q. still fighting. Oh, I had forgotten to say that the 8th, the day before, had been very wet. However, dawn on the 9th broke clear and frosty. Brigadier and I rather worried. No reports from the Grenadiers. Ordered horses to go out and find out what was happening. Wireless operator. 'Message coming through, Sir, from 3/GG.' 'Yes.' '1 Company Q.3.d. 5.6., 3 Coy. Q.5 central. Surprised enemy rearguard. Fifty prisoners. Patrols entering citadel.'

Three cheers, we've done it. Off we go down the main road. Find the Grenadiers radiant, being kissed in every direction. Flags from every window. Mayor. Town band. Bouquets. Grooms smothered in flowers. '*Monsieur, les Anglais et le soleil du bon Dieu sont arrivés ensemble. C'est une autre vie.*' All the time the Germans still fighting behind us on our left and about 2,000 yards E. of the town. 1st Brigade pass through and take the high ground E. of Maubeuge. Boche retires in front of division on our left, being outflanked. We thus become support brigade. Back through cheering crowds—more bouquets. Brigade H.Q. in a well-furnished house. Sleep at last. Sunday moved whole outfit into the town. Monday armistice.

So it was all over. I had expected riotous excitement, but the reaction of everyone, officers and men, seemed the same—flat depression. No doubt psychiatrists could produce some more plausible explanation, but certain reasons seem clear in retrospect.

Winning in war is at all times a heady and exhilarating experience. Even in quite modern times troops used to work off their excitement by sacking the city they had just captured, bursting into the cellars, raping the women, and sometimes shooting some civilians.

The British soldier of today is completely reliable in victory. The day we captured Maubeuge we were smothered with flowers, and even kisses: most of us preferred the flowers, although I do remember one un-garlicky embrace from the sixteen-year-old daughter of the *charcutier* which was ingratiating. The poor girl's pigtails had excited the German soldiery, and she had protected her virginity by hiding in a loft. She had judged that the English would be different: thank God she was right.

We installed Brigade H.Q. in a substantial house belonging to the local lawyer, who was away serving his country. We had been busy preparing to leap-frog through the forward brigade, which had seized some high ground to the east of the town. We replenished our ammunition. The brigadier decided on the order of battle, and skeleton orders were drafted. Our only worry, and it proved needless, concerned our maps. We were warmed up for a pursuit, and we thought we knew how to do it in the best and most professional style. About 5.30 a.m. we got the order that hostilities would cease on all fronts at 11 a.m., and after breakfast sat about waiting for the clock to strike.

About 10 a.m. one large high-velocity shell—I judged to be an 11-inch naval shell—homed into the outskirts. Although it must have been 300 yards from H.Q. it seemed to us, with an hour of war to run, as menacing as a barrage would have seemed a week ago.

No one was hurt. Then silence, a few creaking wheels: a faint chuckling of hens: shutters being wound down. 11 a.m. By noon on November 11th Maubeuge had already slipped back into a normal market town.

By the afternoon we were already bored: a new kind of what the French called '*cafard*' descended. Part of this boredom is because danger has a winding-up effect on human nature and keys up the senses; safety is a sedate sensation. Part of it was because we had lost our profession, in which we had been immersed for five years: part of it because we had already begun to wonder what awaited us in peace-time. The Brigade of Guards had been greatly expanded during the war, promotion was likely to be clogged for years. The youngest of us—I was twenty-five—

thought we should have to get out of the Army. We no longer saw ourselves in positions of authority: clerks, not heroes. We looked up our pass books at Cox's. Had last month's pay been credited? If it had, the balance was smaller than we had hoped.

The brigadier's young wife had died a few weeks before: in the stress of battle he had had little time to brood upon his private sorrow. It now revived.

In the meantime there was only an order for a thanksgiving service the next day. Brigade orders had to be issued. This done, we rode, rather distrait, round the town. 'Hello, do you think there are any partridges near this bloody place? We'd better try for some tomorrow afternoon, after the parade: we've got some cartridges. Anyway, dinner tonight at 8 p.m., we've got a few bottles of very passable champagne.' 'Brother in love and last companion, wine.' Bridge afterwards.

This mood changed quickly when orders for our March Into Germany, to be conducted as a military operation, arrived from Divisional H.Q. Once more movement: new country, victorious troops, Charleroi, the Ardennes, Cologne, once more *la splendeur militaire*.

December 25th, 1918

This on Christmas Day. I must first describe you our house. It is outside just like Buckingham Palace as you see from the enclosed. Inside it is very like Gambrinus.[1] It is one mass of rather dingy gold. This room in which I write is the best on the whole, but it is pretty monstrous as there are a quantity of sham oriental shelves with mother-of-pearl inlay, hung up on a background on bandana scarves, on which are perched some Birmingham-Egyptian china bric-à-brac and vases. Everywhere however is the double window and large steam radiators which make the house wonderfully warm: in fact without the windows open it would be quite intolerable. Oh, I will send you a picture of 'our façade' and also the interior of our dining room. Upstairs I have a wonderful suite with the best grey marble bathroom I have ever seen, quite hideous but possessing every appliance of comfort.

Now about the Huns. It is I think quite a delusion to suppose that they don't know they are beaten. They do. And they hate us walking about in their streets and being saluted by their police

[1] A German beer-house in London.

and uniformed officials and so on. There is no food. I haven't seen or indeed eaten an egg either natural or in something for a fortnight. Their bread and coffee are appalling. Of course this is a magnificent town with some really good hotels where if you pay *les yeux* you can get a moderate dinner. The shops are also full of things to buy—furs, flowers, jewellery, etc., but you never see a German in the shops. All the appearance of wealth and prosperity is merely superficial: they really are badly hit.

It was a curious sensation arriving here. We came the last fifty miles in a German train, cared for by the assiduous German railway official. We were the first troops to be permanently billeted here. Other troops— cavalry—had been on the outskirts, but no one had really penetrated the city. As we left the railway station with the *roulement* of our drums, we were followed by all the small boys of the suburb and marched to our barracks in Cologne proper, amidst a staring and I hope admiring populace.

The billeting had all been done by Germans—not at all well— and we were met by a deputation of ten who explained their scheme in English. It transpired that the officers had all been billeted in barracks. The brigadier: 'Not enough trouble has been taken in doing this billeting. I have not come to Cologne to live in barracks. In two hours you will find billets for 125 officers in the best houses and the best house for myself. If they are not forthcoming I shall take them and shall probably fine the town. You may now go.' Much hat-raising and away went the docile Hun and returned with the necessary billets in about an hour and a half. After this the general reply to all our demands was—'It shall be done.'

It is an extraordinary feeling being absolute master of the resources, labour, morals, music, trains, institutions, restaurants, barracks, banks, of an enormous city of 1,000,000 inhabitants. 'A motor car will be placed at my disposal from 17.00 hours today with German driver.' 'It shall be done, Herr General.'

At first we were regarded with more curiosity than dislike and with this curiosity was mingled a feeling of relief that order had returned. But now I think that the iron is turning in the soul of the Boche and that he is hating the sight of us.

However it doesn't disturb my rococo sleep in gilt bed.

I have been very busy but see an early prospect of some idleness in view. I propose to read constitutional history, political economy and learn a little, very little German. We go to the opera, which is pretty good, almost every night.

I will write you more of what I think about the future in another letter.